DIARY OF A HUNTER

DIARY OF
A HUNTER

D. Brian Plummer

COCH-Y-BONDDU BOOKS

First published by The Boydell Press 1981
Reprinted by Coch-y-Bonddu Books 2002
© 1981 David Brian Plummer
All rights reserved

ISBN 0 954 2117 0 7

To Nicola and Craig
- This is how I once was.

Published & distributed by
COCH-Y-BONDDU BOOKS
MACHYNLLETH, POWYS, SY20 8DJ
Tel 01654 702837   Fax 01654 702857

January

Tuesday 1

January 1980 finds me with fewer dogs and less livestock than I have owned for nearly fifteen years. Actually, it is not a bad thing. Few people with a large number of dogs exploit or train their wards to the full. Furthermore, the tiny pack I now have is trainable and very biddable. My Jack Russells—if one can describe the unique type of terrier I keep as such—consist of Vampire, aged 9, a veteran of hunting almost every type of British quarry, his brother Warlock and his sister Beltane, an amazing bitch with a nose like a beagle and great intelligence. My fourth Russell is Omega, an incredibly athletic animal, bred by mating Vampire with his own daughter. Omega has killed an almost legendary haul of rats and is a delight to watch. In addition to these, I also own a crossbred Patterdale bitch called Pagan. This bitch is bred from a dog belonging to Nigel Hinchcliffe of the Pennine Hunt and my own bitch, a Russell type grand-daughter of Beltane. My bloodline was very inbred and I felt I needed the outcross. This bitch, a black and tan eleven inch terrier will be crossed back to her grandson and I shall keep the Russell type terriers which should constitute half of the litter.

I also have a litter of puppies sired by a smooth fox terrier dog out of my best bitch, Beltane. The fox terrier dog holds an MFH certificate. This litter, three dogs and two bitches is only twelve weeks of age but, God and parvo virus willing, they will join my team of ratters come spring. They are extraordinarily typey and retain the markings of my own Jack Russells. All have straight legs, but two are really deep-keeled and have the short rib cage of their great-great-great-grandfather, my ancient veteran San. I've always avoided outcrosses before, particularly with fox terriers, but inbreeding has produced a number of abnormalities and few desirable traits.

My four border terriers, line bred to Champion Shady Knight, are a mixed bunch colour and personality wise. Two are blue and tan, and two are grizzle. At twelve months old, the blue and tan male is quite a ratter, but the others are non starters as yet. Dave Harcombe is convinced the working blood is being bred out of border terriers. Maybe he could be right. Another year will see, for borders are notoriously slow.

My lurcher crop is small, one merle dog, two brindle bitches, and a blue fawn puppy. Add to these ten ferrets and one almost untrainable eagle owl and that completes the *tout ensemble*. Enough for any hunter and more than enough for me, as I intend to read for another degree this year.

Wednesday 2

New Year has opened with one of the most unpleasant sights in the hunting world, namely a badger caught up in a fox snare. It was an accident, as few badgers are harmful and most are given a reasonable degree of protection around here. Stone, the chicken farmer at the end of my lane, has been greatly troubled by foxes which attack his battery hens in broad daylight since the myxomatosis and over-shooting has reduced our rabbit population. The earths belong to a shoot leased by the Waterworks to some labrador enthusiasts who are not country men. These earths are really old badger citadels, too deep to dig, too vast to bolt foxes with terriers. When the South Staffs Hunt hunted this area, they gave these earths a wide berth if they could, for a few terriers came to grief in them. Hence the foxes have to be snared or lamped with lurcher and 12-volt battery beam. The snares were put down by Robert Parsons and Mick Kirby, two youthful hunters

I

who haunt my place. This morning I found a snare almost bitten through and tangled around a fruit tree near Stone's enclosed garden (a brick-walled 17th century masterpiece). The earth had been gored up by the convulsions of the badger and a late-bred yearling boar was tangled in the fruit cordons. Not a pretty sight. He was probably living in the cavity of the garden wall, a hollow cavity that carried the heating flue of the wall, which, when warmed, ripened peaches. Snaring is a particularly nasty way of taking quarry even though it is sometimes necessary. Rupert Brown, who is producing a huge coffee table book called *Treatise on Hunting for the Common Man* has included a chapter of snaring by a scientist from Cambridge, a Ph.D who has investigated the action of the snare on animals. From his researches, he has concluded that the only creatures which can be snared humanely are hares and rabbits, due to the peculiar structure of the vertebrae. Foxes, badgers and cats (which are frequent victims in snares) die slowly and extremely painfully, but a snare correctly placed will slay a rabbit or hare quickly. I would not question the researches of a specialist, but hares certainly make a fearful squealing sound when caught up in a snare, and sound like small children who have been badly injured. Foxes are frequently snared around this district, now that pelts are fetching £15–£20 on the market, because snaring does little damage to the hide. I am always amazed by the number of foxes a county like Staffordshire produces. Badgers, however, are born suckers with snares; for, being stoats, they explore each and every new object and thus get tangled in the snares. A year or so ago, I caught a badger that had a rabbit snare embedded in the muscles of its neck. It was still alive, though the suppurating wound would probably have seen it off in time. Legislation regarding snaring is on the cards, I feel.

Thursday 3

Thursday evening, and come hell or high water, Thursday nights we hunt rat. Our venue is always the same, our hauls invariably high, which says much for the fecundity of the rat. Harting, a nineteenth century gentleman hunter, says of the rabbit, "What is certain, is that we shall always have him not only in sufficiency, but in superabundance." Then came myxomatosis to give the lie to Harting's statement. I hope and pray that no one will ever tempt providence by making a similar statement about *rattus norvegicus*, for throughout my forty-two years on this earth, I have obtained great pleasure from hunting this, the most despised and revolting of all beasts. Our hunting ground is a chicken farm some twelve miles from where I live, and next to my beloved Yorkshire maggot factory, it must surely be one of the best ratting spots in Britain. Our plan of action is quite simple. We arrive at the farm about 8.30 pm, open the doors of the battery house, release the dogs and instant mayhem usually results. We have taken 709 in a night at this farm and never have we reduced the number of rats—a truly remarkable place to hunt. Tonight, however, we entered Mick Kirby's Patterdale cross dog (a brother of Pagan) and his desire to catch rats was only exceeded by his desire to slay the battery hens. Twice he climbed inside the battery cages to catch a large rat and twice the confinement of the cage and the presence of hens heated him up until he killed three hens. A dog is easy to break of hens until he has killed one; then it is very difficult to wean him of the habit. Dogs need to be rock steady to work in such places as many escapee hens race around the floor and dogs must actually kill rats in the milling ruck of chickens. My veterans are totally steady to fowl and are so at home on this farm that they move from shed to shed ahead of me. Toby and his sister, Pagan are not so steady, as tonight's slaughter proved. Mick's dog is a red, much like the father I purchased from Hinchcliffe, but he is a smaller, neater animal, slightly bitchy in shape but as tough as nails. He entered easily, killing five large adult rats with a quick snap for each one. Oh, that my border terriers were as eager to kill! They have been ratting with us for three months now and though the dog will kill quite eagerly, the bitches are very indifferent and watch the passage of quantities of rats with little more than interest. Possibly, the bustle and banging of a rat hunt is not to their liking. I can't blame them. I also wish it was a more silent sport, but the beating out of the rats to ensure they leave the trays to descend to the floors, is a noisy business. Still, I shall persist with these borders at least another year before writing failure across the "line". I've known borders take 2½ years before they decided to enter to rat, which is the reason why many hunters simply write them off. Once they are wed to rat, they are usually mustard; though I'm a little perplexed about the slow, ponderous attitude and movement of all three bitches. The dog, a large lean slingy type of animal, is very hard and took to rat killing at seven months old. He also took some time to accustom to poultry, but that is another tale that borders on the macabre. An average bag of rats, considering all three assistants were amateurs. 70 rats in 1 hour 37 minutes.

Friday 4

A gusty, windy, starry night, a bit light for lamping, but John Cope decided it was suitable for hunting, so away we went in search of foxes. Night is hardly the right word, for we left the house at 2.30 am and returned by daylight. Fox catching, using a lamp and lurchers is an easily learned skill. It is also easily learned by foxes, who once they have exprienced the dubious pleasure of being lamped, hightail it as soon as a beam flickers around a field. They learn that the lamp means danger and, were it not for their insatiable curiosity, would never fall victim to the lamper. Good hauls (well, I call three a good haul) are easily obtained when one is hunting a new area, but within a space of a week or so, a fox is impossible to approach. They seem to know if one is out after rabbits or foxes and respond quickly to the situation. Make a bee-line for one and you won't see his outline for dust; but hunt rabbits, and after the first squeak of a lamped rabbit, flick the beam around the field and you'll see half a dozen foxes watching you, literally fascinated by the spectacle. We are fortunate in this district, as not only is the village a passage point of numerous wandering foxes, but the area is festooned with artificial earths, small drain-like constructions into which a fox, and, not infrequently, a hard pressed hare can slip when danger threatens. Furthermore, the area has two poultry farms with the usual midden piles of dead hens and garbage and such a place is irresistible to foxes. All one has to do is sit still near the midden pile and flick the beam across the muck heap occasionally to pick out the foxes feeding on the rotting hens. Heck, can

one wonder why fox bites go wrong and fester when foxes feed on such mess? My present fox-hunting lurcher is a bit of an enigma. He is a half bred greyhound collie, hybrid merle in colour and fairly ugly, obtained originally to photograph for my book *The Complete Lurcher*. He proved too heavy for hare coursing, but his cloddy build and gay tail are deceptive. His speed is now fantastic and his courage bottomless. Courage, not size or speed is the prime requisite for a fox-killing lurcher, the desire to get close to a biting, fiery little fox more important than speed and turning ability. Since September 1979, John and I have caught 59 foxes using Merle and a bitch called Penguin, an old and tatty veteran. In October, Merle, aged seventeen months, ran in on a fox after Penguin had bowled and received a very bad mauling, so bad in fact, that he nearly lost one eye. At first, he refused to take fox again, but as his confidence grew, he took more and more readily to the hunt and now is easily able to hold down a fox himself. If one is pelt-hunting the best way to take fox is to lamp them using only one dog, as two fairly strong dogs will make a heck of a mess of a fox skin, making it unsaleable. This morning, we caught three—a yearling male and two adults. One of the adults is a pale silver sable colour almost like a brindled blue fawn whippet. Stone was fairly pleased to see this pale old vixen laid low as she actually took hens from the battery house while Stone was in the battery house feeding the chickens. An audacious act maybe, but foxes pull off some amazing stunts when food is scarce, and at this time, food is very scarce.

Saturday 5

An interesting day. I received a letter from one Aubrey Fryer of Smithfields, Cambridge, Gloucester who disputes my statement that the Smithfield collie is an extinct breed. (I made this statement in my book *The Complete Lurcher*). Mr Fryer, who is a respected judge, and contributor to various sporting weekly magazines, has enclosed two photographs to corroborate his statement. One photograph is of a typical shaggy pastoral type of dog that Mr Fryer has labelled a "Smithfield collie"; the other is of a lurcher bred by

mating the same to a greyhound. Sadly, the collie photograph is very blurred and not at all clear. Curiously, this type of herding dog is common the world over, as a glance at similar breeds will assure anyone. Bearded collies, kommondois, pulis and Catalonian sheepdogs all belong to the same type of canine. Miss G.O. Willison, in her book *Bearded Collies* has photographs of several similar beasts and states that the originals came from Poland and were traded by the owners of a Polish ship for sheep. She says that the

A Norfolk herding dog—one that is actually worked. Briard blood, or perhaps even a Smithfield Collie?

original dogs were wonderfully sagacious and gentle. The ones who were traded (also said to have been sold by Kazimierz Grabski in 1514) said to have almost super-canine intelligence and herding instincts. It is fairly certain this type of dog accompanied the Celts on their migration from Southern Russia westwards maybe in 200 BC.

Mr Fryer's dog looks fascinating. I shall write to him to ask if he will give me data on the origin of this dog and its abilities regarding intelligence and herding. If it is a distinct breed of sheepdog then it needs preserving and the only way to preserve such a breed and maintain its droving qualities is to work it. There is a society called The British Rare Breeds Preservation Society who publish a periodical called *The Ark* (for obvious reasons) who would help him perpetuate this curious breed of dog. I saw one of Mr Fryer's dogs at Lambourn Lurcher Show and an interesting-

looking animal it was. Whether or not it was a genuine Smithfield collie is not for me to say, but its owner assured me that it was bright and capable and he bred excellent types of lurcher from it, mated to a greyhound. For the uninitiated, the Smithfield collie was a droving dog employed to drive sheep from Norfolk to London. Oxen, bulls, turkeys, geese were also driven on these droving runs. Various collie types were crossed with greyhounds and these became known as Norfolk lurchers. In addition to their herding duties, these dogs became pot hunters for the droving bands. I stated in my book *The Complete Lurcher* that once droving finished, it was likely that the droving dog, the Smithfield collie, became extinct. Mr Fryer obviously disagrees with me and sent the photographs to substantiate his claim. I only hope he is correct. It would be a great pity if the breed became extinct—if it is not extinct already, that is.

One of Aubrey Fryer's Norfolk lurcher puppies.

Sunday 6

Who said that Sunday is a day of rest? For me, it has never been. Not only do I have to muck out my stock, but the run of visitors is incredible. My place resembles Piccadilly Circus in rush hour. My day began early with Mr Green of Burton bringing his Patterdale Russell bitch to mate to my stud dog, Vampire. This will produce some very interesting puppies, 50% Patterdale coloured, 50% Russell type. Hinchcliffe's strain of Patterdale (erroneously called Patterdales) produces quite a few black and tan offspring, all small, all smooth-coated. Nigel Hinchcliffe believes his own strain are bred down from bull terrier and Lancashire heeler (a tiny herding dog) blood. Certainly, the black and tan bitches I have bred by mating his stud dog to my Russell type bitches resemble the old heeling strain, but this colouration could quite easily have

been derived from using Lakeland blood. Bull terrier blood is obvious, however, and all the progeny are very pugnacious. I shall keep a good quality Russell type puppy from this mating. I am always a little baffled why the Jack Russell Club of Great Britain are so violently against judicious outcrosses of this type. My own Russells were getting very weak in the jaw and out at the elbows before I used this outcross, and I have no doubt Hinchcliffe's blood will correct this. Furthermore, there is no lack of spunk in these Fell type terriers. The courage of some of these dogs is legendary. It needs to be, to work the earths of the north, I suppose.

I've a great respect for small ferreting dogs of the Bedlington whippet variety, although it is an unfashionable type of lurcher to own these days, now that 28″ greyhound hybrids are all the rage. I spent noon, plus or minus, ferreting with Roger and his whippet/Bedlington dog, Ben. In thick cover, such as we worked today, few large lurchers would be of any use at all, but it is here the tiny dog is priceless. Ben is able to slide through places that would defy a terrier. He is a puppy yet, but I have no doubt that he will make a very useful dog. Such is the craze for large, stately and, frankly often useless lurchers that anyone who put up a small Bedlington lurcher in a show, would be laughed out of the ring, yet as a provender dog these tiny creatures take some beating.

Fudge, (a ridiculous name for a ferret, I admit) my oldest jill, is a treasure, though she has been worked far too little this Autumn and my crop of kits has seen little or no work. Fudge is approaching six years of age and is still full of fire for rats. This is a bit of a rarity, as ferrets worked with any regularity to rat jib fairly quickly. Fudge's mother, a good, quiet, sandy jill, jibbed rat her second time out and henceforth refused to try for them, though she was a really great ferret to rabbit. Her dam was still going strong to rat at four years of age but died of a mauling after a hunt on Bentley Ash Tip, Walsall. Not one of this family has ever bitten me and all are absolute nailers to rabbit. I doubt if these qualities are inbred; some are bound to be, but most are due to proper handling as kits. Perhaps skulking at the mouth of the earth is inherited, though, for I've seen whole litters of ferrets do this. Again, this fault—and by God, it is an annoying fault—could be due to bad handling as babes. For this reason, I would never buy a grown ferret from anyone—or a grown dog, for that matter.

Monday 7

Another fruitless dawn hunt. Two foxes appeared in the beam, but simply turned their heads and disappeared as soon as Merle began to run them. He really is an excelleng lurcher, too slow for hare but once he wed to fox he went like a dream. My snares yielded one large rat, not exactly the best of meat for me, but enough to keep my eagle owl happy. I returned home to find my two border terrier bitches baying at him as he sat there on his block in the run. Contrary to popular tales, owls are remarkably stupid beasts—as are all truly predatory birds—and the eagle owl is no different. This bird was sacred to Athene, the goddess of wisdom, but why I cannot think. He is fractious, unpredictable and very keen to use his feet. In fat condition, he weighs 2½ lbs; but in fat condition he is unhandleable. I've trained a lot of hawks and one or two falcons, but this bird is entirely different from either. Owls of this type, including the great horned owl of America, have no crops and the food passes straight to the stomach; hence training is a little difficult as after a mouthful of meat, the bird ceases to be sharp set. He is very vicious and a killer with his feet. Once, during training, he footed me through the thigh and the grip is quite unforgettable. A few months ago, he flew 7 feet to my first, but he has gone back in training since then as my spinal injury has incapacitated me for two months. I can find no one who has a trained, entered bird. Many boast they have trained owls to take all manner of quarry up to the size of roe deer, but I am very sceptical about such tales. Sufficient to say I am having little success with him. His appetite is phenomenal. When left to his own devices, and fed *ad lib*, he will eat two large rats, but he fasts a day or so after such a feast. This year he has eaten a variety of birds ranging from crows to sparrows—all road casualties, as I am a bit against the shooting of birds. Foxes form his staple diet simply because I catch a lot of them, but he takes rabbit, hare and squirrels a lot more readily. I really must take him up for training again. I hate to keep a useless animal. His weight will need to drop before he will feed on the fist again. Somehow, I just know I will lose with this vicious, unpredictable bird. Yesterday, one of my ferrets got in with him. Fortunately, he was "high" and reluctant to kill her. I feel she would have little chance against those talons.

Tuesday 8

The mild winter is having a strange effect on my livestock. Two of my bitches have come in season, only four months after the birth of their litters and my ferrets are going through what can only be called the pre-rut stage with the male dragging the females around the pen, gripping the back of the neck with his teeth. What causes animals to come into season at particular times? Goodall implies that the intensity of

6

light has a lot to do with it, but temperature may well be the all important factor. So much rubbish is written about dog breeding that it would be unwise to hazard a guess. It is sufficient to say that in an unnaturally mild winter, breeding policies go just a little haywire on my premises.

Ferrets are also curious creatures, breeding wise, that is. This year, I do not intend to breed ferrets, for I have more than enough for my own use, but I say that I won't breed them with some reservation. Some jills will literally pine away if not mated and stay in season for months. A few years ago, Arthur Smith brought me a jill ferret in a very bad state of emaciation. It transpired that the jill had come in season in March and had not been mated. I put her in with a young hob who mated her immediately amidst much shrieking and caterwauling. Within a week, she was fit and well again. Graham Welstead of the British Ferreting Society, is collecting data on such occurrences.

Wednesday 9

I really must do some work on the merle factor in lurchers. There has been very little work done on either the merle factor in collies or, I suspect, in the so-called American Leopard dogs, the dappling of which is probably merle colouration. Merles are bred in collies by mating a merle to a sable or tricolour and no ill effects occur. By mating merle to merle, a very different kettle of fish is bred. Whites occur in the resultant litter, all or some of which are blind, deaf and intractable. One breeder of rough collies, a breed

The communal greyhound and her litter of puppies by Merle.

where incredibly beautiful merles are found, says that she has bred dogs without eyes from mating merle to merle. At first, I thought that the white or wall eyes were to blame. However, it is not so. Even merles with dark eyes throw these terrible defects, if mated together. Various types of merles occur. In addition to the ordinary blue merle, sooty merles, brown merles and slate merles occur. All carry these defective qualities if mated together. I hope to breed a strain of long coated merle lurchers from a hybrid between a working border collie and a working bearded collie. The show bearded collies are a bit of a brainless bunch, devoid of herding instinct, and certainly unable to perform the tasks required of a good farm dog. This new breed of hybrid collies is to be bred from my own blue merle bitch border collie, mated to a very good working bearded collie belonging to Mr and Mrs Foster of Pershore. I used one of their show-bred bearded collies to mate to my greyhound to breed a litter of long coated Norfolk type lurchers, and I had excellent results. Very much planning in the future, I'm afraid, if I'm to breed this super-collie strain to get good lurchers of the type I want.

Thursday 10

Yet another amazing evening at the poultry farm. 76 rats killed and a big improvement in my crossbred Patterdale bitch puppy. As yet, she is only a reasonable rat catcher and a very indifferent hunter. Hunting, or the use of nose to detect quarry, comes slowly in conditions where rats are as numerous as here.

Mick and Roger with (left to right) Vampire, Omega, Rollo and Beltane.

A ruck over a rat—a dangerous time during a kill, as many rats bite like fiends, if not instantly killed by shaking. One dog-one rat, is the best method of killing.

Where a dog has to actively seek out rats amongst rubbish, nose work always precedes killing, but here with cascades of rats flowing down from the poultry feed trays, nose work is slowly learned. My Patterdale cross is a non-hunter as yet, but a very rapid striker. Such a dog is a very useful asset to any team, but it is ridiculous to compare her value with that of Beltane, who is not only an excellent killer, but a super hunter. Tales of her ability to sniff out rats in the most unlikely places are legion and would easily fill this entire book.

As expected, my borders are still very slow indeed. As a breed they are not beginner's terriers, nor are they suitable for those who require instant and easy success. I am somewhat heartened to see all three are keen to "rag" the body of a rat but they are very unenthusiastic about the live ones. I've trained smooth fox terriers that were quicker to enter, and I once had a cairn that was a demon of a ratter at seven months old. Borders are just another cup of tea, I'm afraid. It is all the more curious that the dog, who was the dopey clown of the litter, entered to rat at a very early age. Bitches are usually much quicker to enter than dogs.

All in all, an excellent evening except for the fact that when I arrived home, my house had been burgled and £190 taken. Still, I suppose it is to be expected. Some of the hunting fraternity that come to my house are fairly criminal and must know of my Thursday night rat-hunting mania.

Friday 11

Like the poor, mange, I'm afraid, is always with us. I suppose it has to be, considering that my team of dogs hunt both foxes and rats with regularity. A slightly more alarming point is that as soon as my dogs develop mange, I succumb to a bad attack of scabies. It is consoling to know that some skins are more susceptible to scabies than others. Still, it is a real problem with the dogs, particularly as they are constantly getting reinfected practically every week of the year. Treatment, therefore, never eradicates mange in my kennels. It merely keeps it under control. In winter, there is rarely much trouble with this parasite, but summer and the warm and wet weather causes havoc in my kennels. Some dogs are immune to the disease—my border terriers certainly appear to be. Perhaps their oily coat gives some protection against the mite. Still, when a long-coated dog does get a bad dose of mange, the poor devil is in for a hell of a time. Some strains are more susceptible to this disease. A few years ago, I had a rough-coated strain that was very mange prone.

Dips in Lorexane, Gammexane—in fact in any dip that is predominantly gammabenzene hexachloride—are useful, but this is scarcely a panacea. Some of the mange strains are very resistant to Gamma BHC. Some are resistant to the sulphurous chemicals as well, though very little will stand dips in liver of sulphur; a pity it has been withdrawn from the market. Some years ago, a white emulsion called Benzyl Benzoate was used to treat scabies in humans. However, it is rarely used today as it causes massive erythema or reddening of the skin. It works fine with dogs, however, if the mange occurs only in patches. All in all, if I am to really beat mange this year, I must really bomb the infection with everything I can find. It is an expensive malady to cure, but I can at least economise in one respect. My garden is riddled with wireworms and most mangicides will kill wireworms as well as the mange mite. Thus all surplus dog dip material will be watered on the soil.

Saturday 12

This morning, at 1.48 am to be precise, I had the dubious pleasure of running a badger in my beam. I had salted the area at the rear of Stone's farm with vintage dead hens, the sort that attract foxes by the dozen. I am literally amazed how many foxes will come off country to feed on such filth, for I've taken sixty-one on a stretch encompassed by main roads of 5 miles by 6 miles, a patch called by Moses "The Triangle". Why, I don't know for it is in the shape of a trapezium. Geometry, however, aside, it is *the* place for foxes. Last night brought a badger into the area to feed on the putrid hens. We had taken five fox by 1.48 am and my dog Merle was unmarked apart from a few mouth bites. However, on the appearance of the badger, Merle ran in on him and his unmarked condition promised to be remedied in seconds. I've seen so many dogs ruthlessly mangled by badgers—big deerhound blooded beasts, strong enough to hold down a roe buck don't seem to come off very well against badgers—so my collie cross was in for a bad time. I flicked off the beam to bring him in from the fight, but he had collided with the beast before I switched off the light. Merle was more baffled by the fight than the badger as he came back from the battle with two rips below the jaw, tiny rips but enough to convince him badgers are not worth the taking. If I had encouraged him to worry the beast, I feel it would have been another matter, but he is bright enough to realise that certain prey is *verboten*. Really, looks aside, it is impossible to beat the collie lurcher for all round ability. I will certainly never breed any other kind again.

Sunday 13

Vampire killed a large stoat this morning. A pity, as I was simply exercising the dog when the stoat appeared. He had twenty yards to run before he could tree and escape the dog, but Vampire is uncontrollable when he is on quarry. In spite of my shouting, he chopped it maybe a dozen times before he connected and each time the stoat rolled or jerked to escape the *coup de grâce*. As he neared the beech tree at the edge of Cope's, he retaliated and bit the dog. The outcome of the battle was inevitable, a ten ounce stoat is a loser against any dog. Drabble says many dogs are reluctant to kill stoats because of the musk released by angry mustelids. Personally, I have never found this to be the case; my own dogs become maddened by the odour. During the late 1920s, the rabbit population boomed and the predators increased alongside the prey. Thus the early 1930s saw an enormous increase in the stoat population. The New Forest area of Hampshire has always been famous for stoats. Gladdish Hulkes ran a pack of Sealyhams at stoat in the New Forest and a field of very fashionable people turned up to witness the hunt. The onset of myxomatosis saw off the rabbit, however, and the stoat went to the wall. Recently, it looks as though the stoat population is picking up again.

I found two rabbits dying in hedges around the nearby shoot. Both were badly peppered with shot and both so crippled that they could not run. I hate guns and have never considered shooting to be an acceptable form of hunting. For all the bumph published by shooting books about good shots never wounding quarry, I have found countless small beasts wounded by supposedly excellent shots. Crippled beasts and birds abound after every shoot. Furthermore, the sort of person found on many shoots is rarely the sort who lives a symbiotic relationship with the countryside. I always feel as though such gunmen are infringing on my liberties by hunting this land.

Monday 14

I really must get the fox terrier/Jack Russell puppies inoculated. What with the new bug parvovirus becoming common, inoculation will soon be costly. At this moment in time (I think the next few years will be different) most dogs are inoculated against distemper, hardpad, canicola fever, lepospiroid jaundice and hepatitis. Inoculation really is essential if one is to hunt a dog. The spot where I hunt is alive with leptospiral infection that can slay any puppy. At the time of writing, inoculation costs £5 per dog, a considerable sum to pay out if one is inoculating a whole litter, but I feel it is essential expenditure. If one can buy the vaccine and split the ampoule between two puppies, the cost is obviously halved. Actually a whole ampoule is enough for maybe three puppies, as the same dose would be used to inoculate a puppy the size of a Great Dane or an Irish Wolfhound. All the infections

covered by these shots are lethal. I once lost an entire batch of over a hundred puppies by not understanding the havoc distemper can create. Anyway, the old fashioned notion that inoculation is unnecessary is fast dying out, as is the notion that certain nostrums will cure distemper. I am always a bit sceptical about books that state that such and such a herb will cure distemper or even act as a prophylactic measure against the disease. There is a book by a lady called Juliet Baraclalevi that states that various herbs will stave off most infections and that she has taken dogs (so treated) all over the globe without them experiencing any ill effects from the major diseases. All I can say is that I doubt if her dogs would last a month hunting some of the places my own dogs are required to hunt.

Tuesday 15

I must be decidedly criminal deep down inside, for I find the company of folk who practice illegal sports such as dog fighting and cocking quite fascinating. Tonight, I met a particularly wild and woolly bunch from the Black Country, a bunch who specialise in bird trapping. Liming is still used today (for the honest folk who may one day read this diary, liming consists of the trapping of birds using some sticky substance which clogs the feathers of the bird, making it unable to fly) but the most common method is the taking of birds in a mist net or clap netting. This method enables the trapper to sell an unharmed and unstuck bird to the bird fancier. It is highly illegal but it is also much practised in the district in which I teach.

Goldfinches are very marketable, so it seems, and hundreds are trapped yearly, yet the number of goldfinches in the countryside doesn't seem to decrease. Maybe nature produces a surplus to survive the hard seedless winters and the bird trapper is merely trapping this surplus well of finches.

Certainly, dieldrin and aldrin, two chlorinated pesticides that caused Rachel Carson to write her best seller *Silent Spring* nearly pushed the birds to extinction, but more often than not, given a chance and no restriction of habitat, the bird population of a country will soon get back to normal. What causes the extinction of certain species is baffling. Wood pigeons take a dreadful pounding in my district. They are shot, their nests destroyed, their seed poisoned by bird repellents, yet each year sees the wheat fields opposite my house thick with foraging woodies. The now extinct passenger pigeon of America was obviously not made of such stern stuff. A thesis on the Art of Becoming Extinct (I believe Will Cuppy wrote a book about this) would be a very viable scientific project.

Wednesday 16

My phone rang at 5.30 am this morning and as usual it was an irate poultry keeper who had lost some fowl to foxes. From his attitude, it appeared that he almost blamed me for the damage, and literally insisted that I went across immediately and dug out the caitiff. If one is to keep one's fast shrinking hunting country, such odious chores are necessary, so reluctantly I arrived at his farm at 6.05 am—an ungodly hour, believe me—to find about a dozen Cobbs (white table poultry) had been chopped by a fox. Foxes are not the maniacal killers some books make them out to be, but when a poultry killer gets in an ill-constructed poultry house, it panics and chops at any bird within its reach. Actually, a dozen birds killed by a marauder is quite a light loss. I once saw 126 poultry killed by a dog fox.

Anyway, I had the unwanted pleasure of digging out a fox by torch light and to cap it all, the farmer asked me to skin the fox for him to have the pelt as a wall trophy. After this hassle, I went to school—a hell of a start to a hell of a day. Can't win them all, be damned—seemingly, I can't win any, for when I arrived home that night two of my puppies were involved in a frightful struggle and needed treatment.

Vampire and Beltane with a fox that didn't bolt.

For the first time in twenty years, I have not enjoyed tonight's rat hunt. We took 70 plus rats in 2 hours, but the quality of the sport was lacking. Ratting was to be like a military operation, properly and efficiently conducted; and tonight was chaotic. The problem is that the border terriers simply refused to "pack" and drifted off aimlessly while we were ratting a particular shed, disturbing the other sheds and creating bedlam. There is really nothing I can do to stop this havoc and my temper tantrum in the fourth shed caused me to clout a border bitch, thereby putting her back a week or so. It is madness to hit one of these sensitive animals. They suffer greatly from any harsh treatment. Mine hid under the poultry trays for an hour.

The only ray of hope to escape from the bottom of Pandora's rather gloomy box is that one of the border bitches actually grabbed a twitching rat and began to shake it. Once they get to know what ratting is all about, they will be eager to get in the sheds and will be more than eager to pack. Time alone will help, I think. The dog is a pleasure to hunt and as eager a border as I have ever seen.

Tonight, I saw a senile old doe rat in the late stages of decline, a suppurating eye, a damaged, kinked, scabrous tail and mange-ridden coat. Usually, such does are given a clear berth by the rest of the colony as not only must they appear hideous even to their own kind, but their menopausal rages when approached by a young and virile buck have to be seen to be believed. Twigg has observed that such does tantalise youngsters into approaching them and then slay the youngster with a carotid bite. Seemingly, the female of the species is not only more deadly than the male, but a senile female is deadliest of all. Sufficient to say Vampire saw off this scabrous horror with a single bite.

Friday 18

A letter concerning my most recent book *Nathan* arrived this morning, from a chap in Peterborough. He claims that he has some of the original pit fighting dogs, undiluted by the show-bred Staffordshire bull terriers. Certainly some of the real old fighting dogs were hellers. In the district where I teach, some of the old men can still remember the organised and clandestine contests that took place between the wars. Dog fighting is a loathesome practice, but it has an almost magnetic appeal to some. Funnily enough, "to the death" contests were rare even in the golden days of dog fighting—that is circa 1835. Most of the contests ended with one of the dogs quite simply quitting cold and refusing to cross the scratch line to attack their opponent.

America still has its fair share of pit fighting dogs— if the word "fair" is appropriate when applied to dog fighting. Here, a bigger, more athletic dog than our Staffordshire bull terrier is fought, and the American pit bull terrier is a real demon of a fighter. The dog used in the production of *The Yearling* last seen over Christmas 1979, was a pit bull terrier and I have no doubt the shots of the dog attacking Old Slewfoot the bear, were accurate and the dog certainly did fight that bear. Pit bull crosses are useful seizing or fixing dogs for boar and bear hunters. One was sold for £550 last year and was nigh on a legend in the Bayou country where it was hunted. It resembled a hybrid between a labrador and a bull terrier.

Saturday 19

A hard, bitingly cold and fruitless night, but what is worse a step backwards for Merle, my collie/greyhound lurcher. Not only did I lamp a fox feeding near Lees midden pile, but through my own stupidity, I missed him and Merle came crashing down on a patch of frozen snow, cracking a rib, I think. What is worse is that he is running foxes by scent now and not looking down the beam. This is saddening, for a dog used for lamping must not run nose down, but watch the corridor of light created by the beam. It is a very hard thing to break such a habit, and what with the damage done to his rib cage, he may be *hors de combat* for several days. I touched his ribs shortly after the fall and he screamed, snapping at me, smashing my thumb nail. However, by noon he was allowing the puppies to play havoc with him and did not seem to worry about their rough play. Perhaps he is just winded or bruised by the fall. A pity if he is hurt, as a high wind is building up, and it will be perfect for lamping tomorrow.

The mound of dog bedding and faeces is getting out of hand. Originally, I intended to compost this turd but the quantity doesn't seem to shrink. It is probably very illegal to have such a pile of rotting mess for it must be filled with round worm and tape worm eggs. I shall buy a compost accelerator to speed up the rotting process. Such a chemical gives the bacteria extra nitrogen, enabling them to multiply and break down the heap into useful fertilizer. I doubt if the eggs within the heap are affected by the process, however, and my vegetable crop must be a haven of all things parasitic. Last year, I grew a good bean crop in fox carcasses. Steiner, who was the forerunner of organic cultivation methods, would have been horrified by my methods and so would any reasonable and sensible person, I fear. I shall water my potato crop with old mange dip this year. It should keep away the wire-worms that infest my land, eating every damn thing I grow.

Sunday 20

What a strange crowd of people attend my house. Today, a slightly dubious character turned up at my house and asked if I sold *cocking spurs*. To the public at large, I must appear the raving lunatic, red in tooth and claw. Actually, there is a revival of cock fighting in Britain at the time of writing, and certain strains of game fowl are bred specifically for fighting. The Oxford Club breed only show cocks, but most will fight and are often stolen by itinerants, who quite openly fight game birds on their sites.

In the Philippines, they stage the Philipino Slasher Derby which is well attended by Americans, Chinese and Malays. Here, English or Irish type spurs are rarely used, but the birds are fitted with a superb piece of nastiness called a *golok*. This foot spur is shaped like a sword and cocking mains are still fought in the British Asian communities and *goloks* used. The *golok* is quite simply a sword strapped to the foot of the cock. In spite of my interest in the sport (a tongue in cheek term), may I repeat. *I do not sell spurs.*

Monday 21

One of my fox terrier hybrids is a bit dopey as a result of the inoculation. Actually, the symptoms resemble those of distemper. The inoculate used is quite simply freeze dried distemper virus, a very much weakened bug admittedly, but a live virus nevertheless. Leptospiral jaundice vaccine is a dead vaccine, possibly due to the virulence of any live germs of this type. Anyway, I've never had a puppy die as a result of inoculation and I've no doubt the dog will be hale and hearty by Tuesday.

Omega is in season yet again, and a damned nuisance it is. Nearly every bitch of that family is plagued with phantom pregnancies. Bitches invariably swell up as if they are pregnant, even if they do not come in contact with a dog. They also develop a small quantity of milk. Mastitis is not uncommon when these phantom pregnancies occur. Furthermore, bitches that are unmated come in season three and four times a year. Most are obsessed with puppies, but Beltane will kill any puppies belonging to other bitches. Keeping a family of terriers has its advantages, as one knows the various strengths of the strain. One also gets to know its weaknesses as well. Before I brought in outcrosses, this strain was riddled with cleft palate and water on the brain. Thank God this has been bred out, but now phantom pregnancy is the order of the day, I'm afraid. All strains have their problems; a man is a liar if he says any different.

Tuesday 22

Paul Taylor of Melton Mowbray came visiting with his litter of border collie/greyhound puppies. They really are super. The dam is a trial bred border collie bitch sired by Alan Jones' dog and the sire an open race greyhound dog. This is the only real lurcher as far as I'm concerned. They are totally trainable and very versatile. The deer hound hybrid gives any cross a super coat and a majestic appearance but they are non-starters as far as brains are concerned. For the life of me, I can't understand why the collie cross is not more popular.

I am contemplating a book on rather ragged self-sufficiency. This year I will snare and plant my garden with a variety of food plants. It is easily possible to live on one acre of land, providing one crops it properly. Beans are an ideal crop, as not only do they give a superabundant meal but they are easily salted down for the winter. The country is still in a state where a man might get most of his food from it. Self-sufficiency is the current beatnik "in thing", possibly because of the influence of the programme *The Good Life*. Good life it is not, however, for self sufficiency is usually the polite way of saying "stark penury". I've tried it, and I know. During my eighteen months off the land, I suffered greatly from stomach troubles and my weight fell rapidly. After a while, the human body adjusts to such privations and my health was quite extraordinary during the last months of my ordeal. Perhaps man is courting disaster with his artificial way of life. I doubt if Thoreau or Rousseau would have survived long roughing it, but I've a bit more about me than a fine weather intellectual. Anyway, let's see how I fare. I've obtained a lot of free sweet jars from the shops and I'm all set for the winter of 1980 on salted French beans. Actually, I believe a man could survive on a bean or leguminous diet.

Wednesday 23

The idea of self-sufficiency becomes more appealing by the day. God, I am fed up with teaching, and odds are I will opt out yet again, this time for good. I am a good, if not great, hunter, so survival will offer no real problems. Also my life is becoming far too materialistic. If I had four ducks, a few doe rabbits, I could make it without aid. Hell, it will be hard but I can't take much more of the crap teaching that passes off as education today. With a tight belt, my royalties from books, I can make it.

A grim struggle broke out among the fox terrier/Russell hybrids—a very bad "three way" fight involving the three males. Such fights, I feel, are a result of the litter reaching an age when they are approaching independence and among wild dogs such battles among the striplings would result in: (a) the formation of some sort of social hierarchy such as is found in wolves, or (b) the splitting up of the litters as is found among solitary creatures such as foxes. Thus, when such fighting breaks out among puppies kept in close confinement, the result of such tensions is either a very cowed individual or, worse still, a dead one, for escape from an aggressor is impossible in kennels. I know several misguided people who do not split up an aggressive litter and finish up burying a few of them.

My ferrets are close to season. The young hob is causing a great deal of chuntering in the pens. Usually, this chuntering starts about a month before the ferrets come in season, and is caused by the hobs seizing the back of the jills' necks and going through the act of serving them. A young hob with "ambitions" can badly mangle a jill.

Thursday 24

A very unsatisfactory night's hunting. One of the children of the owners of the poultry farm shot the pens just before our arrival. Subsequently, we caught a half dozen or so rats. All in all, what is generally considered to be a disaster. Roger had better luck hunting rats around the back of the building with lamp and Bedlington/whippet lurcher. This is quite an efficient form of winter ratting, as the undergrowth is low and the dog has space to catch the escaping rats. It is also top-class training for a lamping lurcher.

Early this evening, the phone rang and on answering it, I discovered it was a ferreting enthusiast from Aberystwyth. This gentleman, a Mr Bolton, remarked that several wild polecats have been caught around his area. I believe these to be feral ferrets, ferrets that have escaped and lived in the wild, but Mr Bolton assures me that research carried out by a local zoologist has confirmed that these are the real McCoy. I have always considered the real polecat to be extinct in Britain, but again, I could be wrong. To prove his point, he offered to send me a specimen, preferably alive. This again, would do no more than confuse things, as I would be unable to tell a wild polecat from a meat-fed polecat ferret. Drabble says the skulls are identical and I have no doubt he is correct. Certainly, the fur of the wild polecat is identical with the fur of the ferret.

Friday 25

A gourmet's delight, or is it? Roger and Mike tasted the delights of eating a fox. What is it that Wilde said, so exactly, "the unspeakable in pursuit of the uneatable". Verily, he was accurate. In spite of the fact that the meat was soaked in several lots of hot salty water, it still tasted like very musky beef. Perhaps the quality of the meat improves if the carcass is hung like game. I don't know, nor do I wish to try. The musky meat must be considered edible by some; and the Chinese regard the meat as not only edible, but a great delicacy. I sell quite a few fox cadavers to the Chinese and they pay me £8 for the adult skinned fox. They almost certainly eat them themselves, and do not, as many jokes suggest, serve them in their restaurants. They do not seek to remove the musk, but tend to enjoy it. Ah

well, it takes all sorts, and what with the market in fox furs now down to zero, and pelts fetching a mere £4 as opposed to the £20 they fetched last year, a sale of fox carcasses is most welcome. It is a pity about the fickle fur trade; the weather is very cold and the pelts are in first class condition. The hunts will be delighted, I'm sure, for they have suffered very badly from hunters such as I. This year I have (to date) taken more fox than the combined Quorn, Meynell, Atherstone and Pytchley. My book *The Complete Lurcher* was condemned for its chapter on fox catching. Presumably, it is more sporting to allow the hounds to dismember a carcass than to allow a hunter to sell the skin! A curious world, I fear. Today's haul makes my total 70, using only Merle.

Saturday 26

Arrangements have been made to hunt Paul's railway embankment tomorrow. Ferreting and, with luck, some fox work will be on the cards. Paul Taylor is a railway worker and one of the perks of such a job is the fact that railway workers can get the ferreting rights on the railway embankments. Such banks are havens for rabbits, and providing one doesn't have to dig (digging is illegal on the railway embankments) then the land is usually a first rate place for rabbits and foxes alike. Digging is obviously out of the question as few of the railway officials wish to see the 8.32 disappear into the unback-filled lair of some fox; yet I have seen immense excavations left by fox diggers, excavations that could have caused enormous damage.

A slight mange outbreak is troubling the dogs of Don Scott, a greyhound breeder who lives near me. I am not a vet, but most folk imagine (wrongly) that I am a whizz kid on skin infections. This mange is, I believe, follicular mange, though it is impossible to determine which parasite is causing the damage, without a skin scraping. Follicular mange is incurable and flares up in times of stress. A few years ago, a back-to-nature cult came up with the notion that such illnesses could be cured by whole carcass feeding. It certainly worked with follicular mange. I fed a whole carcass (hen bodies) diet to an infected bitch and recovery was very rapid.

Sunday 27

Ferreted Melton Mowbray railway station with Paul Taylor—a good spot alongside some allotments and a river bank the side of which was undermined with rats—the allotment holders keep ducks so I suppose rats are a compulsory extra. Most of the allotment holders were adamant that swarms of rabbits were attacking the crops, but exaggeration regarding numbers of rodents and lagomorphs is a human failing. Still, there were some easy spots to work amongst the piles of building rubbish that litters such stations. There were no swarms of rabbits, however, and we succeeded in catching two and, sadly, killing one in an undiggable warren. Fudge stuck to it for an

hour and I feared a lie-up. A jill that has worked several seasons, as has Fudge, soon gets used to despatching rabbit quickly, thereby preventing it bolting. Furthermore, lie-ups are more common when one uses an older jill, possibly because an older jill is more possessive over her kill, or maybe quite simply, because an older jill gets more tired. As I expected, rats also lived in the warrens and my young jill ferret received a rip in the neck from one. In some warrens, particularly on rubbish dumps, rabbits and rats seem to live together fairly amicably, though I wonder what happens when a doe rat gets as carnivorous as pregnant does are wont to do. I saw 240 ducklings savaged to death by a doe with a need for flesh, and I have no doubt she would find a nest of rabbits particularly inviting. Still, many warrens often hold a population of rats as well as rabbits. In spite of a poor haul, we enjoyed the day and Peter Easter learned to "net".

Monday 28

What is happening to the standard of the Jack Russell terriers of this country? Tonight, a gorgeous looking woman brought an advanced register bitch for Warlock to serve. She began the phone conversation that preceded the mating, with the somewhat ambiguous comment, "Do *you* mate Jack Russell bitches?" I confessed I did not, no matter what stories to the contrary are circulating at the time of writing. The bitch had a load of defects; not only was she out on the leg, too long in the back, but her mouth was also defective, a slightly crowded mouth, but enough when coupled with the other defects to prevent it from being classed as prime breeding stock. This Advanced Register needs careful pruning if it is to be successful in creating a better type of Jack Russell terrier. What would be better, would be the liberal use of only certain registered stud dogs carefully vetted by a committee of experts, not just used on the chance opinion of an individual. In two generations, the breed could improve rapidly. The licenced boar scheme used by post-war pig breeders greatly improved the stock of pigs in Britain; and a similar scheme would quickly put the Jack Russell Club to rights. Still, while pet breeders buy a bitch to mate to their Pepe, I see little hope of any improvement, and a decided decline in the working ability of the breed. I don't think I'm pessimistic about this, either.

Tuesday 29

A phone call today from ATV—a producer hoping to do a piece of documentary research on rats—easy to say, difficult to do. Anyone with rats in number will hardly be keen on "beam in number 4 camera" type teams on their premises. Furthermore, it is impossible to live catch and hunt terriers with union regulation camera teams. The book *Tales of a Rat Hunting Man* may not be a best seller, but boy, has it had some publicity!

Keith Ruston's photographs of breaking some terrier puppies to ferret have arrived and they really are super, the sort of thing that appeals to women's magazines, providing that is, that they did not realise why I was breaking the puppies to ferret. Actually, I break the terrier puppies as soon as they are eight weeks old or less, and judging from the startled faces of the puppies in Keith's photographs, the terriers are easily bested by an adult ferret. I really miss the mean old ferret that died last year. In spite of his great age, (he was thirteen years old when he died) and his broken and brown teeth, he would very quickly put a young puppy in its place. Using the ferret was a pleasure, and I had only one failure, a bitch called Climber, who time and time again was bitten by him, and just as frequently retaliated. Even as a twelve week old puppy, she would take fearsome punishment from a ferret, and still come back for more. I have little use for psychopaths of this nature, as I hunt poultry farms and need dogs to be rock steady with fowl. I often wonder whether the people who boast uncontrollable killers ever hunt their terriers.

Wednesday 30

I arose early this morning to a bout of vomiting—either the fox meat late last night did not go with the liquorice allsorts, or I am letting school really get me down. Anyway, I did not go to school today, my first day off for two and a half years.

I have a horrid feeling that Merle has served Omega. Such incongruous matings sometimes happen even in the best run of establishments and mine is scarcely the best run. Last year, one of my collies served a border terrier bitch through the wires and with little or no effort she produced two puppies, one a merle bitch. Merle is not a good stud dog, however, and has mated only one bitch (Fathom) to date, but it is the forbidden bitches that stud dogs mate. Funnily enough, and contrary to most dog breeding books, bitches whelping as a result of a misalliance from mating a very large dog do not usually experience a great deal of trouble in parturition. It's curious, actually, that many ill informed people bring a bitch (terrier) for mating and ask for it to be put to a very small dog, not to breed a tiny terrier as might be expected, but because they believe the bitch will whelp more easily. Another fallacy is that a dog that has a reputation for siring small litters is better to use than a dog who sires good sized litters. A large litter of puppies is far more likely to lend itself to an easy birth as each foetus is usually smaller as it has a correspondingly smaller quantity of food and space—small foetus, easier birth is the way these things work.

I had an interview tonight with two chaps from ITV. They want rat shots for *England Their England*, a show concerned with the esoteric world of various harmless lunatics—am I to be complimented by such an appraisal of my qualities! Anyway, the producer is keen on my work *Rat Hunting Man*—a good job really, as I rate it as one of my best. He is coming tomorrow with the object of filming or rather to explore the chances of filming. The poultry farm will test his mettle.

My border dog "slices" a rat. This method of catching is extremely efficient.

A superb rat hunt, the excitement of which was unmarred by the border terriers—we didn't take them. Our TV director is very keen to film our exploits, but in the gloom and humid atmosphere of the poultry sheds, it will be very difficult. Our haul of over a hundred is just about average but the style of the hunt made it spectacular. Beltane marked twenty-odd rats in crevices and filth that would defy the average terrier. I hope just one of her puppies has the makings of their mother. The black and tan Patterdale/Russell bitch is getting to be quite a hunter, waiting near the exit holes and killing the rats as they try to escape. She netted thirty rats using this method, quite a haul for a babe, but she has little nose, and a fiirst class rat hunter is useless without nose. She is a curious fat-bodied frail-boned bitch, who may well be my next brood. Mated to Vampire, she will breed some cracking puppies, I'm sure—¼ black and tan, ½ tan, ½ Russell type.

I shall keep only the Russell type bitches; maybe only one per litter will be bitches of the type I shall want, but it is a mistake to have too many terriers. I have work for eight and no more.

Tonight, I had an offer of a retired greyhound bitch, a bitch of three years of age and damaged. She came into season a week or so ago and may be ready by Sunday. However, even if I try mating her to Merle she may not stand. Greyhounds are difficult to mate and many bitches need surgery before a dog can serve them. This bitch, sired by Patricia's Hope will be ideal for Merle if he will mate her (and if she will stand) The resulting litter—¼ collie, ¾ greyhound—will be ideal for all purposes. I shall let Sarah Daly whelp her, as my kennels are plagued by tinkers.

February

Friday 1

I must whitewash the kennels with a mange-repellent mix—it is a fairly easy suspension to make and, though an old method, is still by far the best. I whitewash with this mix each year and I believe it is the main reason mange doesn't decimate my stock.

> 1 ounce of size boiled in 2 gallons water
> 8 lbs slaked lime stirred into the size
> and water mix until it is a creamy paste
> ½ bottle of bleach mixed into the paste.

This mix will kill all known bugs and bacteria alike and release enough chlorine to slay anything injurious to the dogs for at least six months. Furthermore, it is very cheap to make and easy to apply. Mange mites may become resistant to BHC, but no organism known to man can survive bleach treatment.

I can no longer doubt that Merle served Omega yesterday, so a visit to the vet is the only way to prevent a monstrous lurcher/Jack Russell terrier litter. He injected her with stilboestrol which ills any fertilized ova. The bitch is usually a little under the weather for a few days and comes into season again some three weeks later. I've never known this injection to fail if the bitch is injected within forty-eight hours of the mating—the question is, of course, has Merle served Omega before this?

Saturday 2

Two deer hunters visited me today on the way north. Deer poaching is on the increase in the Midlands and the South. Fallow deer are not all that difficult to take as most are kept in parks. Thus, the taking of these deer in a restricted habitat provides little trouble for lurchers trained to the lamp. The sentences for deer hunters or poachers (call them what you will) are staggering. A local deer poacher received 18 months for taking deer in Altingham Park. Fallow are large beasts and fetch a fair price from game shops that aren't too fussy about where they get their meat. One of the deer hunters said that he received £200 for a red deer he had taken in the Berwyn Mountains. His dogs (some very greyhoundy lurchers) were frightfully scarred and torn, partly through damage done by antler tines and partly because they had been dragged through barbed wire by a stag on to which they had latched. Deer poaching will be the necessary lever the anti-blood-sport fraternity will need to topple field sports. Deer poaching is not only illegal, it is damnably cruel and the sight of disembowelled deer dying puts any decent person's back up.

Merle fought Vampire today. At first, I thought Vampire could do him damage, but Merle turned and pinned him like he does with a fox, securing the terrier with a throat bite. My respect for the collie lurcher grows by the day. No more useful lurcher exists. Vampire is a ferocious fighter and though Merle is over six times his weight, Vampire continues to take the fight to the bigger dog. The outcome of the fight would be all too obvious, for Merle would have had to kill Vampire—a feat of which he is easily capable, as Vampire weighs only 12 lbs.

A particularly good day's ferreting, though our haul was very light. A TV director called Norman Hull came with us and found the hushed whispers of the hunters gave the scene atmosphere. Actually, we'd have had a better haul if there had been total silence. Ferreting should be the most silent of sports if it is to be successful. A rabbit is unlikely to bolt if he finds that above ground things are more terrifying than the ferret.

Roger's small lurcher coursed the rabbits and caught one—both runs were filmed by Keith Ruston.

Fudge, my best ferret bolted each and every rabbit and as soon as they were extracted from the nets, she worked the next rabbit. Such a jill is a treasure, for many will just refuse to work a warren if the particular rabbit they were at, bolted. Fudge simply waits for the rabbit to be killed and goes back into the warren for the next. It takes years to make such a hunter and it baffles me to see the spate of adverts offering well-trained ferrets, lurchers and terriers for sale. Anyone who has a good hunting dog or ferret is reluctant to sell it.

Ben, Roger Parsons's Bedlington Whippet hybrid.

Monday 4

My greyhound bitch stood for mating, and by the most surprising chance, Merle mated het easily, trying for nearly half an hour. The tie position of mating is baffling. There seems to be no biological reason for the incongruous looking act. If anything, such a ridiculous posture makes them very vulnerable to attack, though I have never seen a dog attack another "tied" male. It would be most unpleasant if one did, I'm sure. I shall mate her every day until she refuses to stand. One mating may well be enough, but several matings ensure conception and also trains a stud dog. There is a great disparity between the heights of the two. Merle is 23 inches and the bitch is over 26 inches high. Thus a mating between the two involved Merle standing on a three inch layer of straw. At first, I feared he was impotent as he displayed no interest in bitches, whereas Terry's collie/greyhound cross, a dog only two weeks older than Merle is very eager to mate and has sired four litters to my knowledge. I am pleased that Merle is becoming such a superb stud dog; an indifferent stud dog is a great nuisance. He has already made Fathom pregnant and I might well breed a merle puppy from that mating.

Tuesday 5

If Fathom has conceived on the first mating to Merle, the pups should be born today, but I'm in favour of not counting the first tie of any dog or bitch. He mated her twice and it is my calculation she will whelp on 10th February, rather than today. Once again, the greyhound stood for mating and once again Merle mated her. Everything seems to be either whelping or conceiving. The Jacksons' bitch whelped eight puppies tonight; their sire is Warlock. I'm not happy about this litter, for the bitch is low in hunting instinct, though she is a lovely type of terrier. Sooner or later, the breed will cease to produce good workers. I feel it is inevitable. I believe it is only a matter of time before the Jack Russell becomes yet another lap dog. The Kennel Club is blamed for ruining many breeds but it's the breeders who can decide if a particular animal is good enough to perpetuate a blood line. The Kennel Club itself has nothing to do with the decline of a working breed.

Wednesday 6

Beltane is really looking old these days. I really must mate her again to keep puppies of value to add to my pack. A suitable sire is hard to find, for I must stay clear of the registered Jack Russell terriers, I feel. I could put her to one of Hinchcliffe's Patterdale dogs, for I've bred some cracking little workers from his strain mated to my own. A more likely stud to use is Phelan's black Patterdale dog. This dog works with the Woodland Pytchley and is reputed to be a cracker. Phelan didn't breed him, but bought him from Didricksen, who says the strain dates back to the dogs of Joe Bowman, who ran his terriers with the Ullswater. Quite a few of the Lakeland packs kept these small black or red smooth coated terriers, though nothing is said of them in Lucas' *Hunt and Working Terriers*. Phelan's dog Poker, bred by Nuttall at Holmes Chapel, Cheshire, has a good reputation as a worker and is not too big. Perhaps some of his blood would suit my pack down to the ground. If he has nose. I'll use him, but Beltane should breed nose aplenty in her pups. I never had such a bitch. What a tragedy such beasts get old!

Thursday 7

An excellent night's hunting again. The Patterdale crosses are making incredible rat killers; just the right size, just the right amount of commonsense. A dog needs to be no more than 10½ inches to get under the battery pens. It's a great sport if the dogs are tiny and very game, but the dog that is too big, as most of the

Dog fox killed during blizzard conditions. Merle broke his ribs taking this one.

show terriers are, will be hard put to rat under these conditions. Pagan, my Patterdale/Russell bitch is a cracker and will take some beating when she is older. She caught her first rat at 4½ months— a mistake that could have ruined her, for no puppy with milk teeth should be called on to face a fully grown rat. Some might kill the rat, others, most others, will be over-matched by such a beast. I am now certain that I shall mate Beltane to Phelan's Patterdale and maybe to Hinchcliffe's, if she comes in season again. I've never gone much for breed purity—if dogs are useful, I keep them; if not, no matter how blue blooded they are, I part with them. A good night—100 plus rats taken. Twenty-six were caught in an open, empty shed. A superb night's hunting—it's a pity Mick Kirby could not come. His dog Toby is improving dramatically.

Friday 8

I went to the Woodland Pytchley to see Phelan's dog and after much searching, we found the place. Phelan is terrier man for the Pytchley and keeps a neat team of black and rusty coloured Patterdale dogs and bitches. All are descended from Didricksen's dogs, which were bred by Nuttall and all are about 11 inches high. I liked the heads, really bull terrierish, and the jaws were very strongly made. Most are frightfully scarred as are many working terriers. All in all, a really nice type of terrier, neatly kept and free from mange and other symptoms of neglect. Both the sire and dam of his stud were worked, one with the Hampshire Hunt, the other with Mr Goshen's Hunt—such a pedigree is worth including in my bloodline. As Lucas says, the only worthwhile pedigree is a working pedigree. The pups from this dog and Beltane or Pagan should be superb, but should be and are, are frequently two different words. Still, if he covers Beltane, the pups stand a fair chance of being good.

Found a badger digging in my old potato bed at dawn, this morning. He was doing no damage but the dogs were kicking up hell at the intrusion. Every year, the badgers of Brough's Earths forage further afield. Is food becoming scarce, or is it due to the fact that the earths are overpopulated and the badgers have to encompass a greater feeding circle?

Fell terriers of different types. The farside terrier is one of Buck's fiery dogs, while the nearside terrier is one of Bray's famous strain.

Saturday 9

I'm unable to train my eagle owl and my dogs so I've lent the owl to Bob Green to fool with. Actually, in spite of its fearsome manner, the bird is quite easy to handle. He bites or pecks more in stupidity than out of spite. Bob fetched him today and will probably get him ready to enter to quarry fairly quickly. An owl is a curious type of bird to train and for all those awful talons, they seem to be unable to take large prey. I would be very doubtful if this small male could take hold and kill a very ordinary wild rabbit, yet falconers make such extravagant claims about their birds.

The greyhound refused to stand for mating today and snapped at Merle as he tried to serve her. She is still passing a bloody brown discharge which makes me wonder if she will conceive. Greyhound seasons are erratic affairs. Some bitches take three years to come into season while others are fairly orthodox. I knew of one greyhound bitch who came into season after she was retired (4 years plus, I suppose) and stood for mating for only one day each season. Yet she bred over a hundred puppies during her spell of breeding. With luck, I shall have a pregnant greyhound and with even greater luck, a litter of ¾ bred collie/greyhounds some of which will be merle—this is a project that has taken three years to come to fruition.

At 7.40 am Sarah phoned to say that Fathom had whelped eight puppies, seven assorted brindles and one evenly marked merle. This might be a cracking mating, for Fathom is fast, nimble and has a good nose, while Merle has an IQ near to canine genius. On the other hand Fathom is such a hotch potch of breeds—a mongrel with a liberal sprinkling of greyhound would describe her accurately—that who knows what the pair will throw. A puppy having the qualities of both parents will be an incredibly good bet—an all round hunter and a fairly good catcher of hares. Fathom's sire was one of Bodger Quimby's strain and all these were superb hare catchers, while her mother Penguin had bred some excellent hare coursing dogs. I shall wait and see.

Paul's young jill ferret is becoming quite a useful worker. I lent him Fudge and he tended to use the veteran rather than her great-granddaughter. This is a mistake, though I confess it is one I have made myself. If I have a superb hunting dog or ferret, I tend to use it to the exclusion of all others. Hence, when this hunter dies, it leaves a huge gap in my hunting team.

I really must get my terriers and lurchers tattooed. The dog stealing racket is quite a thing around here. Don, a good coursing man and friend of Granville Madox, has had his best lurcher stolen only a few weeks ago. The thieves simply drove up, snatched the dog and drove off. Granville had his pregnant bitch

Welsh hound puppies—these were originally bred to hunt wolves.

stolen and the thieves whelped her, kept the best of the pups and returned the matron and two inferior type pups to Granville. Even if I breed merle lurchers and these are uncommon and unpopular, there is no guarantee my stock will stay unscathed. Tattooing on the inside of the legs and ears helps, but I've heard of itinerants who cut the ears off tattooed lurchers after they have stolen them. Merle colouring and tattooing and a good security system may just about do it. Tattoos are a bit expensive, but hardly as expensive as losing the dogs. I will contact a fellow called Tony Lynx and get the team tattooed.

Alan Thomas intends to "walk" some Welsh hounds this year—a curious breed only slightly related to their English Foxhound counterpart. Welsh hounds were originally used and bred to hunt wolf, and are considerably noisier than the English hounds. Dermot Kelly, Master of the Meynell Foxhounds, used them for breeding. Some curious-looking animals were bred in the first generations and Kelly took these to Peterborough Show where they aroused mixed opinions. Welsh hounds, like Welsh springer spaniels, are regarded as more intractable than the English counterparts, though a pack in full cry makes up for their intractable nature, perhaps.

Tuesday 12

My fox terrier hybrids look really good. A few weeks ago, they looked as if they were going to be out on the leg and a bit ugly, but now all the knuckle has grown out of them. I like the matched pair of dogs but the small bitch has a very poor head. Beltanne has bred an awful lot of bad heads which is curious as her litter mates have massive heads. The strain is now very inbred, so I suppose it is necessary to outcross the last litter to either Patterdale or fox terrier blood. I really must correct these shocking heads and start keeping very typey terriers.

One of my terriers is very fur bound, the trouble being caused by feeding unskinned sheep's heads. It is not a very serious business in working terriers, though it can cause hell when it troubles toy breeds. Likewise, I feed whole hens and whole rabbits to my terriers. I believe a healthy, strong working dog can cope with small bones without damage. Toy breeds and some of the more elegant so-called working breeds die from ingesting small, sharp bones. Cooked bones are harder and may cause touble, but I've known lurchers on gypsy sites who ate only cooked bones and remained healthy. Fresh green bones (bones uncooked) are rich in protein. Wright's *Book of Poultry* states they have the same protein value as beef.

Wednesday 13

ATV is going ahead with the programme on me. It is called *The Hunter* and I hope I measure up. The programme is concerned with fox, badger, rabbit and rat hunting. Filming will be a nightmare but that won't be my concern. What is the famous show biz quote— "Never work with kids or animals"? Wild animals must be a very bad bet. A huge rat has moved into my hedgerow and is digging in. Fudge is really being missed now (she is still with Paul). The doe has drawn bedding for a nest so it will be one hell of a ferret that will face a doe like this. My young jills would certainly face her and suffer in consequence, for ferrets are madcap creatures when young. The doe must go, however, as a pregnant doe will breed a mountain of rats in a year. The stoats living opposite the house will keep clear of a doe like this and, short of a cat or a fox, no predator will trouble her.

Fortunately, there are other methods of dealing with rats, though. I am reluctant to use poison and the soil is too porous to flood out. I'll possibly suffocate the litter and doe with sulphur poisoning, burning flowers of sulphur in the hole and blocking the sundry exits.

Thursday 14

Not a good night's ratting owing to three factors;-

(a) the youth who hunted with us disturbed the feeding pattern
(b) Roger and I are just not up to handling eight or nine dogs
(c) We are mistiming our arrival and the main bulk of the colony is feeding earlier or later—it is difficult to tell which.

I hand-caught a young buck to show Norman Hull, the TV director and was bitten for my troubles. The bite, a slight nick will almost certainly fester and go wrong. I have cleaned the bite with Dettol and soaked my hand in water, but I feel it will do little good. Live catching is stupid and I think it will be the death of me, if I continue.

Another sliced kill and another bad bite.

Friday 15

A slight fever this morning shivering and a feeling of intense cold—psychosomatic or rat bite fever? Hell, I should be immune to the latter and I'm not suggestible enough for the former.

I have just inoculated my lurcher bitch, a result of mating Tony Ahearne's collie/greyhound dog to Bob McIver's greyhound. The puppy is bright and decidedly greyhoundy. This cross, or series of crosses, takes some beating as an all-round courser and usually has a fair nose as well. She is already fairly well broken to ferret, but has yet to see a rabbit. She will be a treasure as a brood bitch when she is ready, and will certainly see a fair amount of coursing by the time she breeds a litter. My greyhound bitch is fairly certain to be in whelp to Merle so unless I'm careful I may be overrun with lurchers. The whole team will be merle eventually and all will be smooth coated. I've promised Norman Hull I will give him a long coated Merle lurcher. Let's hope I can breed it. It should be easy to do so if Moses mates his bearded collie/grey-hound bitch to Merle.

Saturday 16

A super hunt in the grove nearby and the end of my hedgerow rat. Beltane marked the doe in the warren and dug and killed her. She really is my best-ever hunter and her fox terrier cross puppies will all take after her, I hope. Each one joined in the worry after Mama killed.

The evening produced a good hunt in the grove near my house with all the pups and Beltane running and baying like hounds. One rabbit taken possibly by the pups, but mother killed it. Still, they are what I want. The pity is that they are so bloody noisy. They are certainly the noisiest litter I have ever bred. Each one is hunting like a veteran and all seem eager to kill. Would that I could say the same of my border terriers! They are almost dormant and seem lifeless when out hunting. The bitch Vixen, attacked a young jill ferret this morning, so, perhaps, they are beginning to wake up. Still, a ferret is not a rat, and these borders are fairly indifferent about rats. With luck they'll be entered to fox and badger by Christmas 1980, but heck, they are making heavy weather out of their work.

Beltane, matron of my terrier team, and a superb hunter.

28

Sunday 17

For the first time I have seen a Harris hawk fly quarry. I know little of this type of Accipiter except that it is famed for its fractious temper and its ability to foot innocent bystanders. Although it is slightly smaller than a goshawk it is able to make up its size difference by its superior intelligence—though hawks are near the bottom of the rung in avian intelligence. Against my better judgment, I bolted a rabbit with my young polecat jill and Jeffrey Lloyd flung off his Harris hawk at the fleeing bunny. The take off speed was elec-trifying and unlike the goshawk, it seemed to anticipate the jinking of the bunny. The rabbit ran through a thicket and instead of plunging in in the usual goshawk manner, the Harris hawk rose and footed the rabbit as it bolted from the thicket. I doubt if I've seen a better flight. Story has it that some austringers actually fly a few Harris hawks in train at hare and they never crab as goshawks would do. I really must get to know more about this hawk.

Monday 18

I feel I shall soon get to know the first symptoms of kennel cough. Two of my terriers are wheezing just a little and this is usually the symptom of kennel cough. There is little known about this unpleasant complaint, and there seems to be no cure. Some hunt kennels use inhalants like Friar's Balsam but I feel it does little good. The complaint must run its cycle and the dog must develop its own cure. The complaint is fairly weakening and I've seen dogs look almost emaciated after a bad attack. I've never seen a dog die of this puzzling illness but Charlie Lewis, once huntsman for the Atherstone Hunt tells me that he knew of a man who had a terrier die of kennel cough. I'm of the impression that the cause is a tiny fungus that infects the throat tissues, but my vet believes several organisms can cause this peculiar illness.

Tuesday 19

I am not up to the awful restrictions a TV programme will impose and I am becoming increasingly irritable with the director. It is foolish to think that a man who is not a hunter is able to understand a man who is basically a bit primitive. I find he is asking far too much of my time, my dogs and my fellow hunters. A hunter is a peculiar type of creature much given to solitude if he is a true predator. I am becoming increasingly reclusive and dislike people imposing on my privacy. I think that an even more solitary cottage is to my liking. Phone calls are all too common and visitors all too frequent.

The ferrets are not quite right. I think they will certainly be too light by next week. I like ferrets to be a bit fat in the early spring as the harrassment from my hobs tends to prevent them from eating when they are in season. I shall not breed from my jills this year, as I have no work for an enormous crop of ferrets. Apart from a professional warrener, few people need more than three ferrets. Three ferrets will work all day and every day. A rat hunter needs many ferrets, however, as the duration of a ratting jill's life is short. Fudge is five now and still eager to rat, which makes my previous statement a bit questionable.

Wednesday 20

A hunter has gone to Uist, an island off the coast of Scotland, where there is a rabbit plague. I'm a bit chary about the statement 'a plague', but his wife phoned and enquired as to where she could sell 2,100 rabbits, so perhaps a 'plague' did occur. As soon as they become immune to myxomatosis, we can expect similar conditions here. Undoubtedly, some farmers had good reason to want to introduce myxomatosis into their districts, but it's a hellish death. I first saw a myxied rabbit when I was hitch-hiking through Oxfordshire. The poor devil sat on the pavement and seemed impervious or indifferent to the bustle of the traffic. Later, I came to regard such wretches as food during my desperate winter of 1962–1963 and I suffered no ill effects from eating the myxied rabbits. It played hell when the disease hit Shropshire. I picked up 104 rabbits in a day around Buildwas woods. I've never found a hare with this disease.

Two cats of the nearby farm are down with feline infectious enteritis. No cure—just death, I'm afraid.

Some people believe that parvo virus, a disease that kills dogs is just a form of feline infectious enteritis. Fifteen dogs in the Leicester area have died through this illness in the last few days. I think man has meddled with viruses too frequently and will reap the reward for playing at God.

Thursday 21

I found a few strands of Esparto grass covered with bird lime in the grove this morning, so I gather the bird trappers are working my district again. Finches fetch quite a lot these days, so there is an incentive for illegal trappers to chance their luck. I've never seen so many bullfinches as this year, and the rewards for bird trapping will evidently be good. Good bullfinches fetch £8 a pair on the black market and are easily sold. When I came here, 12 years ago, the area was famous for goldfinches, but the Walsall bird trappers soon reduced the number to practically nil. They are increasing again now though, as there are thistles aplenty around here.

A superb night's ratting with a haul in excess of 200. Never have my team worked better, though kennel cough has broken out in the border terriers. Mick's Patterdale hybrid is really hunting well and catching better than I imagined. I shall breed another litter of Russell cross hybrids by mating Beltane to a dog from Hinchcliffe's stock. I should really use the puppy from Alan's dog Hamish and Omega and try to keep the line pure, but the Patterdale hybrids work so well. I will also send Omega to mate to Phelan's dog.

Mick Kirby's Toby (Patterdale × Russell), brother of Pagan and an exellent hunter.

Friday 22

I found a wounded badger this morning near to Barlow's midden pile, no doubt drawn in by the heat of the dung. Who, in the name of God, would want to shoot a badger? The back leg was all but shot away and the wound was very gangrenous. I hate amateur huntsmen with a gun and a few hours to spare. Anything that moves is fair game to such people. Sadly, I felt that I had to kill the poor devil. A blow on the snout saw off the beast, but the badger is certainly having a bad time around here. I've seen four dead in three months. Not even Brough's Earths, reputedly the biggest in the country, can cope with such a death rate. The gangrenous badger was a sow near to time, I judge, for her womb contained a perfectly formed cub. I reared a cub a few years ago, but never again. It damned nigh destroyed my cottage and became so unpredictable that I had to turn him loose. I found him dead, victim of a road accident, a few weeks later. Badgers turned loose indiscriminately rarely survive. When the badgers around here are finally exterminated by shooting, they will be hard to reintroduce.

Saturday 23

I've cancelled my TV show. I'm just not up to it. I cannot work with a camera team and a director. A pity, but it is so, I'm afraid. I shall let Paul Jackson have my jills to breed as I can't do several litters justice, and I hate to watch young ferrets die off through neglect. My team is up to strength now my merle lurcher from Fathom is ready to join my team. With luck, the greyhound will whelp a litter with a merle puppy. With such a team, I can live off the country for some time. The collie cross is what I really need. I shall experiment with collie hybrids until I get what I want. I shan't have long to wait until I breed what I want, either. Fathom, Penguin and co. will certainly breed me 'nose' into my team, and Merle has brains and guts. A greyhound cross will give speed every few generations. It is early to tell if my greyhound is in whelp to Merle, but he mated her four times, so it is likely.

Sunday 24

What is wrong with me? I am becoming a physical wreck. I need to take to the wild again to regain my old health and vigour, I think. A few weeks of hunting and a natural life will put me right again. I think I shall breed rabbits to keep me in meat this winter. The trouble is that I lived on the damned things in 1968 so I'm a bit sick of them, but I think a spell of self-sufficiency would put me right healthwise. I'm rarely well since I forsook a natural way of life. Three ducks, a quarter of an acre of cultivated land and I'd be able to live off the land, I reckon. Ducks lay a damn sight better than hens, but eat more. However, there is ample forage for the ducks around here, for the land is insect ridden. Ducks will get a good third of their diet from insects, slugs and so on. I'd need to eradicate the rats, however, for ducks are able to draw rats for miles. Furthermore, I've seen rats eat ducklings alive. I'm getting far too damned civilised. I have all I need: land, meat and vegetables and freedom. I need little more except physical health and peace of mind. Ten years ago, I walked the three miles from Lichfield each day carrying up to 1 cwt of dog food on my back. I was fit, well and able to cope with any illness. Look at me now. The three miles looks formidable and I go down with minor diseases all too readily.

Monday 25

I shall buy 12 ducklings as soon as the weather gets warmer. I can easily keep such a number and they lay an egg a day under good conditions and I'd have eggs enough for the dogs and me. They will also feed on any waste meat or meal left by the dogs. Beltane marked numerous rats along the hedgerow so I really must poison them. Ours are not immune to warfarin so it won't be difficult. Rats are a hell of a liability around the place; disease follows them and they are so carnivorous that it is impossible to rear small livestock when they are around.

I've planted a row of broad beans. I'll mulch the land with rotting dog bedding—sounds unpleasant but it rots down to serviceable dung. I've never had trouble with manure made by this vile smelling mess. It's difficult to store these beans so I'll glut myself with them. Pheasants from the nearby shoot play hell with the beans as soon as they begin to sprout, but this year the birds have paid dearly for their appetites. Four years ago, nine pheasants were snared by placing hangs near the bean rows. I feel little shame about killing such pheasants even though the breeding season is almost on us. Likewise, I can appreciate the mediaeval farmer/peasant who killed boars and stags when they raided his fields. I can never understand the rights and wrongs of killing game that is invading my property—at least, I can never bring myself not to feel a warm glow of contentment when I catch such pheasants. Basically, man is a dishonest devil, for no matter what the law says about the catching of such creatures on one's property, it is still simply theft.

Thursday 26

I bought some garlic bulbs today. Not that I like or eat garlic, but story has it that it is readily eaten by the dogs. Garlic is still used as a remedy for tapeworms—I can understand the tapeworm's antipathy to the substance, but still, there are many who swear by this pungent bulb. Garlic was often prescribed for dogs suffering from leptospirosis and hepatitis. It is certainly a diuretic, increasing the flow of urine dramatically. Tom Evans used it for dogs suffering from a pulmonary disorder after distemper or some other complaint that can lead to infections of the lung. Joe Bowman, the old Ullswater huntsman and terrier man, used to bathe infected fox bites in a solution of garlic bulbs boiled in water and he apparently cured some ghastly wounds with this antiseptic solution.

I'm not too happy about the fox that hangs around the end of my garden. He or she (it is difficult to tell from a distance) is always there yet, I keep no edible livestock. Chances are he is simply after the rats that live in the bank near the old brook, for foxes eat quite a lot of rats. Foxes I've kept and fed on rats even eat the tails, a rarity believe me, for apart from owls, hawks and herons, few animals will eat the gristly tail of a rat. But the fox will have to go as soon as I buy ducks.

Wednesday 27

Work on parvo virus is essential. Pedigree Dog Foods have published the results of their survey and terrifying results they are. Heart failure slays the majority of affected puppies and severe gastro-enteritis affects adults. Inoculation with cat feline infectious enteritis vaccine is fairly effective, but it will be very costly. Cat vaccination costs £7 and add another £6–£7 for the distemper shot and an expensive puppy. What in hell will happen to dogs next, in the line of new diseases?

An interview with a brilliant little girl from Radio Stoke. The interview (on dog fighting) is about my new book *Nathan* and is to be sold to Radio 4. With luck it will boost book sales. The RSPCA is to be invited to comment on the book and on dog fighting in general. Personally, I like the book and consider it's the best thing I've ever done. There is considerable antipathy to it in the shows, however, and some stalls refuse to stock it—or any of my books for that matter— for among some of the sporting fraternity, my books (and myself as well, I fear) are considered as being "not nice".

Thursday 28

A poor night's ratting—no excuses, we just didn't do well. The timing was bad, the bitches are in season and the dogs are off colour. We took sixty rats and should have taken 700. Some days are like that. The border terrier bitches are as slow as slow. I've known poodles who would do better than these borders. The red bitch is in season. Perhaps it might be good policy to put her up and get her mated. After she has reared a litter she might be better, but I have my doubts. The dog puppy is superb but the bitches are pathetic. Some bitches that are allowed to rear a litter suddenly galvanise into action. I feel it is a last shot for these; the bitches look askance as the rats pass them by. They are just not interested. One lunged for a ferret last night and I felt elated at the enthusiasm—I would surely shoot a Jack Russell of my strain that was as indifferent as these borders. Let us hope my Russell/fox terrier crosses will be more enthusiastic. How can I possibly justify breeding from these useless borders? Some of the puppies may go to working homes and the result of such misplacing would be traumatic to both puppy and owner. No. I shall let them go another season before breeding from them.

Friday 29

Mr Stone phoned and asked me to dock his puppies for him. Some eleven weeks ago, he brought his bitch to be mated to Vampire. I have rarely mated such a bitch. She savaged Vampire badly and drew blood on me some seven times. She whelped easily though, but sadly Stone left his puppies too late to dock. I shudder to think about docking puppies at two weeks old—the blood and screaming would terrify me. Docking is a pointless and cruel gesture at the best of times and serves no useful purpose. Originally, it was to stop dogs running deer and other quarry and then after that, a dog with a tail was subject to a tax. Now it is simply a fad to see dogs with shortened tails. Sooner or later, tail docking will be banned and there is no reason for anyone to protest when docking is abolished. What a hell of a hypocrite I am—I still dock tails and do nothing to stop this ridiculous cruel practice!

March

Saturday 1

I've loaned all my ferrets to the Jacksons, the net-makers of Reading. Breeding ferrets really is a chore if one is to rear the litters properly. The mortality rate in kits can be ghastly. I've lost many litters of ferrets through E. coli and botulism. Deaths occur at four weeks old and the jills nearly always consume the dead young. I've too many beasts on the premises now and with luck will have a good crop of yearly jills to try out when autumn 1980 comes. This autumn we'll really hunt the rabbits on Paul's railway embankment. Properly worked, the place will yield a great quantity of rabbits at the end of the year. A good hob from Fudge is needed next year. Paul will rear her litter and will keep a big, aggressive liner back from the litter. Fudge is a devil with her young: I've never seen a jill that is as ferocious when she has babies with her. I'm hoping to keep six actively employed jills next year, and with luck, that will be enough. With two dogs to mark the earth, we should find 1981 a really lucrative year.

The law concerning hunting on railway embankments is a curious one. It is one of the few places where a person can be prosecuted merely for trespass.

Sunday 2

My collie/greyhound/greyhound puppy is really superb. Not only is she bright (Terry's dog, her sire is one of the brightest lurchers I've ever seen) but her upbringing with terriers has made her a veritable demon. She will pitch into a fight at a minute's notice. This bitch mated to Merle will breed some terrific puppies. The greyhound bitch is in whelp to Merle. I'd be curious to see the end product. Merle is certainly the gamest, most intelligent lurcher I've ever seen and with extra greyhound dash, we should produce the really fast, intelligent type of lurcher—lurchers of this breeding should be able to take rabbit, hare, fox and even the forbidden deer. I shall not whelp her. Mick Kirby will do this instead of Sarah and if there are any merle puppies in the litter, they are mine. I shall keep nothing but merle puppies from now on. They are so distinctive, that only fools would steal them.

Monday 3

I have reinoculated the fox terrier/Russell puppies with leptospirosis vaccine. I can't be too careful, for I hunt rat far too regularly.

Vampire mated another Patterdale/Jack Russell cross today. I bred two litters to Hinchcliffe's dogs and all are absolute crackers. I've no complaints with any of them. Of the ten puppies the Patterdale male bred to my bitches, all have been absolute demons at work. All have superb noses and all are dynamite at rats. Mating this type of cross bred terrier to Vampire breeds half Patterdale coloured pups and half Jack Russell type—or at least *my* type. I've a stud puppy coming from Mr Miller's bitch and Vampire. If I take a Russell coloured puppy, I shall watch out for head weaknesses. I must get rid of these pathetic little heads in my strain, even if they have to be nearly all Patterdale bred puppies. Unless I get rid of these puny little jaws, my strain is doomed. One method of getting better heads would be mating Hinchcliffe's stud to Beltane producing all browns; two brother and sister

Beige on the morning of her first hare.

matings to give one Russell, two mongrels, one pure bred Patterdale from the mating. This one Russell mated to Phelan's would produce two blacks which mated together would give one Russell, two crosses, and one pure Patterdale. This pup would be ¾ bred Patterdale, but would be pure breeding Jack Russell. It might be what I want:

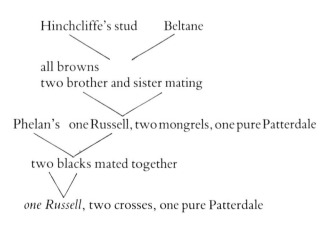

Hinchcliffe's stud   Beltane

all browns
two brother and sister mating

Phelan's   one Russell, two mongrels, one pure Patterdale

two blacks mated together

one Russell, two crosses, one pure Patterdale

★The pup would be ¾ bred Patterdale but would be pure breeding Jack Russell It might be what I want.

35

Tuesday 4

It will be the year of the rabbit, of that I have no doubt. Even this early in March, diminutive pellets, the result of the first ingestion of greens by baby rabbits, are appearing on the grove. The mild winter has not slain off too many rabbits and breeding has continued through the year. Furthermore, no sign of myxomatosis has appeared among the rabbits; perhaps the Uist type rabbit plague will be seen here. Are the rabbits around here immune to this infection or has the motorway provided a natural barrier against migration and the spread of the disease? Ten years ago, I brought in fifty-two mixed bucks and does to repopulate the rabbit-denuded land around my cottage. For the first five years, it was an uphill struggle for them for foxes, disease and worst of all, the inevitable quasi-hunters, the shotgun brigade, thinned them out wickedly. Now at last, I think they will make a comeback.

Wednesday 5

It is easy to see why the sporting fraternity despise the killing of fox with a lurcher and lamp. Last night, I witnessed an incredibly savage battle between Merle and an old dog fox. We lit up the field behind my cottage in the blinding sleet and illuminated a large fox feeding on the offal I had left in the middle of the field. Merle came out of the darkness into the beam and struck the old devil, badly bowling but not pinning the fox. It rolled almost into the darkness, its eyes out of the beam to remain invisible. Merle received a very bad nip and opened up on the fox. Again, he struck it, shaking it like a rat in a jaw to jaw hold, but he seemed to get the worst of the encounter and when I arrived at the fight, I found Merle holding down the fox, but his tongue had been ripped badly by the bite the fox had put in, in the jaw to jaw encounter. The fox was old the skin tatty and mangy and worth £2.50 at the most and the damge he did to Merle will cost the earth to repair. What a callous, brutal person I have become! I do not need this mangy skin, I cannot think of a reason to justify my killing of the old devil, and Merle will be out of action for a while from the wound.

Thursday 6

Yet another good night. The border dog is killing well but as yet, the bitches have not woken up. It is a little disheartening to say the least. Every time I consider getting rid of the bitches, my pride intervenes. I have never had a dog fail and I do not intend these to be the first. Still they watch the rats race past them—one even hid under the largest border bitch that was crouching in the corner. Even for border terriers, these are slow starters.

A letter from Arie van de Berg of Dutch Radio, an authority on rats whose book *Rats, Mice and Men*—a compendium of curious rodent tales and collections of legends—is to be published in Britain this year. I met Arie last year and also the announcer producer Phillipe Scheltema, an amazingly versatile and erudite pair. How strange that the Continentals are so expert in the use of English. Both made me feel very inarticulate indeed.

Friday 7

A good hunt and some bad wounds. We took five foxes, three dogs and two vixens this week, using Merle and Merle only. In spite of his lack of speed, he is a superb fox killer. I have never owned a better—nor, at the risk of sounding conceited, have I seen his equal. He will allow a fox to come to ten feet away from him (I call them in by dint of a rabbit call) before he puts in his try for them. He is almost beside himself with excitement as they slink in towards him, but he is stock steady and silent as the grave. In his present torn and damaged condition, he needs rest and plenty of it. We have already killed 72 foxes with him, though Penguin did most of the work early in the season. Indeed, while Penguin was here, Merle would not join in the rag on a fox. At first, I though that he was afraid of the fox, but after Penguin became pregnant and went to Moses, Merle came to life. He has never killed a fox. I don't want the skins damaged as I sell pelts, but his skill at pinning them is terrific.

Saturday 8

Phoned John Winch of Consett. He wants me to do a book on Fell terriers. It seems a good idea, as this generation will see the last of the old Fell hunters. Buck is quite old, over sixty I believe, and most of the Irving family are getting on a bit. Records and accurate records need to be compiled now if these men are not to pass into extinction unrecorded. Buck certainly needs to go on record. He is nearly a legend in the north of Yorkshire. Newcombe, a controversial figure by any standards, is also worth placing in a book of this sort. Such a book needs to be packed with photographs—more photographs than writing if it is to be of any value. If my publisher is not interested in such a book, I might well finance it—another mortgage on my house? Even if such a book weighs in at a financial loss—and well it might—it must be written. Perhaps I am not the best qualified to write such an epic, but the apathy of many Northern terrier men will guarantee such a book is *not* written.

Sunday 9

I will no longer ridicule any form of hunting. Today a man from Pattingham visited the house and gave us a demonstration with a blow gun. Before his arrival, the lads who haunt my cottage were in the usual fun-making mood with impersonations of Jivaro Indians and shrunken heads jokes. We all expected Harpur to be a lunatic with a strange device, and I must admit I shared their suspicion about him. We are so used to falconers' tales (fishermans' tales with feathers) that we automatically assume anyone who uses an unusual technique is a phoney. Surprise, surprise! Firstly, to own a blow gun, one apparently needs a firearm certificate and after meeting Harpur, I can see why. His blow gun is simply an eight foot length of highly polished copper piping, verdigrised on the outside but mirror polished on the inside. His darts—no, they weren't poisoned—were simply darning needles embedded in a wad of cotton wool. The accuracy of this weapon and also the power is astounding. At twenty-five feet, he fired his dart into a door and I had to use pliers to extract the dart. Harpur claims, and I now believe him, to be able to knock down woodpigeons and even rabbits with this strange weapon. He states that in September he killed a fully grown doe hare with it. It must have been a fairly painful death and I can still picture a hare squealing with a darning needle embedded in its viscera. Harpur is paying us a visit on May 11th to demonstrate the gun properly.

Monday 10

I see the albino badger from Brough's earth is dead. I found his body on the road at dawn this morning. I imagine that he had been hit by a car—for too many people use these lonely roads as a race track. I must have seen his ponderous ginger shape a hundred times in the last year or so—in fact, Penguin bowled him near the grove in November. Sparrow, in his *Terrier's Vocation* indicated that these albinos are rare but this is far from true. When I dug badger regularly, I caught several. In fact, Brockley's artificial earths in Etwall housed dozens over a period of years.

The last of my old dog San's children died today, the end of a useful, valiant but mute blood line. They were ugly, not particularly bright and prone to mange, but they were the toughest terriers I have ever seen in my life. I have trained Fells, bull terrier hybrids and pure bred Lakelands, but the terriers from Hardwick of Blaengarw beat them all for raw courage. My obsession with creating my own strain of terrier allowed me to let the strain become extinct—or nearly so. Vampire and Beltane are distant relations of the old warrior.

Tuesday 11

Killed a large dog fox this morning, bolted it with Beltane and caught it up in the fox net given me by the Jacksons of Reading. The fox hit the net with a smack, thrashed slightly and then remained still, paralysed into a fit-like state. Such fits serve a purpose. They are not the result of a beast pretending to be dead, but they are genuine states of catalepsy. Frequently, foxes come out of the fit quickly, and hightail it off before the startled hunter can realise what is happening. This one did not, for I killed it quickly. The skin is quite good for a March caught male and there are few bites and tears in the pelt. Normally, males duel quite a lot during February, and the skins bear the marks of these battles.

Skin prices have varied a lot this year. Primes in December fetched £25, in fact, one pelt, a bright fawn colour, was sold for £30, but after Christmas these fabulous prices dropped to £5 or even less. I can honestly see the fox becoming extinct if this over-hunting continues. I am as much to blame as anyone, for I have harried them mercilessly this year. If skin prices continue to rise, I can see the "hunts" running a drag instead of live quarry.

Wednesday 12

A busy day or rather, evening breaking my puppies to cat—an essential task as the farm where I rat each Thursday is thick with cats. I can never understand the idiots who allow their terriers to kill cats. The rewards are invariably a blinded dog and an owner who is unwelcome at a farm. Personally, I like cats—I had a

I am proud of this photograph. It was taken during the heat of a rat hunt yet the dogs ignored the cat.

super Siamese once and he was a charmer. The current vogue among terrier men is to proclaim that they are anti-cat and to set their dogs on cats as soon as they see them. Hence I never allow a dog from another owner or trainer to rat at our favourite pitch. I've had idiots with lunatic dogs run pitches for me before, but never again, I promise.

Thursday 13

Terry Ahearne has purchased the Baraclalevi book on herbal remedies for dogs, an interesting book, but very unscientific. Obviously, some herbal remedies are bound to work—herbalism is, of course, the father of modern medicine, but it is foolish and very dangerous to assume herbs have miracle properties that can cure various incurable diseases. Certain herbs are worthwhile, however, and there has been a marked increase in herbal remedies sold in shops. Herbal worming remedies are favourites, but they are not as mild as some people believe. Some, such as Areca nut and Chenopodium can cause bitches to

Sarah phoned tonight and reported that the merle puppy is going to be rough-coated. Personally, I doubt it. Fathom is smooth coated and Merle must be described as an open coated smooth. Still, she is rearing the litter, so she should know. It is a variable litter colourwise. Some are silver brindle, some are black and one is merle.

abort and both knock a dog about quite a lot. I've nothing against herbal remedies, but I think science rather than herbalism is important in conditioning a dog. Having said that, I must confess that I feed whole carcasses of hens to my dogs, so I do believe in natural methods of conditioning.

A hard, cold night that produced a record haul of rats. We took over 400, a good night for March. A lad called Paul Coffey joined our team tonight. He is about thirty and learns the trade very quickly. He has excellent potential as a hunter—probably greater than I had at that age.

An odd and difficult catch.

Friday 14

A kill for my beige lurcher puppy—a drummer, an early bred rabbit but snapped up and retrieved in a trice. She is fast, able and more than willing, a credit to her breeding. As yet, she corners badly, turning and overshooting more often than not, but she is already able to strike at a passing rabbit like an adder. Moses saw the incident. Drab sap (adder) Moses calls this bitch, a Romany name but a surprisingly apt one. She is still very frail and whippety but I am certain she will fill out before Lambourn, when all those who bought one of Bob's puppies have decided to meet. Tony Ahearne's bitch, the sister of Beige, is a gamer animal but not so elegant and graceful, while the puppy Bob McIver kept back is not as lightly built as either, but he is a powerhouse of muscle. Whippety lurchers are usually very fast, but lack stamina.

Whittaker of Bridgnorth came today with a tale that he has seen a black fox. Actually, I doubt if it is black—though Whittaker is a reliable chap. Chances are it is overthick with black guard hairs and that gives the running fox an all black look.

Saturday 15

Yet another north country (Cumberland) lunatic who believes it is unnecessary to inoculate his dogs—boy, is he in for a surprise! It is a common belief among the dwellers of the far north that the dogs, men and horses of the north are a breed apart, rock hard and totally immune to disease. In fact, one of our team says that it is believed by all northerners that every male south of York has been gelded.

A big vixen has taken up residence in Cope's embankment and will have to be moved. This area is a fox corridor and has always been famous for the number of foxes that have bred here. Now that the hunt has ceased to work this land because of the numerous main roads, foxes are very numerous. This one will have to go. I see her most nights in the beam as I exercise my lurchers, but she is always too near the embankment to kill with a lurcher. It is almost a dead certainty she is in cub and that her mate is dug in close by. The bottom has fallen out of the pelt market. I was offered £5 per pelt for this last week's catch. It will soon be not worth hunting foxes if the prices continue to fall.

Sunday 16

Doug Cooper of CTF, a sporting equipment specialist, visited me today and arrived as I was skinning two foxes that I took last night, one of which is a small pale dog fox that beat me hollow last December when Merle had just started work at fox. It's funny, but after one has hunted an area for two or more years, one gets to know every fox in that district. To return to Doug Cooper. Doug has a useful nondescript lurcher called Dylan, a 21 inch dog with pluck to spare. Doug has taken a load of fox with this dog, which is not common for a 21 inch dog will rarely tackle quarry as big as a fox. Doug's dog does, however, and single handed at that—a considerable feat for a tiny dog. More interesting still, is a woolly-coated Norfolk-type lurcher bred by Mick Douglas, a famous Fen man. This dog is not particularly fast but it has incredible stamina and can run all night at rabbit or hare. What is in this strain—and strain it is for these lurchers breed damn nigh true—is a bit questionable. Doug tells me Mick used a Marsh type collie as the starting point, crossing it once with a greyhound, and then mating the progeny to any first-class dog that was winning at Best of Five hare coursing meets. Interesting; I must phone Mick.

Monday 17

Took both dog and vixen on Cope's embankment, bolted with Beltane and taken by (a) a net from the Jackson's of Reading and (b) by Merle when the dog followed closely behind the vixen and she slipped the nets. A ragged nasty fight continued until I half rolled down the railway embankment and finished the dog.

40

A bad bite for Merle, one right through the tongue again, but he is still very game, gamer than I am, in fact. I am 43 next birthday and getting very tired of these before school hunts. Twelve years ago, I rejoiced at going out at dawn and hunting up until school time. Now I am very tired by 4 pm. I can see too many winters of this nature taking a savage toll on my health. By the end of the season (please God let it be soon!) I will have killed roughly 90 fox (or thereabouts) but the task has exhausted me. I no longer take any pleasure in digging foxes and find little fun in lamping them in blinding sleet as I did last night. Roger hopes to hunt fox next winter with Ben. I wish him luck. This year is exhausting me.

Tuesday 18

Warner has invited me to his mink farm again—it's one of the highlights of my year so of course I intend to go, if only to see the various mutations in mink. The big money is in pastel shades of mink and whites, but prime quality standards also fetch a good price. White mink are usually deaf—though there are some strains with normal hearing, so I believe. This causes a bit of a breeding problem as the females can't hear the distress cries of the kits, and hence mortality is extremely high in pure-bred litters. Warner is a genetics addict so he mates the standards to whites and keeps the hybrids which are, incidentally, standard (dark brown coloured) as standard is a dominant colour. By dint of mating two hybrids together, he gets ¼ white i.e.

Standard × White
(SS) (WW)

Standard × Standard
(SW) (SW)

Standard Standard Standard White
(SS) (SW) (SW) (WW)

and hence the problem of litter deaths is reduced.

Wednesday 19

To my discredit, Merle killed a vixen this morning. She was heavy in milk and very slow. Somewhere, a litter of fox cubs are starving to death. I must find them and deal with them. I must also stop hunting foxes until the breeding season is over. I always feel a sense of shame when I kill even a suckling doe rat. I once went eleven days without eating—not a pleasant thing, so the prospect of a litter of any creatures starving to death is a bit terrifying to say the least. They will almost certainly be in the embankment near Cope's farm, but the trouble is it will be too late to hunt for the earth when I get home from work.

A chap came for a book signing today—fame at last, Brian me boy—a fairly uninteresting "can I look at your dogs" type of chap, but one who claimed he kept a six month old carcass of a horse fresh by whitewashing it and hanging it on a tree. A bit macabre but Juliet Baraclalevi says she has also kept meat fresh using this method. The thought of vintage horse is a bit terrifying.

Thursday 20

Fudge, my best ferret, is in season. Now here's a schizoid little beast if ever there was one. She is the tamest ferret and extremely docile even when small children pull her about. When she has kits in the nest, it is a different matter. She is frantically possessive and protective over her kits, and attacks whenever her kits are as much as looked at. I have bred kits from Fudge in a communal breeding project, but it was a disaster. Not only was she preoccupied with dragging her kits back into the nest, but she even took to dragging other adult jills into her nesting compartment. Furthermore, she carries her babies around so often that she damages them and in two litters, she has only reared three kits. A shame, as she is a remorseless hunter and one of the best ferrets I have ever owned. She is the daughter of my old sandy jill, as docile a creature as was ever born, but an absolute coward when facing rats. Fudge is a different prospect. She is a tigress to rat and will even face a doe who has drawn bedding to make a nest. Curiously, she has never been badly bitten, which accounts for her persistent enthusiasm for rat hunting. At five years of age, she is still hunting rat with enthusiasm but at her first beating she will probably quit. Ferrets invariably do.

Friday 21

Hunted late into the morning and returned home at 4.31 am. A brilliant night's ratting—undoubtedly the best feeding time for rats is 1.30 am, but few of the team of men will hunt all night. One does need to be a fanatic to make a first class rat hunter. Tonight, we took over 300 rats—a huge number of rats for a cold wet evening and early morning. My team are on top form, hunting and catching as good as any I've ever seen. One fly in the ointment: the bites on my terriers look ghastly. This morning I found Beltane scarcely able to stand and totally unable to see. Vampire's face is swollen until he looks like a Staffordshire bull terrier. Omega alone is totally unmarked. What on earth allows this bitch to kill so many rats and emerge unscarred? Perhaps the fact that she stays out of the scrimmage ensures that she receives only a few nips. She is undoubtedly the greatest rat killer I have ever seen—even better than San, my old dog, her ancestor. She lacks nose, however, the prime quality for a great rat-hunting dog. Perhaps she is a useful hunter, but she simply allows other terriers to hunt for her.

Saturday 22

A visit from Paul Taylor with his puppy—an interesting hybrid between a blue pied greyhound and my blue merle collie bitch. Like a lot of first crosses between collie and greyhound, the puppy is quite heavy, but I've seen heavier dogs take hare. Speed is certainly not always equated with a light, racy build. Paul's puppy is well trained; in fact, it would be a fool who could not train such a hybrid. It would not have been my choice of puppy, for there was a rather spectacular bitch puppy in the litter, but it is a wise man who can actually pick out the best puppy. In a litter of puppies, it is sometimes best to keep the puppy who blends with one's personality. For instance, I am a boisterous extrovert, so quiet, nervous puppies must suffer hell with me, yet they suit some people. Anyway, Paul has asked me to start Fleet, as he calls the puppy, on the lamp. It is usually easier to start a puppy in the lamp than by daylight, not because rabbits are slower by night or because they are dazzled by the beam, but simply because rabbits feed further out from the warrens at night time and it is easier to approach the feeding rabbits when it is a dark, gusty night. One the debit side, it is doubtful if a puppy finds it easier to pick up a bobbing, weaving bunny by lamp light. Anyway, I shall start Paul's puppy in September or October.

Sunday 23

An interesting question concerning stamina has arisen. In spite of Fathom's lightning bursts of speed and her ability to snap up fleeing quarry from unbelievable positions, she is very deficient as far as stamina goes. Her mother, Penguin, is a powerhouse of stamina, and her father, Burke, was also able to run for hours. Fathom, however, is exhausted after a hard run, though she puts everything into that run. Perhaps her greyhound/whippet shape does not make for a stamina-packed dog or maybe her enormous efforts would exhaust any dog. Salukis are even more fragile but they run for ever simply because they do not put in the awful taxing effort of the greyhound. Certainly, a heavier type of dog seems to outlast a fragile one, and perhaps David's lament over Saul should read "from the blood of the slain, from the flesh (not fat) of the mighty"; for there seems to be a rough correlation between muscle and stamina in a running dog. Still, do I require a powerhouse of a dog for my type of hunting? Is a stamina-packed slower dog a good bet at snatching rabbits and pheasants from cover and stalking feeding hares with catlike stealth? Maybe Fathom's children, sired as they are by Merle, a very heavy dog, will be better prospects.

Monday 24

Watched Thomas Hancock set drop hang snares for rats. These snares are attached to tall poles and pegged in the ground so that the pole is bent double. A rat touches the snare and immediately it is entangled, the stick jerks to a vertical position lifting the rat skywards. It is a fairly nasty type of death and I have seen rats so trapped alive and kicking hours after their capture. Few animals die quickly in snares, no matter how well they are set, and the RSPCA would do well to start a movement to ban the use of snares. The method is a highly effective way of catching rats, but it is damnably cruel. Hugh Whyte, a Jamaican boy in the sixth form has used this method to trap mongoose (or is it mongeese?) near Montego Bay. The mongoose was introduced into Jamaica to reduce the rat population. It did, but it became a pest, eating chickens and reducing the native fauna of Jamaica. All man has to do is to meddle with animal or bird introductions and all hell breaks loose. Some of the Jamaican farmers in the interior regard the mongoose as a delicacy—at least that is what Hugh Whyte says; a mongoose is a relative of the ferret, so that the flesh is likely to be a bit pungent, to say the least.

Tuesday 25

A visit from Walter Clat, the Romany catapult expert. I met him at Appleby several years ago and now he has decided to pay me a visit. Moses says his name is not Clat, but Ingram, for Romanies give certain people nicknames just as the Welsh do. Clat is obviously a corruption of catapult. He is certainly a good shot, but I must admit I've seen better. A great number of skills are attributed to the Romanies, and some books credit them with superhuman abilities at dog training and hunting. Frankly, it is bunkum. I have never seen a Romany trained lurcher that is worthwhile, and never encountered a Romany who was a skilled dog trainer. Brian Vesey Fitzgerald in his book *It's My Delight* writes of Romany dog experts like Arrigho, but I have met several of this family and am not impressed by the skill of these dog men. Furthermore, the Romany lurchers are not the true-breeding strains that are supposed to haunt the camps. The dogs I have seen, and I know many Romanies, are no different from a hundred *Exchange and Mart* type lurchers. Yet one never goes to a lurcher show without meeting a host of people who boast a dog that is Romany bred.

Wednesday 26

Borrowed Jack Legge's hob ferret—a good worker and extremely tame. He has already mated four jills this year. Is this a bit much for so early in the season? Is there a maximum number of jills that a hob should be allowed to mate? He seems in good fettle, in excellent health and very eager to mate every jill I have. The hob is a superb liner and has helped Jack Legge take over 700 rabbits in 1979. I'm not all that confident that these working strains of ferret are any better than pet-shop bought ferrets, but tameness seems to be inherited. I'd breed from an unworked jill or hob providing they were tame, but I'd never consider breeding from a ferret that was wild or ferocious. Terry is breeding from just such a hob, a fiery tempered brute that had run wild. Personally, I think he is just asking for trouble. I can see no possible reason for keeping a savage ferret. My own are all as tame as kittens; and the old wives' tale about a ferret that bites a hand will also bite rabbits doesn't hold good. My tamest ferrets have all been my best workers. Jack Legge's mated to Fudge should produce some super kits—let's hope she takes.

Some of Jack Legge's ferrets. I use this strain for outcross.

Thursday 27

Gary Hudson, my copy editor, came and returned the manuscript for *Lepus*, tidied up with my hideous mistakes corrected. A copy editor's life is not a happy one—not my copy editor at least, for I make numerous errors. After handing me my copy, edited, corrected and what have you, he asked to join the rat hunt, but even though I felt churlish about the business, I had to turn him down. A team of rat hunters working efficiently must not exceed a certain number and we were fielding a full complement that night. Actually, he missed little for owing to mistiming (due to Gary's visit, I must admit) and bad weather conditions that caused a sudden drop in temperature, we had a poor haul and settled for only sixty-odd rats in the entire evening. Timing is all important in a hunt and any mistakes are rewarded with poor hauls. Still, poor hauls usually make for spectacular sport, for each catch is clearly seen. Few rats are caught in the open in this weather, for although rats originate from the temperate zones, they are reluctant to feed in cool pens if they can find a warm food-filled room. Ancient bucks, pariahs of the band, outcasts because of their senility, usually feed alone and unloved (thank God) in such cool places, and it is here giants are caught, for an old buck can be quite a weight.

My research into the life of Joe Bowman, the almost legendary huntsman for the Ullswater hounds, has just begun. There is a biography of this man, out of print admittedly, and difficult to get as it would have been a very limited print. Bowman was an incredible character, as are many of the northern huntsmen, and the stories of some of his famous hunts are still related in the Lakes.

Bowman bred and worked a strain of red fell terrier, a game and elegant strain of dog if all the accounts are true. Many believe that this strain of terrier gave rise to the border terrier, but this seems unlikely. Not only do many fell hunters still boast that their strain of Lakeland/Fell (the words are interchangeable) are descended from Bowman's strain, but Bowman was a hard if mercurial man and such a man would find little satisfaction in the temperament of the border terrier. Also, Bowman was quite unique among huntsmen of this area, for he kept accurate records of the breeding of his terriers and such was the fame of his strain that the pedigree of border terriers would probably include references to Bowman's Ullswater strain of dog. Ann Roslin Williams' book *Border Terriers* also states that it is unlikely that Bowman's dogs were border terriers.

Joe Bowman.

I failed to see the old jack hare on the Whittington pastures this morning. His black ears invariably flick up as I go past on my morning walk, but this morning he did not appear. What has happened to him is sheer speculation. He has been there as long as I can remember so he is probably senile and therefore heir to all the misfortunes that can befall an ailing and ancient hare. Foxes and even badgers would make short work of a sick hare, for few hares are allowed to die peacefully and simply take part in the cycle of life and death that is part and parcel of the countryside. More than likely, he has fallen prey to the lampers who are starting to work this area quite regularly now. Hares have little chance on the lamp and a moderately fast dog, providing he is game and prepared to strike at his hare will make mincemeat of one on the lamp. It seems almost a pity to kill such a "fixture" but then I must appear very hypocritical for I have poached and lamped many such hares from other districts. But it seems different when a hare from my own area has been killed. I ran him regularly with Burke, Penguin and even Bear, but with no success, for he knows this area all too well and take advantage of every cranny and niche to throw off the dog. A pity that he seems to have departed. He gave me great sport.

A distemper outbreak in Cannock. Let's hope it stays there. All my dogs are inoculated but an outbreak can cause bedlam in the young dog population. Personally, in spite of the Baraclalevi book which states that distemper inoculation causes harm, I would not be without it. I can honestly say that I have never lost an inoculated dog. Ferrets die like flies during a distemper outbreak and act like miner's canaries as a warning to the dog population of the kennels. I even inoculate the ferrets since I had a distemper outbreak six years ago. Perhaps if distemper inoculation was made compulsory we could stamp out this frightful disease. I am amazed at how many Fell terrier men do not inoculate their dogs as they believe that their dogs are so tough as to be immune to the disease. They live in a fool's paradise. The very isolation of the Fells has ensured distemper has not become common in their district. When a fell becomes invaded by distemper, the dogs, which have little or no immunity, die like flies.

I really need a new lamp; my old one has taken a lot of use this winter. The glass is split and the battery is almost beyond charge. Still, it has been a damned good lamping kit. It was purchased from CTF of Sutton, and has taken considerable "hammer". It has, in addition to a split in the glass, a series of fox bites along the edge of the beam and the box is also scored with fox marks. If I replace the lamp, it will be with another CTF outfit.

Badgers are digging up my garden, probably for the wireworm eaten potatoes that I have left in the ground. Four years ago, the badgers from Brough's Earths, a sett threequarters of a mile away, turned over the bins regularly in their search for anything edible. At one time, I had to catch stray boars before they wrecked my garden. Now the badger population is dwindling and it is almost a pleasure to find them foraging on my plot.

The seasonal mange in my terriers is late in arriving—or do I speak too soon? By now, the first pustules of sarcoptic mange have manifested themselves; and by late April daily dipping in BHC is absolutely essential. By some unbelievable miracle, has the outbreak missed me this year? I doubt it. Perhaps the strange winter has something to do with the late outbreak.

April

Tuesday 1

What a load of madmen are joining the ranks of hunters—madmen who are certain to give field sports a hell of a bad name. Today, I heard of a chap selling a sheep killing lurcher for £150. The taking of sheep with lurchers is on the increase and sheep are such easy quarry! I know quite a few Midland lurcher men who regularly go into Wales and slay a few sheep to fill the deep freezes and sheep rustling in the Midlands is far from rare. One of my policeman friends—I still have one or two!—says that it is the poverty brought about by the recession that is causing these sheep thefts, but I doubt it. Boredom through unemployment is a more likely cause. It costs quite a lot of money to buy a sheep killing lurcher (viz £150) and a lot of money to keep one well fed and I doubt if forays after rabbits, deer or sheep would cover the cost of such outlay on dogs. Furthermore, the psychology of poachers leaves a lot to investigate. Two of our noted sheep stealers are employed and earn good wages, yet they still go into Wales after sheep and harry the deer quite a bit as well.

Wednesday 2

Omega is obviously in whelp, but to what? She has not shown colour and I've seen no dog mate her. She is very fertile and a dog has but to look at her to make her pregnant—well, that's a slight exaggeration. If the litter are obviously Jack Russell or even Patterdale crosses, I shall certainly keep them as Omega is a treasure. Even if the border terrier dog is the sire, they will make a useful though unplanned litter. I have a horrid fear that Vampire, Omega's sire and grandsire is the father of this litter. Time alone will tell. Whatever her condition, she will rat with us tomorrow night.

The inevitable mange has manifested itself on Beltane yet again, making dipping in a fairly strong BHC mange dip essential. This usually slows up this hellish infection even if it doesn't cure it. All the rat hunting team looks decidedly motheaten as summer approaches. Benzyl benzoate has little effect on this bug as the whole of the bitch's belly becomes a vile, suppurating mess if not treated with a BHC dip. There must be several strains of sarcoptic mange. Alan Thomas has a strain that is entirely different from mine and responds to dipping in *Alugan*, the proprietary name of a chemical that has no effect on my strain of mange.

Thursday 3

Our rat hunt was marred by another savage fight, or to be more exact, the usual bloodbath when Vampire sets about another dog. This time, it was the border dog who, for some small, inconsequential reason somehow offended Vampire. The result is predictable and unpleasant, a savage attack, a furious battle, a totally incapable border terrier desperately trying to avoid the cyclone that besets him, and finally the strangling off of Vampire. He is getting old, too old to be much use after this year. An ageing stud dog is like a middle-aged lovesick swain, ever eager to prove that he is not past it, so to speak. When he was younger, he was a heller, lightning quick, a devastating rat killer, and so fast at slaying that he could take on most. Now

47

Vampire after a terrific pounding when killing rats in a poultry house vent.

Omega beats him to the punch, or rather the bite, every time and even Beltane makes him look slow. He will continue for years yet, absorbing punishment like a sponge, asking no quarter, nor giving it either and as he slows up he will take more and more bites killing his rats. He finishes up each rat hunt looking a bit like a butcher's shop and next morning sees his face swollen to bull terrier proportions. He is too old even for a veteran rat dog, hobbling around a barn after the odd rat or so and for the job in hand, he is well past it. A hundred-odd rats a night exhausts a young dog, but Vampire is still too game to show the white feather. He is irritable with faster dogs, eager to fight any dog who can beat him to the rats. By midnight, he is tired, ill and scarcely able to stand, yet he will not give in. What a valiant dog he is! On good days, he behaves almost like a youngster, on bad days I contemplate

putting him down. Tonight, his face is a red ruin, covered with bites that even antibiotics cannot cope with, and lately an incurable mange has manifested itself. "Mithridates, he died old", I think Housman said. This will be the fate of my old warrior, I think. Like Jack London's dog hero, he will die in harness.

I dropped Omega back in her pen tonight and noticed she was a little more excitable than usual. Within minutes, she had whelped a brown and white puppy, followed by a brindle and—wait for it—followed by a merle. He must have served her through the bars—a useless litter, the hallmark of an amateur dog breeder, but within minutes they had been sorted out homes. Harry Lees has booked the brindle, Roger the fawn tan and Keith Ruston is having the merle. What use will such a puppy be—a collie/greyhound to Jack Russell cross?

Friday 4

I shall certainly mate Beltane when she comes into season but not to a Patterdale. Alan's dog Rollo now seems a good bet, or maybe Vampire, Beltane's brother. My team *are* old, too old to last all that much longer, so I need direct descendants, not crossbred Patterdales; and I can mate the progeny to Patterdale types. I'd settle for a whole batch of Beltane-Vampire puppies that, with luck, will have her nose and his thrust. Last night exhausted the team of oldies and convinced me that I need a lot more youngsters to run on. I need a young brood bitch as well, one that will breed me top grade stuff even if she is a non-hunter herself.

Fathom's litter are superb, or so Sarah says. She phoned tonight to report on their progress. She has several collie marked puppies that she is a bit chary about selling—why I don't know. Brindles are the easiest colour to sell without a doubt, but colour is not important. In November, I saw a white lurcher, a rough coated bitch that was absolutely dynamite on hares and also a good lamp dog. The idea that dark dogs are the best for poaching is a bit of an old wives' tale. A dark dog or a brindle is just as obvious to a vigilant gamekeeper or farmer. Early Norfolk lurchers were invariably pale straw coloured or a very light wheaten, yet these were the traditional poachers' dogs.

Saturday 5

Graham Welstead, founder of the British Ferreting Society, has a friend who has supposedly bred a litter by mating a wild polecat with a white jill ferret. Question—how do you tell a wild polecat from a flesh fed ferret? When ferrets are meat fed, they exactly resemble wild polecats in coat, colour and skull structure. With luck, these will be exhibited at the Game Fair. Graham has done a lot for ferrets and the once humble, totally expendable, under-researched animal is having at least a crack of the whip in terms of stock improvement, stock management and disease research. I've a lot of time for Graham because of this and he justly deserves his once monthly photograph in *Shooting Times*. Anyway, I'm not certain whether the polecat/ferret mating will produce a better litter than a simple ferret/ferret mating. After all, a ferret is simply a domesticated polecat and there is little to gain by bringing in wild blood—that is, assuming the polecat sire is a true polecat and not just an escaped ferret. If a wild polecat is used, will the young be wild and unhandleable? Haagedoon implies yes, but I think he is wrong. Hesselrigg, a German naturalist, tamed a litter of wild polecats and found them as docile and loving as a ferret.

Sunday 6

Boy, am I getting them—tonight I had a visit from a chap who asked if I could dig him a litter of wild rats—yes, I'll say it again—wild rats. He has a yen to tame a batch so he says. They are so easy to get and so repulsive to keep that I can't imagine why a man would want to tame such a beast. Anyway it's illegal to keep a rat without a licence from the Home Office and sometimes they will need to have the beasts spayed and castrated before a licence is granted. Personally, I am filled with loathing at the thought of keeping the creatures and I really can't see the interest in keeping a beast of this type.

I obtained a litter for Paul Summers only last year and let it be hinted, I doubt if he had a permit to keep them. We took a dozen babes scarcely able to feed and, horror of horrors, he bottle-fed them. They were all, except two females, very wild and panic-stricken when approached and I believe he released the ten savage brutes as soon as he realised that they couldn't be tamed—not a good practice, for he should have killed them. The two females he kept were allowed the freedom of the house and were very affectionate— or so Paul says, for I could not bring myself to go to a house where rats ran over the owners of the property. He was photographed with them licking his ear lobes, an act that would give me nightmares.

What became of them, I do not know. Few will live longer than a year even in captivity and I should like to see what the effect of keeping such a fecund creature celibate or unmated is. I suspect that metritis and pyometra would contribute to an early death. Actually, death by accident is more likely. Frances

Pitt—a really superb naturalist—and Phil Drabble both kept tamed wild rats but in both cases the rats came to sticky ends. There is, in fact, always a tendency for the wild beast to revert quite quickly as soon as it escapes and the result of a wild rat escaping when it has lost some of its fear of man, its natural "edge" so to speak, is fairly predictable. Still, the prospect of having a rat, tame, wild or feral, gives me the creeps.

Monday 7

Paul brought a *Shooting Times* magazine today—they are now becoming so expensive I have to save up to buy one. In it was an editor's note about a pair of chaps from London, out on a somewhat abortive poaching expedition with lurchers and lamp. The pair were caught, charged and fined a total of £200 each. Expensive rabbit and boy, I can see why. The cause of the crippling fine was the fact that one of the men carried a sheath knife and was charged with possessing an offensive weapon. Is this a case of the courts trying to make an example of poachers? Certainly, poaching is on the increase and certainly convictions are coming in by the bucketful, but I doubt whether such staggering fines will stop the poaching. In the papers today, there was a case of a pair of youths mugging an old age pensioner—they were given a suspended sentence—yet the poaching of a rabbit (and let's face it, the carrying of an offensive weapon was a bit of a "curly" one) cost the miscreants £200—a curious business. "The law is an ass, Mr Bumble."

Tuesday 8

Once again, the familiar phone call from a man with a young daughter, requesting that I catch him an otter cub. These phone calls are all so common after a showing of *Ring of Bright Water* that I no longer even check to find out if the phone call is an RSPCA ploy to trap the unwary. It is the result of one rather spoilt otter-struck child, pestering her father. Anyone with the foresight to breed either British otters or even marsh otters from Iraq—which, incidentally, breed quite well in captivity, so Henrik Schreider the South African naturalist assures me—would make a fortune, providing the release of this delightful film coincided with the birth of the cubs. Here's the rub, however: an otter cub looks really appealing on the silver screen but it is a very different round-the-house prospect. Otters kept in a confined space very soon remind one that they are quite simply large ferrets, for they literally stink the place out. Furthermore, it is not possible to house train otters, so the otter appeal wavers a bit after a few days. Nastier still is the fact that otters have a capricious temper and unlike ferrets, bite quite savagely when angered. To try to take unsuitable food from an otter is supposedly quite a feat. At one time, I contributed to the decline of the otter by catching and selling cubs, but I have stopped, quite simply because of my disgust at seeing captured wild animals fretting in unnatural surroundings.

Wednesday 9

Tinkers—and a groan escapes from my soul. I arrived home to find sundry dirty children in my run and my milk stolen yet again. I am really fed up with these intruders. A few night's ago, the Tinker Council spokesman appeared on the television and expressed concern about the fact that people resent tinkers visiting their district. A short spell in Huddlesford would convince him why people object to the itinerants. Some cause little or no damage, others are demons. I've seen my garden completely destroyed by the hordes of unruly youths who come with this band and, more than once, these people have used my porch as a toilet. My dogs attract them like magnets. I am pestered beyond the bounds of reason and when I refuse to sell, my dogs mysteriously disappear. I dislike any restriction of human liberty—I am an eccentric myself—but something has to be done to curb the tinker problems.

Thursday 10

One of the hardest night's ratting I have ever known. The dogs were totally exhausted when we arrived home. We took upwards of 200 rats, but we spent from 9.0–1.45 to catch them. Pagan is quite badly torn as she ran in on a ruck, but she is undeterred by the trouble. The border terriers still look unlike doing any work. Apart from the dog, they seem uninterested in rats and spend their time simply wandering aimlessly around the sheds. When they will decide to work, I just don't know. The bloodline must produce the occasional worker, and why is the dog so good and the bitches so indifferent?

The trailer is finally too small to accommodate all the dogs. Fitted with divisions, it could be used to carry twelve dogs instead of six. A partition made of wood is necessary. I've seen people in shows take over 20 terriers in small trailers but this is not only cruel, it is also a bit pointless. I doubt if I could control 20 terriers on a rat hunt anyway, but stories of the Monmouthshire ratting pack are often heard and the MRH (Master of rat hounds) fielded 28–35 terriers, or so I'm told. The best of luck to him, I say.

Friday 11

Phoned Mick Douglas of Norfolk about using his best bitch to mate to Merle and he seems quite keen on the idea. His strain apparently descends from a bitch called Rust, a collie/greyhound bitch mated to any top class coursing dogs that are free from the saluki taint. Mick is an incredible character who lives in a state of near penury in the marshes of Norfolk and is known over here simply by the nickname "the Fenman". He rarely wears shoes and seemingly only leaves his marshes for a once a year trip to Lambourn show. His dogs are flawless runners and are unbeatable on the hare killing contests that are sadly in vogue at the time of writing. To my knowledge, no one has taken money from him in the coursing contests on the Fens. Doug tells me Mick has an Arts Degree and I'm not surprised for, in spite of his broad "stuffing advertising" Norfolk accent, he is very articulate. At first his tales of marsh hunting seem a bit tall, but on investigation, his stories prove to be true. Rust, his ancient and rather tatty old bitch, once killed fourteen hares in single-handed courses in one day, a feat that was witnessed by Doug Cooper, a very truthful person. Personally, I've never had a dog that could do this. Fathom is very fast, very nimble and great at snatching prey, but she burns up like a torch after two runs.

Saturday 12

I have mated my merle border collie bitch to a bearded collie dog, the property of Mrs Foster of Pershore. The bearded collie dog is a big outgoing brute with a heavy coat, a far cry from the shy, skulking collie I have mated to him. Why I have done this, is a mystery to my friends, and why I should spend £25 on a stud fee when I am flat broke is a bit of a puzzle to me. It is very doubtful that I will sell the litter and if I get £25 a puppy I will be very well pleased. I should like a merle rough bearded collie male or female, but coat length is a bit of a difficult thing to guess at. Really, I have too many dogs as things are, and I need more like I need a hole in the head. The merle factor fascinates me, however, and if I am correct, the litter should yield roughly 50% merles and the rest black or blue. If I am correct, I will write off the cost of rearing the litter to experience. Moses says that the Romany name for a wall-eyed merle is a moon pie, incidentally.

Beltane snapped at a little owl as it rose from the grass this morning, killing it quickly, but not before it footed her in the nose. Any owl is a ferocious beast if it is hurt. Eric Hoskins lost an eye through an encounter with a tawny owl. Normally a bird the size of a little owl would not put up much of a fight, but the poor devil ripped Beltane's face quite badly before it expired.

The communal greyhound whelped today. Three males and a bitch, but the bitch was born dead. Mick has easy sales for these: one is already sold to a Corporal Horton who poned me from Germany for a ¾ bred collie greyhound puppy. Another, a black collie marked dog, is almost certainly sold to Eddie Jones. These three-quarter bred puppies are quite greyhoundy as a rule and much faster than the half-bred first cross puppies which are usually fairly ugly, but I am not certain that the second crosses are better lurchers. True, they are faster, but it's a swings and roundabouts business and some three quarter bred collie greyhounds are as intractable as pure greyhounds and have the collie's sensitive nature. One of Mick's puppies is a gay merle pied, a curious browny tan type of colour, not a blue merle. Merle is a lot more variable a colouration than I had hitherto thought. Brown, red and beige merles are all easily bred simply by mating a blue merle to a tan, red or beige animal. To breed the best blue merles—merles free from any muddy tan colour—a blue merle should be mated to a black or a blue.

Sarah returned Fathom together with a curious looking merle coloured puppy. If I didn't know better, I'd say the puppy was rough or broken coated. He is certainly the ugliest lurcher puppy I have seen in ages. His coat is very bad, the sort that picks up water and mud or becomes entangled with briars. Nevertheless,

One of Merle's puppies.

I shall keep the puppy. Jane, a six year old girl from my neighbour's house has nicknamed the creature Woolly Bear, a name I feel will stick. Fathom is very fat, but within minutes of being back she caught and retrieved alive an adult moorhen. She really is a great little hunter. With the enormous rabbit population in the district, I will have an exciting and fruitful summer training her and her puppy. In spite of his ugly shape, Woolly could turn out to be a superb little hunter, having his mother's instinct and his father's brains. Looks should not influence the lurcher breeder too much, but they do, and the present interest in shows will almost certainly result in beautiful but not very useful lurchers being bred. Still, few of the show fraternity wish to own a scruffy poacher's dog and if any dog fulfills any purpose or gives any enjoyment, it has justified its keeping. The show world is not for me, I fear.

Tuesday 15

A very mangy fox was dug out by Cope and me on the disused railway line. I've never seen such a mangy brute. Many foxes die as a result of this disease or rather by the sepsis introduced by the scratching of the dog, for many foxes itch themselves to a state of frenzy with mange. St Leger Gordon believes more foxes die of mange than are killed by hounds, and he might well be right. This one was red raw and had numerous deep scratches on his skin, scratches that were suppurating badly so it would be only a matter of time before he expired anyway. I killed him and left the unskinned body—a bit wasteful but it is not the sort of creature one skins and to take it home for the ferrets would be courting disaster, for fox mange is infectious to ferrets and dogs. I always feel guilty when I kill simply for the sake of killing and I try to salve my conscience by giving some reason why I did what I did. Mange is very bad in the local fox earths and unless there is a good clear out of the local earths by badgers or rabbits, next winter will see some very poor pelts on my drying board. I'm also a bit doubtful as to whether or not I've been infected with mange from this fox and so tonight I will bath in a benzene hexachloride sheep dip solution—a bit kinky but better than mange.

Wednesday 16

Bob Green is doing well with my eagle owl. I need to read up on eagle owls but there are few books on the subject. Bob says there are many species, and that my own is a Bengal eagle owl. The European eagle owls are bigger than the Asiatic owls and therefore incapable of taking large quarry. Bob went to see a chap in Nottingham who specialises in these birds. He has a large female that is easily capable of taking hare, but unlike my owl, is very tame. I have heard of these owls taking foxes and judging by their enormous feet, the task is not beyond them. I doubt whether they are easy to enter to such quarry, though I am constantly suspicious of falconer's tales concerning the ability of birds to take huge ground quarry. Obviously, there must be some practising falconers who hunt their birds, but I rarely meet them. At one time, I trained goshawks, not particularly successfully, I must add, but well enough for them to take a large number of rabbits, and I met an enormous number of falconers who told amazing stories of birds they had trained that had dwarfed my feeble efforts. On examination, however, most proved to be lies and I became convinced that the prime qualification for falconry was to be a good raconteur.

Thursday 17

A funny sort of night's ratting though, if I needed proof my dogs were broken to rat, this is it. Together with a neutered ginger tom, Joan Hancock's pet, Vampire hunted and flushed a rat from the tractor engine in the yard. The whole team ignored the cat. I just can't understand how anyone can boast about cat-killing lurchers and terriers. Such dogs must be hell to own, and they are a certain ticket to refusal at any farm that has cats and most farms have.

Eddie Jones, an educational executive officer from

53

Wolverhampton, came ratting with us tonight. He is surprisingly agile for a man near retirement. He gives up his job in a year's time and goes rough for a while with the dogs. Eddie wishes to buy a lurcher puppy and perhaps the one-fourth collie, three-fourths greyhound puppies of Mick Kirby would suit him. Anyway, I can see Eddie giving them a good home and the proximity of a black stud dog of this breeding is suitable for the syndicate. We are certainly reluctant to bring pure greyhound blood into our already greyhound-saturated strain of lurcher.

Friday 18

Sheep stealing is on the increase again and the locals blame the tinkers. For once, I must defend the itinerants. I saw beams of light cutting Brown's farm last night and I confess I thought it was lampers out after rabbits. It was obviously sheep thieves. It is on the increase hereabouts and a good sheep worrying lurcher or greyhound can earn a huge sum in a night. Sheep do not expect dogs to attack them and thus a dog aided by a beam of light is a frightful weapon against sheep. I was offered sheep for the freezer (I haven't one) in Penkridge market, £10, no questions asked, and the would-be seller didn't even know me. I think another year may see desperate bands of thieves roaming the countryside pillaging. It is a frightful prospect, I must admit, but I feel such a time is coming. Brown's lost only one sheep so I should imagine a small time sheep thief is working this patch. Really, if the economic crisis continues, bands of "sturdy rogues", Elizabeth II versions of Elizabethan times, will be a nuisance around the countryside. Everyone I meet seems to be unemployed and bored—and boredom is "murder" to many of the hunting fraternity.

Mick and Roger with the fox terrier × Beltane hybrids. Note the long weak heads.

Saturday 19

I shall not breed any more fox terrier/Russell crosses. Something is not quite right with this mating, something intangible. Somehow they lack punch and drive—an essential quality for a rat hunting team. If I can find a very hard Jack Russell strain, I may use it, but I rather fancy my outcross blood will come from Patterdale stock when I have to outcross. These outcrosses are usually iron hard and will face a lion. Frankly, much as I love my own strain of Jack Russell, a cross bred pack would not worry me in the slightest though my team would lose its classy look.

My hob ferret is not covering the jills properly. He mates them furiously and they certainly go off season but they do not conceive. Question, is he sterile, senile or what? He is certainly overused and was overused before I borrowed him, but I've known hobs serve ten jills in a season. Let's hope Fudge has conceived to him—if she hasn't, the ferreting will be fairly poor this winter. Really, anyone who states that they need more than three ferrets to work a winter is kidding themselves. Three decent jill ferrets, and maybe a liner hob, will get an enormous number of rabbits. In pre-myxomatosis times, one might have needed a load of ferrets. Now there is no justification for such a mess of ferrets.

Sunday 20

Thank God the tinkers have left. I wish they would take their filth with them. They really are a curse in the district. Our lane looks like a rubbish dump and there is no way one can make them adhere to any codes of conduct. They go where they will, when they will. Their dogs worry sheep and kill cats. They set badly placed hangs and forget about them—hence dogs and cats are hung up and often die a lingering death. I took a terrier out of a snare tonight. I found a gin trap this morning, set of course, and it now hangs on my wall. The Government must legislate against these people.

They make life in the village a living hell. I am constantly pestered for ferrets, dogs and scrap. When I refuse to sell my property is looted when I am at school. I have no redress. The police cannot enforce the law on these people. The Government seeks to protect them with curious legislation and the police are requested to turn a blind eye to crimes. It is a lunatic situation and it needs rectifying. These people thumb their noses at our laws, our moral codes and get away scot free. I am extremely bitter that this should be so.

Monday 21

Yet another falconer with an Imperial eagle and a set of lies that would delight a Baron Munchhausen. Yet another story of foxes slain by these gigantic, beautiful and, frankly, useless birds. Imperial eagles are carrion feeders. They flock around Spanish tan yards and seem positively inert, yet in the hands of the falconer/raconteur they become cyclones of fire and initiative. I've heard so many tales of them slaying Alsatians and suchlike that I am just a bit sick of it. There are a few falconers who actually do fly birds at quarry but they must be very thin on the ground. It is a sport that attracts exhibitionists by the dozen. At various meets, I have visited, the most bizarrely clad band assemble, so eccentrically dressed that I feel embarrassed. Today's fibber boasted a prodigious haul of foxes and deer with his eagle. I checked the tales out via a friend—no one has seen this man catch anything with his eagles.

Tuesday 22

An interesting experiment—at least, for someone who has never tried it before. Peter Davies, 25 years old and an ex-pupil of mine (God, I feel old) has visited my house frequently since he left school. Now married and settled, he still comes and takes a delight in exploring us "simple country folk" and our ways. Today, in spite of warnings, he tried the flesh of the hedgehog and is in no doubt that the taste of the beast is vastly over-rated. Vampire caught one at dusk as it was leaving its lair and Peter insisted that he tried the verminous little beast. Nasty, believe me. Hedgehogs are regarded with awe by the Romany and in spite of stupid stories to the contrary, few of the Rom speakers eat them. The extracts of the flesh, the fat, the peritoneum, the dried and powdered liver are still used by some Romanies as cure-alls. Manfri Woods, in his book *In the Life of a Romany Gypsy* believes it is a medicine beast, a beast put on earth to cure the ills of others, just as the tench is a medicine fish. Toothache is supposedly cured by sucking the baked foot of a hedgehog—personally, I think I'd rather suffer the toothache.

Paul Taylor's dog catches and retrieves a rabbit.

Wednesday 23

I must really consider the prospects of introducing Fell terrier blood into my very inbred strain of Jack Russell. I should like to introduce a smooth coated Fell dog, but most strains are either bent-legged, long backed or else are the result of Russell crosses. The good quality Fell dogs are invariably rough coated and to introduce such blood is rather asking for a non-descript strain. I feel such blood would certainly not harm my strain of Jack Russell and might just possibly keep the same agility, speed and toughness that characterises them. If the Jack Russell Club of Great Britain developed an interest in the science of genetics rather than the petty bickering that was rampant when I was chairman, then the breed would improve in leaps and bounds. Certainly, I should never use outside Jack Russell blood to improve my strain as there just aren't any strains that have the qualities I require.

Ray Baxter sent me a photograph of a polecat pied ferret—a curious looking beast. It's strange why more mutations haven't occurred among ferrets as man has been breeding them for at least 2,000 years. Mink, a newcomer to domestication, has a whole load of mutations, but one never sees an odd coloured ferret—not until Baxter's, that is. Let's hope it breeds. It will be interesting.

Thursday 24

My second encounter with a Pharaoh hound—a breed incongruously named because they resemble the dogs carved upon Egyptian tombs. Alan Thomas brought up a young chap with such a dog only a year ago, a young chap called Tony Harte, and I was astonished to find how bright and tractable this dog seemed to be—he would have put most lurchers to shame. I am a little sceptical about exotic beasts, as I have had considerable experience with borzois and salukis, considerable but not favourable experience, I must add; but this dog from Wales was a different cup of tea. Tonight's dog, owned by a woman, was equally well trained and the lady managed the handling of the dog without the Barbara Woodhouse affectations. I doubt if the breed is fast enough for hare, though I could imagine that there are Pharaoh hounds who could wear a hare down over the right country, for the breed appears to have terrific stamina. It is with rabbit that the breed is supposed to come into its own and possibly with partridge and other ground-nesting game birds for the breed has lightning quick responses. However, as a poaching breed it has its limitations for it is notoriously noisy when pursuing quarry. Some people have crossed the breed with greyhounds to produce a more suitable hare hunting dog, but I have heard few reports concerning this sort of lurcher.

Ratting good—haul 238 in 3 hours.

Friday 25

Gwyn Williams of Lluest, a reliable observer and childhood friend, has reported seeing a buzzard catch and eat a huge grass snake. Buzzards came back to the valley shortly after the Forestry Commission started the replanting of the hills with larch and similar conifers, which is a bit curious as rabbits are far from common here. Buzzards are extremely adaptable creatures, however and make out on most food. I've seen birds of this type scavenging on ash tips eating stuff in a state of very ripe decomposition. My own buzzards (I've trained two) fed on worms and beetles when I failed to catch meat for them. Before myxomatosis, buzzards ate rabbits, but once the myxi wiped out the rabbits, they changed their habits a great deal—or did they? What did buzzards feed on before rabbits came to Britain? Certainly not rats, for they arrived later. Were the buzzards deprived of rabbits, their staple food in the days before 1953, actually merely reverting to their old ways, their pre-rabbit diet, rather than simply switching diets from rabbit to whatever else was going? The same applies to stoats. What did they eat before the rabbit and the rat? Tegner once told me he believed a now extinct rodent once provided food for both these predators.

Saturday 26

If I ever achieve my own strain of lurcher, it will be through Steel and Merle. Steel is a rather beautiful bearded collie/greyhound hybrid and Merle is a border collie greyhound, an ugly but highly intelligent dog. David James says collie crosses will eventually breed true to type. If so, I will endeavour to breed a rough coated black or merle type animal from the border/bearded collie greyhound hybrid. They should level out at 23–24 inches which is about the right size for the all-round dog. The deerhound introduction, to produce tall, elegant, rough coated dogs, has just about done for the lurcher. No longer are canny, sagacious collie blooded dogs prized, but the show type dog—the dog that will enter the Kennel Club lists as The Lurcher—is simply a rough coated greyhound, as brainless and noseless as a track dog. If I desired a rough coated dog (and frankly coat makes little difference) I would use a bearded collie hybrid to bring in this coat. Deerhound blood, from a dog untried and untested in the field of battle for which they were intended, does little to help the real lurcher. Question—how many lurchers will I eventually have? I already have too many to train properly and would hate to finish up with a huge team of dogs like the dog dealers at lurcher shows.

Sunday 27

Yet another mating for Merle. He is agitated by the presence of Steel in season and refuses food if he is not allowed to mate her. A stud dog needs constant work to stay in good mental health. Furthermore, constant use seems to improve a stud dog's technique so that I am no longer forced to spend six hours at a stretch fruitlessly trying to mate Merle to sundry bitches. His last client, a blue greyhound bitch the property of Harold Hodson Walker, finished up as a hysterical wreck after Merle fruitlessly tried to mate her. I shall not put him to public stud: the colour would be far too common, if I did.

My artichokes are through and thriving, but a diminutive rabbit has taken refuge in my woodpile and is just beginning to get a bit of a nuisance. This morning, I found small pieces nibbled out of my cabbages. If this continues, he will have to go, but catching a rabbit in such circumstances is often hard.

Foxes musked my bean trench last night, no doubt drawn in by the stench of the cadavers buried below. I feel that I have fetched coals to Newcastle by lamping foxes miles from home. These foxes haunt my garden and breed just twenty yards from my house, but it would not be expedient to catch them.

Vampire's puppies—the heads are deceptively strong. Vampire usually breeds weak, "snipey-headed" offspring.

Monday 28

Vampire has mated a very hard little Patterdale bitch—smooth with some hairs around the knuckles of the legs. This type of dog is often bred by Bill Brightmore of North Lancashire and the strain has a reputation for being extremely hard and game. I would not object to a puppy from this mating to bring into my own strain of terrier.

Beltane is beginning to come into season. I shall mate her to Vampire, I think, not Rollo or a Patterdale. Both are old and though they are still useful, it would be lunacy not to perpetuate the bloodline by mating brother to sister. I really need two new studs anyway. Contrary to opinion, little harm comes to the puppies of this incestuous type of mating although I have seen some hellish deformities from such close inbreeding. I will almost certainly have a litter of putty nosed puppies, or at least one with a putty nose, for Vampire and Beltane's mother was putty nosed. A quarter of the litter should therefore be putty nosed—not black as the standard requires.

Tuesday 29

I had a dead foal given me today. The trouble with feeding horse meat is that the fresh meat causes scouring. Barry Dainty, a first rate kennel man from the Meynell hunt, used to hang a dead horse for two weeks before feeding it. This, he assures me, is the best way of stopping the laxative effects of fresh horse meat. I've fed dead foals before, but always with bad results. Last year, my dogs scoured so badly, that I nearly lost Omega. But I just don't fancy a horse carcass hanging for several days. The bitter irony is that in spite of the fact that I pride myself on being a good rat hunter, the area around my cottage has great potential as a rat haven. I have only to leave a bag of meal in the porch for a day or two, to hear the gentle pitter-patter of tiny feet when I open the door. In an area as crisscrossed with streams as Huddlesford is, it is unlikely one will ever be entirely free from rats.

Wednesday 30

Two chaps, no names, no pack drill, have spent the day looking for potential sparrow hawk chicks. There is certainly a pair in the district for I see the female regularly and only last Sunday the musket or male swept in and snatched up a feeding sparrow opposite my house. Twenty years ago, sparrow hawks were easy to get and every wood boasted at least a pair. Now, they are a rarity. The persecution by game keepers did little to slow them up but the advent of chlorinated hydrocarbons such as *Aldrin* and *Dieldrin* really slew them. In spite of protection by law, they are still shot and I found a dead female only a month ago. Mick Wilkinson of Willington succeeded in breeding sparrow hawks in a small aviary—a heck of a feat for the birds are naturally paranoid and desert nests as soon as danger threatens. Actually, there has been a marked increase in predatory birds bred in captivity. Thirty years ago, a pair of kestrels produced chicks and it made the national papers. Now, peregrines and eagles have been bred in captivity. It is perhaps the only hope these birds have of not becoming extinct in our crowded world.

May

Carnage! Roger and I arrived back from hunting and Roger kennelled his team in the ferret pen. The result—one dead ferret, one very badly damaged hob. Sadly, a ferret that is badly savaged by dogs invariably dies. To my dismay, I found the hob I had borrowed is the one that is severely damaged. To have one's own stock badly damaged or killed is bad enough, but to have another man's property killed is upsetting to say the least.

Changing the subject rapidly, a good night's ratting, upwards of 250, and caught with ease. A huge number of half grown rats were feeding in the first shed—a fair indication that the place will have a good stock of very huntable rats in the midwinter. Actually, our constant thinning of the rat population does little good. We merely disturb the social structure a little and cause minor ripples on the huge pool of rats. Otherwise, we merely act as rather inefficient predators in places that house such a vast rat population. We could easily kill a thousand a week in such a place—as, indeed, I have done—without doing any real damage to the rat population.

The hob is very badly damaged and will probably die. Several ribs are broken and one testicle has been practically torn away. Roger killed his jill as she was so badly damaged that it was unlikely she would have lived more than an hour. Unbroken dogs and ferrets are a bad combination. Mine are broken to ferret, but Alan has little chance to do this. Hence his terriers are a bit of a liability when they come up to be entered.

If the hob lives, it will be a bit of a miracle. I have never seen a ferret so badly damaged. In cases of severe injury, beasts should be kept warm; hence I have built up my fire and boxed the ferret in the hearth, but I will be very surprised if he lives. Shock usually carries off any ferret who is even slightly ripped. Frankly, if this was my property, I should put it down, but I am obliged to persist with treatment. It will be quite an expensive treatment if the hob is alive by the morning.

An offer of a saluki to train—a desert bred one at that. A friend has brought in a mated bitch from the Rub Al Khali, a fiery hell in the middle east. The bitch was in whelp to a famous chirk hunting dog, trained to hunt gazelle with the assistance of hawks—probably the last chirk hawking saluki in the world. I am tempted to try to train such a beast, but the memory of a similarly bred hound called Emir made me reject the offer. Emir was an outstanding coursing dog, a wonderful hare courser and a runner of deer, but he was totally intractable and completely unreliable with sheep. Few insurance companies will insure salukis against third party damage for salukis, Afghans and borzois have a well earned reputation for being notorious stock worriers. Emir was the most adept sheep killer I have ever seen. In no time, he bowled one and took out its throat. When he was returned to his owner, I vowed I would never keep another saluki and I shall keep my vow and refuse this desert bred puppy.

A litter of black Patterdale type puppies, sire a black dog bred by Frank Buck, and the dam a bitch sired by

Maurice Bell's dog Britt, has been bred in Leicester. Excellent prospects by any standard. Buck's stuff invariably is. I met him five years ago, but I doubt if he would remember me.

Sunday 4

I see from an extinct copy of *Shooting Times* that Henry Tegner is dead. A pity!—a great naturalist, a keen hunter and for my money, the tops as a writer. Where is the present generation to replace these "greats"? Will the 21st century be devoid of writers of his magnitude. The greats are all either old or dead now—Brian Vesey Fitzgerald, my one time hero was very ancient when I last spoke to him, and now Tegner is dead. It saddens me to think of Tegner being dead. He was first rate, not only as a writer, but as a conversationalist. I met him years ago after his lovely book *The Molecatcher Says* didn't do as well as he expected. I can't understand why this book was remaindered—and Tegner told me it had been. It was a superb little book describing the tales told by a rustic naturalist with an abnormal gift for translating Latin! Tegner was an educated, articulate, gifted man, a man able to convey his ideas to an across the board audience and a fitting epitaph to the passing of this great writer would be the lines from Kipling's much ridiculed and much parodied "If".
"To walk with kings
    Nor lose the common touch."
I shall miss Tegner.

Monday 5

I see one of Moses' pups is up for resale. What a shiftless, useless sort of person the run-of-the-mill lurcher man appears to be, quitting and selling a puppy as soon as the first obstacle is encountered. I am ashamed to breed lurchers as I am confident that more than half the litter will change hands a dozen times or more, coming to rest in a coalhouse in Liverpool or Doncaster. The greyhound blood gives the lurcher a stoical indifference to changing homes, but woe betide the collie-blooded dog that must suffer such change. This puppy of Moses, a whelp from Steel and Grip, two genuine working dogs, was sold to an idiot who boasted he knew everything about dogs—the hallmark of a 100% fool. Moses simply shrugs his shoulders and accepts that such flash in the pan freaks buy his lurchers, but I would be a bit upset at selling dogs to obvious clowns of this type. In the right hands, the puppy would be a cracker, as it has speed, brains and nose but the fool who buys and sells dogs rarely trains anything and seldom gets a good, well-trained dog.

Tuesday 6

A letter from a man claiming that he has crossed a fox with a dog. There are such people the world over. I've followed up every story of fox/dog crosses including the tale of an amazingly fox-like dog bred from a Bedlington terrier bitch, but not one has proved authentic. This chap, from Gloucester, seems adamant that he has bred such a litter. His bitch, or so he says, a collie cross was regularly courted by a dog fox when she was in season, and although Collis did not see them tie or mate, he is confident the dog fox sired the litter. Haagerdoon says such crosses are possible, but I doubt it. Anyway, a visit to Gloucester seems on the cards. Every year sees a spate of these litters of fox/dog hybrids. I'd feel very much more confident of the parentage of the litter if a tame vixen had been seen to tie with a dog and produce a litter, but this is never the case. It has been proved scientifically that such crosses cannot be produced—yet I follow up every one I hear of.

Yet another fox, a vixen with cubs, has taken up residence near Stone's wood, and once again, I have the odious task of shifting them. The cubs are the size of half grown kittens and spit fiercely when caught. Billy Giles says he'll have some to release in the foxless area where he hunts, and no doubt he will fetch them. I hope it is quick. I hate messing about with wild animal youngsters and the smell of the foxes on my premises drives the dogs barmy. Furthermore, my own forte seems to be to pick up sarcoptic mange from foxes.

Giles came up as soon as I phoned, but I can't honestly see him restocking his area with foxes. The district is rabbit-free, and too clean to harbour a great number of rats. I think these cubs stand as good a chance of starvation as they do of being pulled down by hounds. Last year, the hunt Giles supports cost £30,000 to run and caught one and a half brace of foxes—which works out at roughly £10,000 a fox.

Quite a nasty bite tonight, and through my own stupidity, I fear. I blocked the bolt holes with my foot and Roger grabbed a rat as it tried to climb my leg. It sank it's teeth into the nearest object possible and hung on even when Pagan shook it to death. The nearest object was myself. The pain was excruciating and the

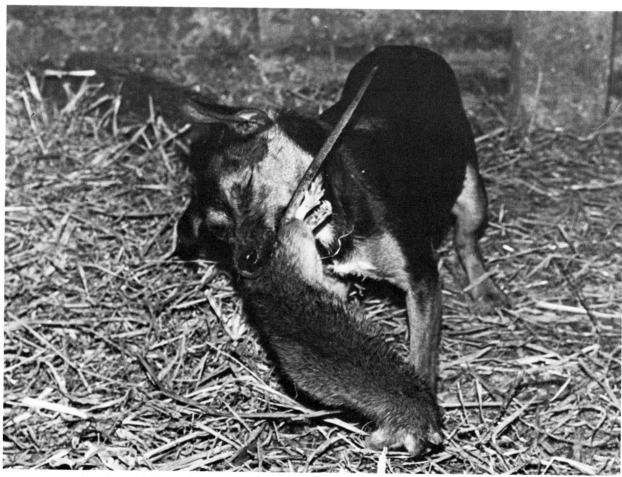

My Patterdale × Plummer type Russell kills its first rat at 5½ months. I rate this hybrid as one of the best, most easily entered type terriers I have bred or owned. I've bred 47 of this breeding and not produced one failure.

rip has to be seen to be believed. Anyone who under-estimates a rat bite is a fool. It takes a hard terrier to endure savage punishment of this nature. A good night's hunting, apart from the bite, that is—324 killed. Roger's dog Ben, a Bedlington whippet hybrid, started killing tonight. Such small whippet lurchers often make terrific ratters, as they are sharp as a razor.

On the subject of sharp, my bite has swollen badly.

My knee is twice its normal size and I spent the night awake, unable to sleep with the throbbing pain. I have been very lucky with rat bites. Most fester, but not one has caused permanent damage. As usual, I will spend Sunday night fevering and Monday will find me weak as water. Why in hell do I follow such a dangerous pastime? The world must really regard me as an eccentric.

Friday 9

My interest in mating a wolf to a dog is still great. Some six years ago, I took a mongrel collie bitch to be served by Dr John Naylor's Siberian grey—a fertile male who has sired a whole load of nervous wolf cubs. I had always regarded the wolf as being a dominant primordial creature, but the grey was decidedly frightened of humans and as it transpired, dogs as well. The wolf is overrated as a devourer of little pigs and Red Riding Hood grandmothers. In legend, he appears as the sinister assassin of men, the beast with more than animal cunning, the prowler in the dark,

ready and waiting to snap up the unwary and the foolish. In reality he is a bit of a fraud, and his repu-tation for cunning has come about because of the fact he is so shy of humans that he will simply watch a man from afar, way out of gunshot and certainly way out of range of hand-thrown missiles. I have never been close enough to a wolf to shoot one, and it is only by the merest chance that any hunter gets a stab at killing one. Gaston Phoebus mentions that the wolf is the most difficult beast to hunt.

Saturday 10

One of our local farmers has a sheep with a quarrel (crossbow arrow) embedded in its neck. What lunatic is hunting sheep with a cross bow? Crossbows are deadly weapons and have an enormous range. As deer-killing weapons, they have been used with good effect—"good" from the awful carnage they cause, I mean. A quarrel was responsible for seeing off Richard the Lionheart as he rode out of range (or so he thought) of the castle archers at Chalus. He died a lingering death. Today, the crossbow has become a lethal weapon in the hands of the poacher, as the recent

Shooting Times photographs show. Personally, I find it nearly impossible to aim a crossbow accurately. I have one and have practiced much but to no avail. I cannot hit the side of a barn door with a crossbow bolt. Still, I know really competent archery exponents who find it an amazingly accurate weapon. Sheep poaching is reputedly the "in" thing in Wales and not simply because of the economic decline, but because the poachers actually treat sheep capture as an exciting form of hunting—exciting that is, because of the risks involved rather than the nature of the quarry.

Sunday 11

As promised, Harpur appeared with his bag of tricks, namely darts and blow gun and once again amazed us with his skill. As a target marksman, he is almost invincible, I am sure. If I had doubts about his hunting skills, they are now gone. He killed a woodpigeon with his blow gun and the needle went damn nigh through the bird. The Jivaro use a jelly-like substance called curare to tip their darts, but I doubt if the Jiravo

blow gun man is as efficient as Harpur. Harpur's copper pipe is given a shine like glass before use and his cotton wool wads must make the most efficient darts.

Where do I get the idiots I know? I am amazed by the lunatic fringe who come to my place. Today's sample boasted he had worked in a hospital and obtained an amputated hand that he promptly fed to his ferrets. My God, what a disgusting ghoul! I dislike freaks of this nature. They give legitimate hunters a very bad name. I am still puzzled how he got my address. Amputation of a limb is bad enough, but the knowledge of a fiend throwing one's appendages to ferrets is sickening.

Monday 12

Andrew Lucas has a young badger cub, which at this moment in time, it is an enchanting pet, maybe five pounds in weight (a late-born cub). But a few months will see it a huge brawling brute causing havoc in the house and leaving an oily musk over the floor. I reared such a cub ten years ago. Never again, I vow. Beasts of the field should be left in the field for they have no place in the house. Mine tore up the quarry tiles in my kitchen and went berserk with settees. Andrew is convinced his will be different and he has read all of Drabble's delightful books on badgers and is still undeterred. It would be interesting to hear how he would house train a badger, a task, believe me! Most dig latrines where and when they will, but as I've said—the best of luck, but it's 100–1 on that next year will see a very upset Andrew seeking a home for his badger.

Tuesday 13

A letter from Alec Dowton, the last of the great Dowton family, so I believe. I met him at the Appleby Fair maybe ten years ago, and we have kept in contact. The Dowtons were a family of travelling herbalists—often confused with tinkers and gypsies, but a different breed. My sister Margaret was cured of whooping cough by the Dowtons (a disease that was said to have killed no end of children in 1921). The Dowtons were an amazing band, and though I once ridiculed their odd skills, I no longer do. Years before the medical profession realised that onions were beneficial for heart complaints, the Dowtons had said that if one kept a string of onions in the house (and made use of them) heart attacks would be unknown in the family. The family used to sell potions of wild violet and ransomes to cure mange in dogs and John Cobby of the South Wiltshire Hunt said that the stuff worked. Alec has some curious beliefs though, for he is adamant that mandrake roots are either male or female and the two planted together will copulate like human beings. Mandrake used to be a regular ingredient of chest remedies during the 1930s, a time when the dreaded TB carried off most of my father's family.

Wednesday 14

The teacher from Rugeley who bought one of Moses' puppies, came and brought his puppy with him. It is very suspicious of strangers—most collie blooded dogs are, but the puppy will probably make a useful hunting dog. It resembles a greyhoundy bearded collie and if I ever wanted a model to illustrate the typical Norfolk lurcher, this would be it. Another puppy from the same litter was brought back to show Moses only last week. It is a steel-grey ticked puppy, the epitome of what the average man considers a lurcher to be. The coat is long and harsh and the face has a collie expression. It is already catching small rabbits and certainly looks fast enough to run down hare. The litter has been a good one, though the one I picked for Martin Knowelden looks none to clever, I must admit. Martin's puppy has turned out to be the only smooth in the litter—he asked me for a rough coated puppy—and is a bit undersized and lacking in muscle. Still, it is early days yet and I've seen saplings, ugly ungainly saplings at that, turn into beautiful and useful animals. I will certainly keep a puppy from Steel next mating.

Thursday 15

The ghoul who fed hands to ferrets phoned and asked if he could come rat hunting, but I made an excuse to turn him away. He didn't miss much as it was a fairly poor night. A pity really, as my depression is quite bad. I am certainly not suited for the stereotyped life school imposes on me, and perhaps as Moses suggested, I would be more at home in a vardo than in a regular job.

One of the dogs (I think it must be Merle) is very badly infested with tapeworms. I find tiny segments of the worms in faeces each day. It is curious and perhaps disgusting to the person who does not keep dogs as to why a dog keeper spends so much of his time looking at the stools of his wards. Faeces tell a person much about the health of his dogs. Black slimy faeces indicate either incomplete digestion of an unpalatable protein such as is found in lights, or perhaps internal bleeding. Pale grey faeces give an indication that the dog is feeding on either a lot of bone or even a hint that the dog is heading for one of the unpleasant hepatic diseases such as leptospiral jaundice.

Friday 16

Went to Salop to see a litter of German short-haired pointers with a view to choosing one for Jeff Dyke—though what the heck to look for, I just don't know. It is a common practice to believe that any dog breeder is instantly able to recognise a good 'un in any breed. True, one can pick out obvious defects like undershot mouth or a badly reared litter but after that, it's a job for the breed specialist. I trained a batch of German pointers about ten years ago, so I suppose I should know a bit about them—I should, but I don't, I'm afraid. These dogs point game and then go on to flush it in the manner of a field spaniel, but they also retrieve the game. Hound blood features highly in the makeup of the breed, and while they are considerably tougher and more versatile than our own pointers, they just cannot compare with the versatility of the springer. I'm perhaps just a bit prejudiced here as I did my apprenticeship, so to speak, with springers when I worked at Tom Evans' board kennels, but most German shorthaired pointers have a slightly lack lustre look that puts me off.

A letter from a man in Utah, who says that he and his father have hunted the Oorang strain of Airedale at wolf boar, bear and (illegally, I gather) at javelina, a type of peccary. He has the utmost faith in this rather houndy strain of Airedale and would put them against Plott hounds, Louisiana curs and any of the Redbone Bluetick type hounds in the sport of hunting large prey. The Oorang strain of Airedale is descended from a rather houndy type of Airedale dog called King Oorang, and he was really tested against heavy game. Ben Lilly, one of Teddy Roosevelt's huntsmen, never rated the Airedale, however, as their terrier blood made them eager to flash into attack without thinking, and with bear, boar or cougar, the one mistake is usually enough to finish a dog. I am surprised to find that this strain still survives and more astonished still to find that it is still worked. Five years ago, one was used in Louisiana as a fixer dog, at razor backed swine, and this received a great deal of publicity.

Saturday 17

A rare turn up for the books. At two o'clock we had arranged with Bob and Keith Ruston to photograph eagle owls flying at rats. Bob keyed up Golem last night by fasting him until he was keen, but a ferret escaped from its pen and killed the owl. It is baffling that such a bird should be slain by a ferret for Golem's feet would have pulverised the largest hob I have seen. I can only assume that the owl must have been used to the presence of a ferret and, unaware of its killing ability until too late. Either that, or the owl must have been under par. A ferret is really a ferocious little killer and it is impossible to break one to any form of small livestock. I saw chickens feeding in the ferret pens of Abbott Brothers of Thuxton, Norfolk and the ferrets ignored them. I doubt if they would have been quite so friendly if they had not been overgorged with a dead calf that also lay in the pen. A ferret on the loose is a nuisance to end all nuisances. The death of Golem certainly leant an air of gloom to the day and no photographs were taken.

My collie bitch is quite pregnant—it will be a huge unsaleable litter if she is so obviously pregnant at this stage.

Fathom took a pheasant this morning—an adult hen. It is a pity as it must have been sitting eggs or covering chicks when she caught it. A lurcher of the old type, a beast able to hunt up as well as hunt by sight, must be a great nuisance if allowed to run free. Penguin, Fathom's dam, an equally mongrelly type of beast, was a great killer of pheasant poults during her heyday. Anyway, tonight will probably find a clutch of very frightened pheasant chicks huddled beneath a hedge awaiting the attention of the next foraging rat, stoat or wandering cat. Charles II issued instructions that predators were to be kept down to allow the pheasant to breed and flourish. Pheasants certainly get a tough time in the wild.

Ian Bullock, a schoolboy in my school, has a ferret that is showing the classic symptoms of pyrometra and metritis. These diseases of the womb are common in ferrets who are not mated. These jills stay in season for months and few survive if not served. I have a feeling the jill will die even if mated, but it is a hazard of keeping non-breeding jills. Paul has dropped another jill with me, an in season white who is very wild. Apparently, she was found in Melton Mowbray station and trapped under a bucket by a signalman. Small wonder she is wild!

Monday 19

Perkins, a farmer from Coton some four miles away, called today to see if I would clear his farm of rats, rats which had slain two dozen Khaki Campbell ducklings. I went to his farm at 6.20 to examine the kills, but he had put them in a bin and I had to sort through piles of filth before I found them. They were not as hideously torn as a rat victim should be so I suggested that the caitiff might be a stoat. Perkins was adamant it was rats, but his farm was remarkably clean and rat free. Against his better judgment he allowed me to put down a Fen trap in a tunnel, and later we found a dead dog stoat in the trap. Fen traps are fierce pieces of equipment and I've had several fingers broken setting them. They were designed to replace the gin after the 1953 Act made gin traps illegal. The spring is tremendously strong and though a trapped rabbit caught with a Fen is totally unsaleable, the trap kills them instantly. Tunnels of any sort fascinate the mustelids. A ferret will deliberately crawl inside the folds of a carpet or into any form of tunnel it can find. Perhaps they are simply curious about the contents of such a cavity; but curiosity not only killed the cat, it has seen off whole armies of stoats, weasels and ferrets as well.

Tuesday 20

A rare visit from John Farley, one of the best northern terrier men I know. Farley keeps and works a team of Fell terriers or Lakelands—call them what you will—that he claims are descended from the dogs of Joe Bowman, the famous Ullswater huntsman. What a great strain of terrier it is—although such dogs are certainly not appreciated in the south. Farley's dogs commit mayhem on foxes when they go to ground—Rasp, his ancient one-eyed bitch saw off two hundred and six during her long, eventful life. I trained a puppy from this bitch ten years ago and the terrier—Farley called him Rock, a common name for a terrier in the Lake District—was a demon. He would literally demolish a fox in minutes, though I confess the battle took place in silence for he was dead mute. Rock eventually met his Waterloo on badger, for his refusal to give an inch was his downfall. He died during the subterranean battle with Brock. Dogs of this strain are far too hard for badger hunting and most come to grief after an encounter with a badger.

Wednesday 21

I have no doubt now that Merle is infested with worms. He passed a long string of segments this evening. Few wild canines are without tapeworms and fewer still seem troubled by them, yet a dog can look very down after a bad infestation. The worm anchors itself in the gut by means of a hooked head like object called a scolex. I doubt whether the worm absorbs that much food for it neither moves nor does it ingest food like an ordinary animal, it simply floats limply in the passing food, absorbing the predigested nutrients in the would-be faeces. The real danger comes from the toxic chemicals the worm secretes. These chemicals are produced partly to prevent the worm getting digested by the host, and cause considerable damage to the dog. Merle is not showing any signs of low condition as yet, but it is only a matter of time before he develops that most curious of phenomenon, a staring coat. He already has a tendency to a capricious appetite, perhaps one of the first symptoms of going downhill. Anyway, he must be wormed.

Thursday 22

A hard fox dig in the early morning and though Beltane did not suffer too badly—a mere rip on her nose—my own arms and legs ache terribly. Next year, someone else can have this thankless job of digging foxes locally but I've said this every year and the next spring finds me digging again. Hunting is a dangerously addictive type of drug, and I am hooked on it. I arrived home exhausted, my legs weak, my arms sore but two hours later I was preparing for the rat hunt.

The ratting is very good. Paul Coffey took his first live catch tonight, a big buck rat which Dave photographed. Live catching is easy but very dangerous, for it places the rat in a position where it can squirt or drop a pool of infected urine at the live catcher. This urine is more venomous than the bite, for it is usually rich in in the spirochtes of leptospiral jaundice or Wiel's disease. Perhaps I do wrong encouraging the lads to rat hunt, for sooner or later they all try for a hand catch!

Friday 23

Lowrey has bred another litter of servals, a tall leggy cat of the African savannah, a bird-killing, hare-slaying cat that is easily tamed. Five years ago, an advert appeared in *Fur and Feather* advertising a litter of these cats, and Carol and I went down south to see them in the hopes of buying one of the kittens to train as a hunting cat in the manner of a cheetah. I didn't particularly fancy any of his litter as they were too far advanced to tame and spat like Furies when approached. The female that bore the litter had three legs only as she had been caught up in a gin as a kitten, but she was more tame than a Siamese female and doted on her owner. The male was a different proposition and flew at the bars of the compound. He was as tall as an Alsatian and had a head that looked like a Scottish wildcat. I ordered a kitten from him asking him to socialise it for me, but the year of its birth coincided with the passing of The Dangerous Wild Animals Act that made the keeping of such beasts difficult and their use as hunting dogs impossible. Hence I never had my serval. A pity really, because cat temperament doesn't deter me as much as it does some people.

Saturday 24

Something really has to be done about the new element that seems to be invading working terrier shows. The present craze seems to be taking Staffordshire bull terriers to these shows and goading them to make them fight each other. Paul Richards, a good lurcher man, visited a show only today and showed his rather timid but useful lurcher bitch. As he passed near the Dog Fighting Brigade, one of the Staffords struck at the lurcher ripping the shoulder muscles and latching on like a leech. The idiots' set seem to find this hilarious but it has ruined the lurcher for a few months. What a crowd of clowns and what in God's name are the show organisers doing about the bringing of such dogs to the show? Ten years ago, I really enjoyed seeing such shows, particularly the Fell and Moorland shows, where hosts of interesting Fell terriers could be seen. Now, I avoid the shows like the plague. I have no desire to see my dogs dismembered by these quasi-pit-fighting dogs.

Sunday 25

The rabbit living on my premises is a hell of a nuisance. He is already making fearful inroads in the beans and has ripped off the centres of two score of cabbage plants. He will have to go, but how. It is impossible to ferret him as he lives rough. He is most unlikely to be snared as he rarely uses distinct runs and anyway the land is well hunted by my neighbours' cats and cats fall easy victims to snares. Fathom runs him daily, but he has only a few feet to run before he is in cover. It is impossible for a lurcher to catch such a rabbit, yet caught he must be. The land is riddled with wireworms, so potato culture is difficult and now it is cursed with a wayward rabbit that prevents any chance of a cabbage crop. If I cannot catch this rabbit, I will put the area down to semi-free range poultry for a year. At least the land will yield something. What an indictment on a man who professes to be a hunter: a *rabbit* is ruining his chances of self-sufficiency! I must pull myself together and catch the rabbit, and forget such defeatist talk.

Monday 26

A fox has killed a fowl or so for the Taylors, and as usual, I have been called in to kill it. How easy to command, how difficult a job to accomplish. Most of the vixens have taken their cubs into the corn fields by now, so digging the brutes with terriers is a bit out of the question. Furthermore, the family are ardent hunt

A snare set for fox—the correct height and correct size.

supporters, so the thought of snaring the fox is a bit off for them. Likewise, the family would be upset if I lamped the fox and killed it with a lurcher. How little the average country man knows about foxes. I will have to snare it if I am to keep the rabbit hunting rights on the land. Fox snares are quite expensive and can only be used once. Thus the skin of a fox taken in summer coat will scarcely make it worthwhile buying fox snares. Foxes around the Taylor farm have taken a savage beating these last two years. I have taken twenty-three from the neighbourhood using terrier and lurcher. Nature obviously abhors a vacuum and foxes simply creep into districts that have a regular food supply.

P.S. At 12.05 I found a vixen in the snare I set this morning—a lean scraggy, elderly old girl who probably spent the season barren.

Tuesday 27

I have been asked to shift a badger at Anthony Lewis's farm, an odious, lengthy and rather tedious job, and to be honest, not one I enjoy. Badgers do little harm though this one has undermined the whole of a corner of wheat land and I doubt if the combine will be able to work the place without falling into the tunnels. Still, I must steel myself and get the creature dug out if I am to keep the land for use as coursing country. At one time, I harassed badgers quite mercilessly, but I reared a cub and after that my passion for badgering the badger ceased. The licence laws for taking a badger are a bit curious. At first, it was thought that the 1973 Act was a very stringent Act indeed, but it allows anyone to dig a badger providing the land owner has given his permission and is prepared to state this badger is causing a nuisance and needs to be moved. If I do dig this badger and I must, I'm afraid, I will take it alive and release it near Hopwas Woods. This area is easily capable of supporting quite a lot of badgers. At one time, this area had a good population and was one of those much badger watched districts. However there has been a reduction in their numbers recently, due perhaps to digging them, but I suspect due more to the changing methods of farming and possibly to a distemper outbreak that blitzed the area six years ago. Like stoats, badgers have little immunity to this deadly malady.

Wednesday 28

My supply of tripe is coming to an end, or at least it is becoming quite scarce. At the moment, I feed cow's tripe and supplement it with a box of chicken entrail, heads and fat every Thursday. Most of the dogs thrive on this diet though Beige, my collie/greyhound/greyhound hybrid looks a bit sticky on this food, I must admit. No matter how I try the bitch will not put on weight. She varies between emaciated and very thin. Some days she looks decidedly pathetic. Of late, she even looks out of coat. I am not working her recently so there is no reason to assume that she is over-exercised. Fathom fattens on a quarter of the food that reduces Beige to a skeleton. I must consider feeding meal to help out the tripe situation and maybe to fatten Beige. I once fed meal to my terrier pack; not only was it very expensive but it reduced the condition of the team drastically. Purina, a derivative of soya bean, is perhaps the best meal I have used, but it costs the earth. Happidog or Wilson's is good and reasonably priced. Personally, I have had little luck using Vitalin; the dog's faeces become a bit loose and the meal passes through them.

P.S. One badger easily dug after 20 minutes and released in Hopwas Woods. It was a yearling sow: a bit of a rarity these days to find a sow on the move at this time of year.

Thursday 29

Is Moses having me on yet again? It seems like it for today he mentioned that he has bred and hatched a clutch of phantams—hybrids between a bantam hen and a pheasant cock. They appear to be almost identical to pheasants in colour, size and, story has it, taste. I have seen many poultry hybrids in my time including the turkey/chicken cross called a churkey, and muscovy mallard sterile hybrids are commonly reported. Whether or not Moses is telling the truth is a bit open to doubt, I feel for he is a great teller of tall tales at the best of times. His present craze is Maran pullets, which lay dark chocolate brown eggs, some as dark as milk chocolate. He has promised me a hatch of chicks, but Moses' promises are a bit like pie crust—made to break. Back to the phantams: Moses intends to release them with the pheasants as they seem very

keen to fly and are as nimble as pheasants. Even if such species could be produced, it is doubtful if the progeny would breed. I'd be interested to know if any of the pheasant breeders in Britain have ever bred and kept pheasant poultry hybrids or even crossed the various breeds of pheasant.

Martin Knowelden, my illustrator and coursing companion, hunted with us tonight. A good to modest rat hunt, but nothing spectacular. A pity. I should like Martin to have seen the place in its full splendour. We took 200 give or take a few, but it was not a good night in terms of style. May is never a great month for rat hunting on this particular poultry farm, as the rats are invariably nesting in the hedgerows at this time and feed on stuff near to the nest holes, if they can. In spite of the fact that *rattus norvegicus* is a beast

Moses with spaniel bitch at Radburne.

used to cold weather (originating around the north of the Caspian Sea) he is not particularly keen on coming out on a chilly night to feed. Indeed, even in poultry pens *rattus norvegicus* will choose a warm pen in which

to feed. So many of the natural history books write bunkum concerning rats and their behaviour. After reading some books on rodent behaviour, I wonder if I am hunting the same animal as the one they describe.

Friday 30

Wormed Merle after a huge discussion on the correct vermifuge to use. There are many worm medicines on the market today, the most popular of which is a chemical called Dichlorophen that not only stuns the worm but removes its coating of protective slime, allowing the intestinal juices of the dog to dissolve the parasite. However, nothing other than some liquid slime passes into the faeces and the owner is left in some doubt as to the efficaciousness of the remedy.

The proprietors of such medicines, and make no bones about it, such remedies do work, state that the obviously improved condition of the dog indicates the remedy has worked, and add that unlike many worm remedies Dichlorophen does not make the dog off colour. Still, despite my scientific training that should tell me the Dichlorophen treatment is best, I like to see the expelled worm. Thus, I use a substance called Scoloban, a worming medicine obtainable only from the vet's, containing the extract of Areca nut, an extremely old remedy made from betel nuts. In India, these nuts, mixed with slaked lime, are chewed as the Indians believe it makes the teeth white.

Saturday 31

Went home to my mining valley in South Wales to see some old friends. Gwyn Williams is following in the footsteps of his illustrious uncle, Tom Evans and is keeping springer spaniels. Indeed he is now captain of the Welsh team—quite an achievement as there is little enough game in the valley to test a dog of this calibre. The valley has been reforested—God, what a hideous ecological mess! When the trees were first planted, the villagers felt that the wild life would come back to the scarred and blitzed hillsides. In fact, many deliberately brought in badgers and rabbits from Carmarthen and released them on the hillside in the hope they would breed. For a while, things looked hopeful but as the rows of alien conifers grew, tightly packed for maximum cropping, the undergrowth that would have nourished a host of game died off and the hills became even more devoid of wild life than before. A rubbish dump, it allowed to mature, is far more capable of supporting animal life than a modern forestry plantation. Perhaps a hardwood forest is less financially productive than a stand of conifers, for it takes far longer to grow, but these stands of softwood trees are actually denuding the countryside of its wild life.

June

Sunday 1

Fathom is getting a nuisance. Each morning I turn her out at 4.30 to exercise herself and each day she returns with a catch undamaged but frequently illegal. A month ago, scarcely a day went by when she did not materialize with a screaming kicking drummer but the undergrowth is so thick that she finds difficulty in catching rabbits. Subsequently, the morning token offering has consisted of guinea fowl, the greys, the pieds and the whites, obtained from God knows where and a small team of Light Sussex bantams. It is useless to thrash her for her misdeeds for she is a natural chicken thief, what the Romany call *kanniechor*. Lately, she is catching a great number of collared doves. At first, I thought she had found a spot where they were feeding, but so great is the number caught that I feel she must know a farm where these doves are bred. The guinea fowl pieds certainly come from Alrewas, five miles away, so to catch them and retrieve them, Fathom must cross the busy A38. Should I ever contemplate life in a vardo, such blood will be useful, but at the moment it is a great worry. Woolly Bear, her son, is likely to be a similar type of thief, for his extra collie blood will make him more sagacious still.

Monday 2

Merle is now free of worms, I think, and starting to pick up in condition. It is amazing how quickly a dog who has been cleared of worms resumes his former good health. But he failed to mate the greyhound bitch brought him this evening—a pity really, as she was a superb black and line bred to One and Only. Greyhound bitches often have very small vaginal orifices and dogs that are not skilled studs often fail to mate these bitches. I've known quite a few bitches who need surgical operations before they could mate. Still, what the hell—if she had stood, been mated and conceived, half the litter would have been merle and the rarity value of such a colour would have plummetted. Within ten years, merle puppies will be fairly common, and I will once again be beset by lurcher thieves. At the time of writing, few thieves will touch a merle lurcher as the markings are as distinctive as finger prints. I've never seen two merles who look alike, let alone identical. The variation seems limitless. At Lambourn, three years ago, I saw a black merle, an almost black dog dappled with jet black markings; Keith Ruston photographed the dog, a curious hybrid between an Italian greyhound and a Shetland sheepdog—a strange animal with a hell of a reputation as a rabbiter.

A litter of Merle's puppies: note the considerable variation in merle colouration.

Tuesday 3

Omega is off colour and vomiting freely. This morning, she ingested a plant Moses tells me is mandrake, a plant Moses' tribe used to peddle around the pubs in Guildford to cure chest disorders. It became illegal to do so after the 1939–1945 war, as mandrake is poisonous. My whole garden is infested with poisonous weeds, and my cabbage plot resembles a witches' paradise. Bryony, henbane, aconite and monkswood abound. Moses is fascinated by these weeds, for he has considerable knowledge of such plants, even though his stores concerned with them are bizarre. For in-

stance, he too believes that there is a male and female mandrake and the roots of the respective plants grow until they intertwine—a curious and common sort of belief, though fungi breed similarly. Anyway, when I returned from school, Omega looked a lot better though her kennel bore traces of severe vomiting. The dog's ability to immediately throw up any substance that the stomach finds disagreeable must save countless canine lives. All the same, I must get rid of the witches' grove at the bottom of my run.

74

Wednesday 4

I saw a heron eat a weasel this morning—a good, old fashioned, no-fight type of contest, not the desperate struggle described by natural history books. Few birds or mammals will take on an opponent that will damage them. A lion that is slightly hurt by a gazelle or zebra each time it brings one down, is very quickly *hors de combat*. Likewise, I have never seen a stoat tackle a fully grown rat. Granville Maddocks, MFH of the Atherstone Hunt, saw one only this winter. He was working out his books while his car was parked in Shelfield (there was a torrential hail and rain storm that made driving difficult) when a rat ran screaming and shrieking under his car and crouched there. The rat remained beneath his car for ten minutes, bleating piteously, but shortly afterwards a stoat appeared and ran the scent trail of the rat, killing it beneath the car, accompanied by the cacophony of rat screams. Funny, that; I've seen stoats hammered by suckling doe rats and I've watched a buck drive a stoat out of its warren and away from the lairs.

Thursday 5

After weeks of trying, I have at last caught the rabbit that was destroying my vegetable plot. He has played havoc with the crops, destroying £20 plus of vegetables. Heaven knows, I've tried to catch him. I've used snares, traps and harassed him with dogs and ferrets yet he has managed to escape times without number. Terry spent an entire day trying to catch him and Roger and Mick have had repeated attempts. Yet, until today, he evaded all efforts to catch him. By the merest chance, he was taken. Fathom flushed him as he sat feeding among the beans (he has destroyed two rows of runners) and he bolted under the shed. I tried to flush him with Jack Legg's hob ferret, but the ferret killed the rabbit, sandwiching it against the spars of the shed floor. He weighed 1¼ lbs, a tiny sliver of a rabbit, yet the havoc he caused has been considerable.

A good night's ratting, but not a very great number to show for our troubles. To get a huge haul in June, one needs to hunt the farm after midnight. The haul was low because we were forced to leave before midnight as my uncharged beam ran out.

My border terrier dog chopping a rat.

Friday 6

Another vixen was killed by Merle; this just about sees off the litter, I should think. The skins are worthless, but the litter has caused a lot of trouble locally. Three kittens were killed by the vixen and her cubs, one of the few instances of cat-killing foxes I have ever encountered. Foxes need to be fairly desperate before they will tackle a cat. Cats are tough creatures, more than capable of putting the fiercest dog to flight. No fox in his right mind would run into that set of claws and teeth.

Wolves are equally frightened of creatures that cause them hurt, and usually leave even house cats alone. In Poland, I heard of a few cats that were taken by wolves but such killings are rare. Wolves are not as fierce as people imagine. The mongrel collie I tried to mate to Naylor's Siberian grey frightened the old devil by her skittish behaviour. The wolf is certainly terrified of dogs and few will approach farms where there are watch dogs. In Zakopane, I heard a tale of a hunting pack that killed a chained Alsatian, but I have doubts about the tale. Wolves need to be nearly mad with hunger before they will attack a dog.

Saturday 7

Correction—yet another cub killed by Merle. This surely must be the last. This cub, a young dog, was as big as a large cat. I really hate slaying fox cubs with a lurcher, but unless I clear these I cannot hope to keep the land on which I hunt. I need work for Merle and as he is not nimble enough for rabbit nor fast enough for hare, the only other legal quarry left is fox.

My collie bitch is due to whelp today. She is as full as a balloon. Last season, Paul Taylor of Melton Mowbray had her and mated her to a track greyhound. She whelped eleven puppies, six merle, five black, an easy delivery but not an easy rearing. On the second day, two weedy black puppies died and the bitch reared the rest. On the thirty-fifth day of the rearing I visited Paul and, like a prophet of doom predicted the bitch would keel over with milk fever. She went down with a thrashing fit the very next day. Such problems often cause the death of a bitch and sadly, I am convinced that not only is the condition recurrent in later litter rearings, but the bitch puppies of the litter also have problems when rearing a large litter.

Sunday 8

The Whaddon Chase Show near Milton Keynes and I signed books at the CTF stall. I am astonished to see how many people have read all my books. The type of lurcher that is winning at the shows is fairly gigantic. Ten years ago, a dog *above* 26' tall would have stood no chance at such shows. Now a dog *below* 26″ tall has little chance of winning. Deerhound type dogs, dogs as near as damn it pure deerhound, thirty-one inch giants are in vogue at the moment. For the first time in years, I saw a merle coloured lurcher, more greyhound than collie with the far away look of a sight hound. Whaddon Chase will soon rival Lambourn in size. It is well organised, well planned and quite good entertainment.

On returning home, I found my collie had whelped litter of eleven puppies, five merles, six blacks—or what appear to be blacks: some will obviously be slate blue. It will be a difficult litter to sell; few people want collie crosses even though they were a planned litter. Perhaps obedience competition addicts will appreciate this breeding; they will almost certainly be bright and lively puppies.

Monday 9

I shall go to Lowther Show this year. It is on 10th–11th August. Apparently there is an enormous selection of Fell terriers shown there and I do need data on this breed to do the book. A chap at Whaddon Chase gave me a circular concerned with Lowther and it may be exactly what I want. Not only will it be a great place to see the various types of Fell terrier but it may also be the spot to pick up a suitable outcross bitch for my own strain of terriers. Russell strains are rather poor when compared to the Fell dogs. If one finds 3 or 4 puppies in a Russell class that look good then one is lucky. Fell dogs, however, are usually pictures of conformation. At Whaddon Chase (hardly the best spot for Fell terriers as it is too far south) I saw only one Russell I would have used for my own team of terriers, but there were over a dozen high class Fell terrier types.

Tuesday 10

My collie litter are growing well. Each one is a fat, torpid blob, an ideal state for a puppy, but such rapid and sound growth is thwart with danger. The bitch reared her last litter very well and went down with milk fever. Normally, milk fever manifests itself when a bitch is lactating heavily but Blue, the collie went down with the complaint on her 34th–36th day of lactation, when she had very little milk. Bitches usually lactate most heavily during their second and third litter rearings so I can be fairly certain that she will go down this time. Still, it's an occupational hazard of dog breeding.

I'd be more than interested to find anyone who had researched the physical peculiarity known as the wall eye, the total absence of any pigment in the iris of the eye. Partial wall eyes, partly devoid of pigment, called "tic eyes", are fairly common in merle lurchers and I've seen a wall-eyed puppy that was collie marked black and white. Gypsies dislike wall eyes; they call them moon pies and quite a lot of travellers avoid going to farms where moonpie collies are on guard. The absence of pigment does not, as far as I know, interfere with vision and the puppies are usually bright blue-eyed. Anyway, I'll know later as I will undoubtedly have a wall-eyed puppy in this litter.

Wednesday 11

A visit to Warner's mink farm and surprise, surprise, a trip to the new enclosure to see the litter of silver foxes he has bred. The cubs look delightful and it seems almost a pity to kill them. The vixens breed quite easily, though not as easily as dogs, Warner assures me, and like all foxes they are none too choosy about their feed. Warner feeds them mink food that is slightly "past its best". I was instantly taken with the litter, but they come under the Dangerous Wild Animals Act, so it appears. Thus a a public health licence would be needed to enable the would-be fox breader to keep these beasts. Actually, red foxes taken young enough will breed quite freely in captivity— I've bred them many times but the fox makes a skulking uninteresting type of pet. If the pelt prices continue to rise, the breeding of red foxes in captivity might well be a worthwhile activity, but the fur market is very fickle and next year pelts may be worth next to nothing.

Thursday 12

Eczema has appeared on Roger's puppy in a wet patch on the hind legs. This puppy, the progeny of Beltane and a fox terrier dog, has an identical condition to that of Witch, Beltane's sister (and also Beltane's mortal enemy). I am puzzled as to what causes this condition. Obviously it is an inherited disposition, an allergy to maybe wood creosote or meat. It causes little harm and no pruritis (itching) so I am reluctant to treat this ailment. Anyway, treatment for eczema is a bit hit-and-miss and it can be a lengthy and expensive process before one arrives at what actually causes the eczema.

Still no signs of the border terriers starting work. I think that I will have to quarter them at Hancock's and let them see nightly work with Thomas. When I think of some of the borders I have owned, I could curse myself for these. Yet, in spite of the lack of hunting instinct, they are terrible fighters and spend hours each day locked and ripping each other. If I had a key to unlock their hunting instinct I might have some very useful animals, but somehow they just don't want to work; or is it I have merely failed with the three bitches?

Dog and bitch border terriers. The bitch (left) is one of the most useless terriers I have ever owned.

Vizla—A Hungarian dual purpose pointer-retriever breed.

Friday 13

A vizla has come to reside in the village with his dolly-bird owner. I'm not all that keen on these pointing, retrieving breeds of dog, but Weimaraners, Vizlas, German shorthaired pointers and Brittany spaniels are very much in vogue at the time of writing. The nearest the British came to producing a pointing/retrieving breed was in the production of the springer spaniel, who often gives a rough and ready sort of point before it crashes into cover. Dual purpose hunting dogs are the average on the Continent for the working man has long had shooting rights in Germany and so a dual purpose dog, one who would both point, flush and retrieve was the order of the day to those who could not afford two shooting dogs. Against this, I must say that I have never seen a really stock steady German shorthaired pointer and all the Weimaraners I have encountered were fairly run of the mill huntingwise. I once saw the falconer Laurant de Bastyai with a vizla and was not at all impressed with the dog. Still, one does hear of hunters who use these breeds successfully even in good competition.

Saturday 14

To Cheltenham to see the only pair of Galgos in the land—at least that is what the owner, Peter Saunders tells me. Galgos are reasonably true-breeding Spanish hunting dogs of the lurcher type, the sort of dog that is procured by crossing a heavy-coated bearded collie with a greyhound. These are dogs used by the ubiquitous Spanish gypsies who haunt the dry regions of Central Spain—though the pair I saw came from Alicante. Judging from the bright eyes and eager, willing attitude of the breed, it is reasonable to assume that some form of sheepdog has been used in its creation. The breed is probably a Spanish counterpart of the original Norfolk lurcher and closely resembles the dogs bred by Aubrey Fryer. I gather Mr Saunders wants to register the breed—the end of another useful type of dog? So what—the lurcher is hell bent for the show ring and total uselessness. I've not a lot of time for the show world though it gives some people pleasure, I suppose.

On a more practical note, the artichokes look like small sunflowers and if Moses is right, they will decoy pheasants from miles around—and then as they say in the best Batman cartoons—ZAAP!

Sunday 15

A visit from Harry Lees. He has been asked to judge the Cottesmore Lurcher Show with Lt. Colonel Ted Walsh, an odd couple if I might say, both decent chaps but as different as chalk to cheese. Harry is an amazing raconteur and one of the favourite people at my house. It is really impossible not to like Harry, and Walsh also seems a likeable chap. I wonder how he will take Harry's very earthy anecdotes, particularly the one about the farmer who hit him with a gun. Harry is a competitive coursing man and wants a different type of dog from the type I require. I have little use for straight sighthound type dogs, but these are the type that do best in the coursing field. My own type of dog is one with a tractable disposition and I would sacrifice a mite of speed for this trainable nature. Harry has in training a puppy from Omega and Merle, a tragic mismating, I'm afraid and one that should never have happened. Still, Harry seems pleased with it and it is already facing cover well enough. Keith Ruston's puppy from the same breeding is a tiny mite and able to get to ground with ease. Harry's is bigger and a bit bolder. What they will do, I just don't know.

Monday 16

I had a young leveret brought me this evening and offered to me free of charge. The poor little devil is still suckling and has little chance of surviving. Why on earth people seem to want wild things for pets is baffling. Hares are naturally wild and nervous, and when taken as leverets and reared in captivity, they either become nervous wrecks, ready to race away if even looked at, or else become vile tempered little beasts only too eager to attack the owner—and the attack of an adult hare is pretty formidable, I can assure you. I've been *kicked* by hares and I certainly didn't enjoy the tussle. How does one sex a tiny leveret? I found it very difficult to determine whether the mite was a male or a female. The ancients are certainly to be excused for believing that hares could change their sex, becoming jacks or does at will.

Perhaps the ancients are right for there is now remarkable evidence that certain primitive human tribes change sex regularly. Back to hares—of course I refused the babe. I hate rearing any wild beast in captivity and I've had little luck when I've tried. I've reared hares and had some bad times with them as adults—not again, thank you. Once is enough.

Tuesday 17

I need a lot more data on Harry Hardestey, the famous Fell hunter. Nearly every classy looking working Lakeland terrier seems to date back to Hardestey's dogs, in particular to a dog called Turk. Tyson's dogs are directly descended from dogs he had from Hardestey, so Winch's dogs will be from the same source. Some of Buck's Lakeland/Fell terriers are supposedly from Harry Hardestey's bloodline, but I'm not so certain of these for Buck breeds a distinct type of Fell terrier. Newcombe wrote an article in *Shooting Times* about the Fell terrier and used a picture of Frank Buck and one of his black bitches—very classy, a bit long in the back maybe, but absolutely first class in conformation. Dave Harcombe, compiler of the *Working Terrier Year Book*, is quite keen on these Fell type terriers and has become very disenchanted with border terriers. Certainly, one meets many people who own failed border terriers these days. Twenty years ago—boy, this dates me—a border terrier was a first class working prospect, but now things are not so bright. My own bitches are certainly near-idiot and I know many who have dogs and bitches that will not look at a rat, let alone go to ground. How long will it take before this craze for conformation ruins the hard little Fell terriers? Not long, I imagine: many seen at the shows never see work yet they will undoubtedly win and be bred from.

Wednesday 18

A hob ferret was handed to me this morning. A nice type of ferret, but riddled with mange. Of course, I could not take it in. Such mange would ravage my entire crop of ferrets and also infect my dogs. Ferret mange, like dog mange an ever present guest at my premises, is caused by the mite that causes human scabies and more than once I have been infected by a mangy ferret someone has brought me. It is very hard for the lay person to appreciate that if one owns a kennels or even a small team of hunting dogs or ferrets, that one does not welcome every waif and stray creature to one's doors. Some people even materialise with sheep worriers and savage dogs and attempt to sell them, but most people are all too glad to get a nuisance off their hands. Curiously, these people are amazed if one does not want to take a dangerous liability that could easily destroy the equilibrium of a whole kennels. To return to the hob. The finder, a woman of maybe fifty, lamented on its filthy condition and proclaimed it had been living wild for weeks. Ferret escapees do well at this time of the year and usually a few days living wild will produce a healthy, sparkling ferret free from mange, foot rot or what have you. This ferret had all the signs of a beast that had been kept in a filthy hutch and not fed or cared for. It had probably only just escaped.

Thursday 19

Yet another superb night's ratting. Alan Thomas's dog, a son of Omega and Hamish, has joined the team, but is showing little hunting instinct. Few terriers catch on the first time out. The travelling in the trailer, the stench of poultry, the fluttering of the hens and the carnage of the rat hunt is a bit disconcerting to the newcomer. I never write off a dog, for some are very late starters. When the border terrier bitches will start is a bit of a puzzle though. They are apparently absolutely useless, but I am certain they will get it together one day. I received a nasty bite on the knee from my border terrier dog who struck at a rat racing up my leg. He missed the rat, but put his teeth in my knee. It is a fairly frightful rip and gives some indication of the power of this border terrier's jaws. If the bitches would even try, I'd put up with these bites and gladly at that.

A small problem—maybe not so small. Paul Coffey, travelling behind the trailer, ran full tilt into me, smashing the doors and bending the axle of the trailer. No dogs were hurt—a bit of a blessing, but the trailer is in a hell of a mess. Fortunately, Trevor Edwards, an ex-pupil of mine, has joined the team and he has a large wagon to transport the dogs, so hunting as normal is the order of the day.

Friday 20

Harry Lees has been asked to judge the Cottesmore Lurcher Show—a pity, really as I should have liked to show there. It is very bad policy to show dogs where a friend is judging. Whenever I judge, I literally beg my friends to keep away. It creates bad feeling if one does not give a friend a prize and animosity with the crowd if one does. It's a hiding to nothing, judging shows where friends are showing.

We now have a set of T-shirts, the ultimate in vanity. They depict a huge rat and a caption "I have hunted with DB. Plummer." Curiously enough, my friends go wild for such shirts. What a strange animal the hunter is! Few of us can honestly say we are not exhibitionists and fewer still can really admit to not enjoying favourable publicity.

Andrew Cocks, my publisher, tells me the Jack Russell book is selling well. It's quite a nice book, but not one I enjoyed writing. *Rat Hunting Man* or *Nathan* is still my favourite book. *Lepus* is quite a good book, I think, but I'll wait until it hits the market before I comment on its real value. The critics are kind to me. Few of them lash my books and fewer still give me the miserable pathetic criticisms other sporting writers seem to get.

Saturday 21

Moses materialised with his Italian greyhound—a tiny, high stepping, fragile little beast—not the sort of beast an ex-gypsy cum gamekeeper might be expected to own. It is tiny even for an Italian greyhound and cannot weigh more than seven pounds in fat condition. Surprisingly, it is very tough and has great hunting instinct, hunting by nose and pushing rabbits out of cover like a veteran. I am astonished that such sporting instinct still survives in such a beast—after all, the breed has not been worked seriously for three or four hundred years, and even then it was a court lap dog rather than a pot filler. Yet this diminutive little beast hunted up quarry like a first class lurcher and was quite fearless of nettles and briars in spite of its fine silky coat. Moses says it has been used for ferreting, but I have no doubt it would find a rabbit too big for its tiny jaws. Nevertheless, it marks well and goes to ground like a terrier, entering seemingly impossible small cracks and crevices.

Sunday 22

The artichokes are now nearly in flower. Let us hope that they will attract the pheasants as Moses assures me they will. What a disreputable sort of person I have become! A few years ago, twenty maybe, I would have been hurt had any one accused me of poaching. Now I have the reputation of being a poacher and I seem to be going out of my way to be anti-social.

Shooting Times reviewed my book *The Complete Lurcher* and called it a "handbook for poachers." At the Badminton Horse Trials, one lurcher stall refused to sell my books as they did not approve of them. I am almost certainly losing my respectable readership—or am I? Is the rogue element not fairly strong in all of us? I am a school teacher yet I am deliberately planting artichokes in order to attract pheasants from the nearby shoot, hoping that the morning run with Fathom will reap pheasants that are feeding on my patch of land and are therefore legally if not morally mine. Moses assures me pheasants will come from miles to feed on artichoke tubers. If he is correct, I will certainly be able to test my theories on the poaching of game birds.

Monday 23

A fellow from Banbury came with a huge Lakeland—a bitch more the size of an Irish terrier. It is probably an amazingly game type of terrier but where could one use a beast of this size? The show world, the world of working terrier shows favours such dogs, but it is insane to expect a beast of this size to work fox. True, they are able to get to badger, but terriers were designed to work at middle-sized earth-dwelling quarry, not just badger. Furthermore, an eleven inch dog will usually do just about any job below ground. This chap wanted to know of, as he put it, "another good Lakeland stud." Perhaps he is satisfied with the dog. It certainly would not suit me.

Fathom brought home a fully grown partridge this morning. As usual, it was alive. I turned it loose and it whirred back into Cope's field. Fathom seems mystified when I let her prey fly off. It must seem a little thankless, to say the least. In spite of her chicken thefts, she has become a superb little hunter, ever eager to catch anything available. Fur, feather and fowl are all grist to her insatiable mill. She must be kept up until the poults are on the wing. Woolly Bear, her son, is settling down a little and is no longer the absolute clown he used to be. I must start to train him shortly. It is nearly impossible to teach a dog to sit, lie and stay if he is not lead trained.

Tuesday 24

A slight panic and an unnecessary one. Steel whelps in about a week and she looks decidedly under the weather. I once lost three bitches through toxaemia, the inability of the liver to cope with vast amounts of toxic breakdown chemicals produced by the growing foetuses, and this has made me very careful of pregnant bitches who are off colour. Toxaemia must carry off quite a few pregnant bitches and there is not much a vet can do about the condition. Steel is such a gluttonous omnivore and to find her off her food is a bit of a surprise. By 12 midnight however, she returned from the walk ravenous and frantic for the food she had refused. She is a grand old brood bitch, worth her weight in gold.

A greyhound has been offered by Harold Hodson Walker. I need a stud greyhound like a hole in the head at the moment. I am terribly overstocked and if I am not careful I will finish up with a huge flock of useless animals, untrained and scarcely entered. I must not have another dog or ferret brought to my premises. I have nearly enough terriers to last out the decade.

Wednesday 25

Beltane whelped three days early—a pathetic litter of three dogs and one putty nosed bitch. One of the dogs is very undersized, a result of
(a) breeding from an elderly bitch
(b) mating Beltane to her own brother, though the last litter to Vampire was not weedy
(c) working the bitch to rat right up until the day before whelping.
Personally, I believe it is simply due to the fact that

Beltane is thirteen years old and should be well past puppy bearing—at this age she should also be well past hunting, but I would miss her sorely if she went, for she has the most unerring nose of any terrier I have bred.

Alan Thomas's dog, the result of mating his Hamish to Omega, has a serious stomach condition and has vomited for three days. As yet there are no obvious signs of dehydration but he is showing great lassitude and is most unwilling to eat or drink. He has had an antibiotic shot and has been encouraged to drink an electrolyte/glucose solution but the treatment has not helped. He is still bringing up a frothy white vomit and becomes weaker by the day. Heaven knows what awful bugs he has ingested during the rat hunts.

Thursday 26

I shall cancel tonight's hunt, the first for some time. Beltane has a premature litter (one has already died) and Alan's dog is sick. The team would thus be too small to make any impact on the rats, although the border terriers would benefit from such a hunt. They really are the slowest starters I have ever encountered.

I will certainly put Alan's dog into intensive care tonight. The vomiting has not abated and if it continues it will almost certainly see him off. Perhaps another day might put him right, but at this rate he will need to be given antidehydration treatment. His father was slightly nephritic and died as a result of a gut infection—not a good omen for the young dog I fear.

The ferrets are looking lean and well. The diet of starlings (provided by Peter Hancock) and doves caught by Fathom from some place that is obviously breeding collared doves, is superb. The jill is very lean but obviously pregnant. There is certainly a relationship between fat condition and tameness. Jills in this condition are quite frequently very touchy, yet fat overfed animals are usually quite tame. I really don't want any of this bloodline in my ferrets. Touchy animals are a misery to hunt and not a pleasure to own.

Friday 27

The dogs are decidedly restless after last night's lack of hunting. It is easy to understand why terriers make such lousy pets. Those whose hunting instinct is strong must be exploited to the full if they are to be of any use as house pets, those who are not hunted become irritable, neurotic pests. Half the stock worriers in the district are either border collies or Jack Russell terriers, both essentially working breeds.

A few weeks ago I gave the manuscript of "The Dyatt Jack" to an unknown typist—a nice piece of work—the manuscript, I mean. Since then she has disappeared together with my tape recorder. I need a big T-shirt with S for Sucker printed on the front. Not only have I lost a tape recorder but also a superb piece of writing. Well, superb by my standards. What a curious little creature this woman must be—willing to profit from one stolen tape recorder. I shall rewrite the article and simply write off my tape recorder to experience. A pity, for I grow attached to my property. Perhaps I have been too long amongst the Romanies, but I feel no good luck will go with this woman for this deed. It was a really good article concerned with how Fathom caught the famous Dyatt hare—one of our local legends.

Saturday 28

Steel, the bearded collie greyhound bitch is due to whelp today. I must really ask myself, do I need these extra lurchers? They are an added expense and I simply do not have the work for any more dogs. If I told the truth, Fathom is the only lurcher I really need. At first I contemplated disposing of Fathom's bloodline and keeping a pure breeding collie/greyhound line from Steel and Merle plus an infusion of greyhound blood from time to time, but in spite of its mongrel nature, I would not want to part with Fathom's family. They are true lurchers, sagacious, cunning and great providers. I will chance being overstocked and run on puppies from both Fathom and Steel and postpone making my decision until both families have been tested. Steel is balloon-like and it should be a very big litter. As a brood bitch (and since her crippling accident, she is little else) she will take some beating. She rarely loses a puppy and her stock is very typey.

Still no sign of Steel whelping. Dawn found her as usual, bouncing against her pen. Fathom brought yet another guinea fowl home this morning, alive, unharmed and as usual, stolen. It is a problem above all others now and no longer a joke. If she killed her stolen swag, it would solve quite a few problems, but the stolen poultry are always alive. I can no longer justify turning her loose to exercise. Sooner or later, I will be prosecuted for her thefts and she will be shot. I cannot see an end to the trouble. To date, she has "stolen" 24 chickens, 16 guinea fowl and 53 doves and pigeons. Add to this one tame black and white rabbit which may or may not have been running wild and the enormity of her crimes becomes obvious.

I spent the evening shooting rats with Thomas and starting Sally Hancock's greyhound at catching rats. Greyhounds are natural killers but their size and stupidity does little to help them in the places where I hunt. I have seen greyhounds nail rats with the best of them in open spaces, and Terry Aherne has a whippet that puts most terriers to shame. I dislike guns, but I owe Thomas a few favours. Rats shot in the head or spine die fairly quickly though the convulsions are hideous to watch, but body shot or worse still gut shot rats are usually pitiful to watch and may die slowly over a period of weeks. Several times, I have seen rats with paws rotting away with slimy gangrenous pus. Even rats deserve a clean death.

Eddie Jones' Celt, Merle × greyhound. Note the knuckle of forelegs—bone that will "grow out".

84

Monday 30

At 4.0 pm I arrived home to find Steel about to whelp. She produced ten puppies, four black and six merles as easily as shelling peas. This now confirms my theory on the inheritance of the merle factor and I am now convinced that I must only introduce black or blue blood into the strain. If a merle bitch puppy—there is only one merle bitch which is rough coated—1986 will see a true breeding strain of rough coated, fast, intelligent lurchers, all 23–24″ tall and all superbly athletic. Eddie Jones has a black three-quarter bred male, and a good black stud put out to an enthusiast—

not a meddler—will be enough to keep me going for years. If this blood is tested in the fire, (the real fire, not the world of the two minute chop and change hunter) the strain is sure of surviving. This litter *must* go to anyone who will really test it. A few dashes of greyhound blood brought in through either pure bred greyhound or better still, a dash of genuine three-quarter bred greyhound/collie blood will suit me fine. I must find permanent homes for suitable stud dogs. That is my first priority.

July

Tuesday 1

The Steel litter is doing well so is Blue's crop of puppies (bearded/border collie) but the collie bitch is looking a bit under the weather. I am unhappy about this bitch; the temperament is not quite right and she is neurotic, much given to running the length of her pen and retracing her steps. She frequently loses weight at an alarming rate as a result of this hyperactivity and she has to be kennelled in a small pen to prevent total exaciation. After this litter has been weaned, I shall keep the most placid and pass on the bitch. I often wonder if the bitch would be as neurotic if she was worked to sheep regularly.

Another grim struggle in the moonlight. After the Coventry Writers' Circle meet, I went on a 3.0 am hunt with my merle lurcher. Another fox was taken, a young male maybe a year old, but it was a savage battle, for Merle is out of condition. Fathom watched the whole battle without batting an eyelid. She is terrified of foxes or perhaps totally unaware that they constitute quarry. Dogs with a large proportion of greyhound blood are usually very easy to enter to fox but Fathom is such a mongrel that she lacks most of the fire of the pure greyhound. She is still the best all round lurcher I have ever owned, however.

Wednesday 2

Yet another tragedy. My collie bitch went down with milk fever this morning, rolling staggering walk preceded a violent thrashing fit. This complaint is caused through the leeching of soluble calcium salts from the body. I do not believe she will survive the ailment. Richard Jones, my vet, a first class man with small animals, says that she has also suffered a heart attack. It is useless for me to keep such an animal. She will not survive the life in my kennels.

Thank God for Moses and his wife. In Romany they would be called juckmar, or dog daft, besotted with small puppies. Carole, Moses' wife has agreed to rear the puppies for me. A blessing, as they are only two

weeks old and will require constant attention. As I am still at school, such a task would be beyond me. Dogs are taking up far too much of my time as things are. I found only ten puppies when I took the batch to Moses' house and on returning heard a squealing and crying coming from beneath the shed. I had omitted to take one of the black puppies up to Moses. Steel heard the crying and snatched up the babe, carrying it to her kennel. She will rear it easily. Fostering is usually fairly easy with dogs. All a bitch has to hear is a puppy crying in hunger and maternal instincts simply flood in, I'm glad to say.

Thursday 3

An excellent night's hunting. I took thirty live rats by hand. We arrived late and set to work as soon as light faded. Within an hour, we had over 200 and sad to say, we missed far more than we caught. I saw Omega kill a pied rat, a rat that had fairly plentiful white mark-

ings. Such mutations must be fairly common in a place with such a high rat population. Freaks must abound for a short time, at least.

Bob took back thirty pounds of rats to feed the ferrets—a cheap nourishing meat, and as anyone who

86

Thomas Hancock's puppy chances a grab at a rat—and was bitten for her troubles.

has reared a litter of ferrets will know, rearing a litter of ferrets can be a costly business. Young ferrets will eat between ¼ lb and ½ lb of flesh per day. Thus a large litter of ferrets will eat 6 or 7 lbs of flesh per day, and could cost the ferret keeper one heck of a price. I once saw three litters of ferrets strip a young store pig in three days and saw a half grown litter eat a hare in a 24 hour orgy of eating. Rats are really good food, a bit disgusting to the average man, but excellent meat. Ferrets fatten well on rat and eat the lot except for the very tough skins of old bucks and the rat tails. With the exception of owls, I have never seen any bird eat a rat tail.

Friday 4

My search for a male wolf to mate to a dog continues. I am now fairly convinced wolf/dog hybrids do not exist. Paul Taylor of Melton Mowbray is arranging a mating for me. His house is half a mile from a miniature zoo and it is difficult to sleep when the wolves herald in a new moon. Dogs are not closely related to wolves, I am convinced of this. In spite of considerable research, I have failed to find anyone who has actually bred a wolf/dog hybrid. Every lead has come to a dead end. Dr John Naylor, an authority on the wolf, is also certain that it is nearly impossible to cross a dog with a wolf. Perhaps an advert in *Exchange and Mart* will produce the required results. If not a mating, at least a stud wolf that will be capable of mating. What to do with the hybrids is the problem. Who on earth would want such a cross?

Saturday 5

A Saturday rat shoot finishing at 2.0 am on Sunday. A superb night's entertainment even though the hauls were not high. A .177 pellet does little or no harm to a rat, and though I am fairly certain there are a host of people who have killed rats with a .177 pellet, there must be a host of wounded rats after a shoot using these pellets. I have no doubt that .22 is the only suitable calibre gun for rat hunting, and even then a lot of rats escape. I dislike guns and gunmen and I merely carry the beam and flush rats during these hunts. Dogs are strictly forbidden on these hunts and for good reason. The casualties would be enormous,—canine casualties, I mean. Those present were Thomas Hancock 14 years (an excellent shot), Makham Singh (18), Hugh Whyte (18), Lakbir Singh (17).

One of my fox terrier/Russell hybrids seems to have incurable mange. When Liz was here the word incurable seemed never to have been used. Now, with my myriad commitments, it is a word I tend to use all too frequently. I must cut down external activities and spend more time on stockmanship.

Sunday 6

Myxomatosis—the first signs have appeared in the district, heralding as usual the end of rabbit hunting. It is a mixed blessing, but I feel no man has the right to introduce it deliberately. Fathom fetched three rabbits home this morning, not one apparently infected. At first, I marvelled at her hunting ability, for a rabbit takes some catching at this time of year. Later in the day, Woolly Bear, her merle broken-coated son caught one and retrieved it gently to hand. Diseased rabbits are ideal to start a puppy. Not only are they on the way out, so to speak, but they are too doped to put up much of a show against a young lurcher. Woolly overshot it at first, but soon snapped up the rabbit at the second attempt. If I work him hard for the next few days, before the disease wipes out the rabbit population, he will soon get the hang of rabbit catching.

The bearded collie lurcher Steel is rearing the litter well, although she killed the collie puppy I fostered with her. Fostering is a risky business, to say the least.

Monday 7

Yet another rabbit for Woolly Bear—an easy catch after a not so easy chase. The rabbit was diseased, of course, for myxie is now absolutely rampant around here. At 4 am there are a load of rabbits around here, all seemed slightly dopey and quite a few squashed cadavers of rabbits litter the roads. The magpies, crows and rats will feed well for a few days, and then there will be no rabbits to speak of. A pity really, as the stoat population around here has built to quite a high level now that the rabbits seem to have made a comeback.

Moses brought the collie litter to show me; they seem fine if dirty. It is nearly impossible to clean up a litter of puppies by hand. The bitch is back to normal again, but I will pass her on to a pet home. With a heart condition and a susceptibility to milk fever, she will be a liability to me. I will find another bitch to attempt my dog/wolf hybrid—one of her puppies, I think. There's a superb merle in the litter—well worth keeping.

Tuesday 8

Live rabbits are thin on the ground but the cadavers are plentiful. Another day should see off all the rabbits—a pity really, they were very numerous and I had a lot of entertainment hunting the rabbits with my lurchers earlier this year. It will take a year for the district to recover from the disease, and the ecological change wrought by the infection will have a far more lasting effect. A massive rabbit population usually has a deleterious effect on the land, the pools of urine and the enormous mounds of faeces (each rabbit passes 360 plus pellets a day) causes the fodder grasses to die off and he replaced by spurry and other rank weeds.

I have nearly finished the Knowelden commission and it is not too bad, I think. Am I losing my edge as a writer? Certainly too many people visit my house and disturb my concentration. If I complete two books a year, it will be as much as I can manage. I must break with this sporting type book if my literary career is to take off—but what else do I know about other than hunting?

Fathom took a young drummer as she leapt across a stand of bramble. Ian's dog, Fathom's half brother, immediately ran in and killed it. He will certainly make a useful animal, but he is reluctant to retrieve.

Wednesday 9

A hard morning's course and Fathom was made to look stupid by a hare that appeared on the edge of the Alrewas turn. No excuses, the hare appeared some twenty yards in front of her and Fathom was in first class condition. It was simply too good for her. How on earth men can boast dogs that will catch and kill 9 out of 10 hares is beyond me. I rate Fathom fairly highly as a providing dog—she is the correct size, weight, and shape—but I have seen hares that have put her to shame.

Woolly Bear, Fathom's rather ugly son, is improving daily. He is hunting quite well, using his nose quite a lot, and jumping very well. Today he scrabble-jumped 5 ft 6 inches easily. He is also losing his shapeless look. With luck, he will put Fathom to shame by the time he is three years old. Lurcher adverts that offer an all-round dog aged two are a bit puzzling. I have never owned a lurcher that was any good until it was three years old. It takes that time for a dog to learn the necessary bushcraft. Or do I expect too much of my dogs?

My hob ferret is sterile, without a doubt. Eleven jills have been mated by him, but not one has conceived. Even the apparently pregnant jill is a sham. It will be a long cold winter as far as young ferrets are concerned. Still, I have four mature jills down with the Jacksons at Reading.

Thursday 10

I arrived home to find Fathom running loose and a young leveret on the doorstep. Where on earth did she get it? There are no hares this side of Alrewas. The other place where hares are to be found in the district is the Dyatt Estate. Either way, she will have had to cross the busy A38 to get to these hunting grounds. I am puzzled as to how she has survived so long. The sixty-four thousand dollar question is, however, what else has she stolen during the time she was out? I searched the place thoroughly but no stolen loot has materialised. It is a constant worry, I must confess.

The rat hunt was very savage and long. We started at 10.32 pm and finished at 2 am. We took 200 plus but the dogs suffered terribly. Beltane has puppies and should not really be worked but she is upset if she does not accompany us on hunts. She received an awful rip that caused her eyes to close. Vampire is a terrible mess and Pagan is no better. Alan's dog is practically unmarked and the border dog has a few rips on his face. Omega was slightly bitten but she rarely swells up since the huge abscess on her throat burst. We started the two fox terrier cross bitches and though they settled very well, neither attempted a kill. Next litter I will bring the puppies here as soon as they are inoculated and simply allow them to see a succession of kills before they are given a chance to try for a live rat.

Friday 11

Not a good evening's hunt though Woolly is really becoming a useful dog. He took off after a healthy adult rabbit in the field opposite the house this morning and although he missed, he stayed with the fleeing rabbit for a most arduous course.

I received a letter from Peter Evans, a lad who met me at Whaddon Chase show. I arranged for him to hunt rat with me, and he is taking me up on my offer. As a boy, I received so much discouragement and was ripped off so many times by unscrupulous dog and ferret sellers that I go out of my way to help youths. Sometimes, I come unstuck and help to promote a pompous knowall, but more often than not I think I help some lad along with the sport.

The hob I borrowed from Jack Legge is not covering the jills. Today Paul phoned and Fudge has "missed". I don't really need young ferrets, but Paul does.

Buying ferrets at the Game Fair is hardly my scene, but it seems to be in Paul's mind at the moment. Normally, one can pick up baby ferrets at the livestock market for 25p or perhaps a bit more. One changed hands at the Game Fair for £10—a bit ridiculous if you ask me.

Saturday 12

Bullock's puppy, the result of mating my cur bred lurcher Penguin to Terry Aherne's collie/greyhound dog is catching. Today, it killed a myxied rabbit at the end of the grove. Admittedly, it is not a great feat, but myxied rabbits provide an excellent start for a young lurcher. Not only is the puppy, now aged six months, hunting well, but he is very obedient. Woolly is roughly the same way bred and the end product is the same. Collie blood is essential in the ideal lurcher and I

now regret the years of deerhound greyhound breeding I spent trying to produce the ideal coursing dog.

A very boring rat shoot. It is ridiculous to take too many on such a hunt. Saturday night rat shoots should be used to accustom puppies, kept on leads, to the bustle of a hunt. I will stop taking hordes of people on such a trip. Basically, in spite of my eccentric ways, I am keen on discipline and the undisciplined multitude on Saturday did not appeal to me.

Terry Aherne's collie × greyhound × greyhound bitch—a litter sister of Beige.

The Cottesmore Lurcher show—and I bought a Fell terrier puppy, as straight-legged a babe as one could imagine. Very few pure bred Fell terriers are bow legged and most are hard enough for the Thursday night rat hunt. I left a deposit of £5 with John Dean and sent the rest by post. I will mate this bitch to Vampire or one of his sons and breed out the black colour later. Alan Thomas is also interested in bringing in this Fell terrier blood to improve his stock. The Jack Russell as a whole could be vastly improved by using these northern terriers. Not only are the dogs well shaped, but they are certainly not wanting in courage or hunting instinct. If I was starting up again in Jack Russells (God forbid) I would certainly use copious amounts of Fell terrier blood. Some of the Lakeland terriers I have seen at shows are absolute stormers. At this moment in time however, it is considered very infra dig to use Fell terrier blood on ugly, scruffy little dogs that are collectively known as Jack Russell terriers. Why, I just can't think. Anyway, I am now once again the owner of a Fell terrier puppy. Who knows, if the puppy has nose, brain and guts I may introduce this blood into my own strain of Jack Russell terrier.

Jack Russells with obvious fell terrier ancestry. Not only are these terriers good lookers but also excellent workers—a little big for the Midlands though.

Monday 14

My litter of lurchers is growing well. Steel is lactating like a Jersey heifer. I have a horrid fear that milk fever might be on the cards with this bitch, and I live in dread of seeing another attack. I just couldn't take the fuss of rearing a litter. The forthcoming holiday, which I desperately need, I might add, would degenerate into a nightmare if I had to hand rear a litter of this size. A fostered litter needs constant attention if it is to live, let alone thrive and the time spent with the litter must mentally exhaust anyone. Two hourly feeds would be necessary at this age to keep a litter on form and that means day and night feeding. I pray to God she will rear this litter herself. I am literally pumping food into the animal. She gets the equivalent of the needs of a bitch six times her weight and that's just in dry meal. In addition to this meal, she also gets whatever meat, chicken innards, tripe, etc. I can get, yet she still looks exhausted, fat, but very tired. With luck she will rear the whole lot by herself but I have this sneaking dread of milk fever.

Merle and Steel's litter aged three weeks and four days—Mara nearest camera.

Tuesday 15

A hurried feeding and then to Birmingham to have my car repaired. I really must trade this thing in for a new one. I can just about afford to have a new Fiat using my old car as a trade in. Actually, I do a terrific mileage in any vehicle. This one has clocked thirty-five thousand miles. The clutch is slipping, and the steering not right. Furthermore, I must confess that I do not look after a vehicle.

Beltane's litter was a mean, pathetic little brood. Not only is she not very good at rearing them, for she is old and has very little milk, but she is indifferent as to their welfare. At the thought of a hunting trip, she leaps up and down on the litter and is unworried by the hurt squeaks. What a superb bitch she is! When will I breed her like—certainly not from her as her progeny leave a lot to be desired. Perhaps this litter, sired by her maniac brother will do the job, but I have my doubts. I really should have kept more puppies from this bitch. Hindsight, however, is remarkably easy. I would not object to an entire brood of Vampire/Beltane puppies in spite of their tendency to be putty nosed.

Wednesday 16

Quiet night—caught the last of the myxied rabbits with Fathom. The dead now litter the fields. During the early part of the year, I thought it would be the bonanza year for rabbits. Now the place is a desert. A heck of a blow. Question—how will I start Steel's litter? I shall reduce the number of lurchers I shall keep back from this litter for I have no work for the number I now keep and it looks as though I am overdogged now that the rabbit crop is reduced. There is one merle bitch, a feathery, whiskery-faced bitch that may be worthwhile. I shall certainly dispose of the two pale merle dog puppies.

Pagan is showing colour. Question—shall I mate her to Vampire or to Alan's dog? Vampire, mated to Pagan's sister produced a bad fronted litter of puppies, but Alan's dog is untried and untested. If I mate Pagan to either Vampire or Alan's dog then the result, colourwise, will be the same. 50% of the litter will be white Russell type and 50% will be Patterdale coloured, black and tan or tan. Paul Coffey will take some of the coloured puppies and Trevor some of the others. I think Vampire, as he is ageing rapidly and I may not have a chance to use him again. I will settle for a suitable bitch, and, boy, will it be well bred work-wise!

Thursday 17

An interesting lady, Mrs Janet Evans plus her son Peter, joined our Thursday hunt. She is the wife of a Cambridge doctor and rather surprisingly, unafraid of the cascade of rats. We had our photographs taken in various lunatic poses and with good luck, she should have a few useful prints of the hunt.

Moses intends to return the collie litter on Monday. They are five weeks old and eating well, altogether a fair job of rearing. Question—should I keep a dog or bitch for future lurcher breeding? Strictly speaking, a bearded collie mated to a greyhound usually breeds a somewhat lighter type of lurcher than a border collie mated to a similar greyhound. I have bred both and the somewhat taller bearded collie tends to produce a lighter, but less intelligent type of lurcher. Steel, before her injuries, was a beautiful and very fast lurcher. Whether or not the bearded collie/border collie hybrids mated to greyhounds will produce a shapely intelligent lurcher is open to question, however. Time alone will tell.

Friday 18

One of Steel's puppies, a blue merle, looks decidedly off. The puppy is a bit lean and cries a lot, but the anus is very wet and sore—a fairly sure sign some thing is wrong. Steel is very weary of this litter and is reluctant to clean this sickly puppy. It's an odds on favourite that tomorrow will see the death of the babe. Cause of illness—I haven't a clue, it just seems to fade by the minute. Perhaps a virus, a stomach weakness or quite simply the possibility Steel has stepped on the puppy or maybe lain on it. If another one looks sickly, I must get the vet in. I hope it isn't an infectious disease that is causing the trouble. I'd hate to lose the litter, not only have they been costly to rear but I am quite fond of the batch. Tomorrow will tell, I'm certain.

My collie bitch has a huge abscess that has just burst. As it is below the jaw, it is impossible for her to clean it. It is already flyblown and a day or so will see maggots in the wound. I shall leave these maggots to clean out the abscess—which though the thought of maggots eating out a septic wound is revolting, it is usually quite effective. I've used this method before and I have had good healing as a result of these maggots eating away the filth within an abscess.

Saturday 19

A reasonably quiet day apart from two savage fights, one between the two fox terrier cross puppies and the other between Vampire and the collie bitch. The latter was particularly ferocious and resulted in an ugly six-inch gash in the bitch's throat. I am not particularly angry with Vampire, for the bitch has gone out of her way to upset him, leaping as this cage and engaging in a maddening barking whenever she sees him. A collie bitch makes a very bad pet—a working collie bitch with herding instinct, that is—for they find mischief when they are idle and cause a great deal of trouble. She has served me well, however, in spite of her recent hypocalcaemic problems and when the rip is repaired I will find her a good home. I will certainly keep one, if not two, of her puppies particularly as one has a pale blue eye that will almost certainly turn "wall." This is a fascinating freak eye colour and while it looks bizarre, it brings about no problem regarding sight, though some hill shepherds refuse to keep wall-eyed puppies, as they are supposed to frighten the sheep.

Sunday 20

A chapter of accidents and a burned out clutch plate that necessitated my walking from Measham—a town 23 miles away. I am certainly not as fit as I was during the hectic days when I did nothing but hunt. My trip was to Spalding, Lincs. to fetch a fell terrier puppy from John Dean who has some really neat Lakeland type dogs. Dean's were of moderate size and could easily be worked to fox even in Lincolnshire where the fox earths are reputedly very small. I am certainly going to the Lowther Show this year and there are usually some exceptionally good Lakeland type dogs shown there. Some are huge, however, and I do not believe such dogs ever see legitimate work. These giants are often 17″ at the shoulder and could not possibly follow a fox to ground in a normal earth. Still, I do need to go to this show to get data on the Lakeland and Fell terriers. I had plenty of time to contemplate my future books as I walked the 23 agonising miles from Measham. I injected the ailing lurcher puppy with an antibiotic and gave it a shot of saline solution to prevent dehydration. Within two hours, it was looking much better. Dehydration kills puppies rapidly. Hope to God this isn't an outbreak of Parvo virus.

Monday 21

I arrived home at 2.37 am and settled into a fitful sleep but at 3.0 am I was awakened by Merle's hysterical barking. Normally he is a very sensible dog and is usually very silent. Clearly something was wrong, so I went to investigate and found Steel, my nursing lurcher bitch, in a thrashing hypocalcaemic fit. I dragged her indoors and was staggered to see the amount of slaver the bitch produced. At 3.21 am I phoned for the vet for the subscutaneous injection of calcium boroglutinate (I had given the bitch 50 ml) was not working, but by the time the vet arrived the stuff was starting to be absorbed and Steel was coming out of her thrashing turn. I think I have a feed problem, for she refused her meal on Sunday 20th and I left her a huge piece of tripe. Did the sudden change of food bring about the hypocalcaemia, or was the rejection of the meal an indication that the condition had already begun? I know so little about dog ailments, and each and every day some small incident convinces me of my ignorance.

No sign of the dreaded hypocalcaemia reappearing in Steel, thank God. I do believe I have beaten the damned disease in her. She has not even tottered since her injection of calcium boroglutinate and I feel very pleased with myself. Pride, as usual cometh before a fall and I am tempting fate by writing this, I feel. Still, I cram Steel with food in the hope that this will avert a further problem. Her puppies are feeding, but badly, as few well-reared puppies seem to want to eat at three weeks old.

I intend to get rid of my collie bitch. Her disposition makes her a nuisance and I can ill afford a passenger in my overcrowded kennels. Jacquie Fallon, who breeds or rather keeps border terriers, is finding her a new owner, and brought one Judith, a truly beautiful woman, to see the bitch, but the collie's nervous temperament is a bit off putting. Still, with luck she will find a home that will take her. Her puppies are doing quite well and I shall keep a Moonpie bitch—a blue merle with a wall eye—to replace the collie in my lurcher breeding programme.

Wednesday 23

Andrew Lucas phoned and is at his wits end what to do with his badger cub—what a surprise! In spite of all our predictions, Andy seems surprised that the beast has torn his home apart. The house stinks of musk. It is very strange that people who live in musk-filled, dog-scented, fetid houses seem immune to the smell; or at least they fail to notice it. I dislike dogs in the house, they invariably taint the furniture, curtains and even the floors, and a badger is far worse. The scent from Andrew's badger lingered on my clothes and hair for days. Now to find an idiot who will take the beast off his hands.

John Dean of Spalding phoned at 12.0 to ask if I knew where he could buy a good fox-catching lurcher. With the price of pelts likely to reach £30 come November, it would be a fool who would sell a 100% guaranteed dog. As a money making beast, a fox-killing or simply a fox-catching lurcher would take some beating. Yet, I knew of people who pay £40 for a grown dog and expect the beast to be a nailer. I can honestly see the fox becoming a rarity if this hunting continues and legislation may well be necessary to protect the flagging fox population.

Thursday 24

The Game Fair is at Welbeck this year, a spot near Mansfield. Each year, the event gets larger and in spite of the depression, the Fair attracts a huge number of people. I see enormous numbers of lurchers and terriers at these shows and obviously the breeds are getting more popular.

Gun dogs of all breeds abound, including rare exotic breeds like Munsterlanders, Brittany spaniels and Vizlas. I wonder how such sporting dogs compare with our springer spaniels and labradors and also why people see these exotic breeds in preference to the tried and tested native dogs. Munsterlanders look very mongrelly, as if they were the result of a large and heavy collie having mated to a blue roan spaniel. Vizlas resemble short tailed red bone hounds. Perhaps I am naturally conservative by nature, but for the life of me I cannot see the advantage of these breeds. The ones I have seen work have certainly not compared with our native rough shooting dogs.

All in all, a superb first day, bright, very hot and a delightful atmosphere pervaded the whole event. What a contrast to the dreadful fight at the Hampshire Long Dog Show, an event that seemed to inflame a host of gypsies and tinkers and caused one of the worst fights on record.

Day two of the Fair and another roasting day with temperatures well into the 80's, at least in the tent where I signed books. *Nathan* is selling extraordinarily well. It is my favourite book and one I really enjoyed writing. As a result of this book, I met a chap called Farrer who rats a team of three Staffordshire Bull terriers, an unenviable task as a Staff, well heated after a ratting session must take some handling. Like the triplets song, "the other two would rather be one."

Ferreting equipment is really getting scientific. Welstead of the British Ferreting Society also mentions that there is at least a ferret-orientated vet willing to do research on ferret ailments. Such research is long overdue, for the average ferret gets a hell of a time. Few vets know anything about diseases of ferrets and the universal specific, an antibiotic injection, invariably sees off the ferret. It is essential that money is ploughed into ferret research, and I hope Welstead's band do just this.

I am neglecting my dogs sorely through my days at the Game Fair. Still, it is only once a year and after tomorrow who knows when I'll go to another show. The puppies don't look too bad, but the little Fell terrier has lost some of its usual sparkle.

Last day of the Game Fair and I'm not particularly sorry. I've really enjoyed the event, but I'm rather glad to return to my lonely life. I don't like crowds, and though I am a naturally easy-going person, I enjoy my own company.

I met Corporal Hooten yesterday with the puppy from Mick Kirby, the result of mating Merle to a very beautiful greyhound bitch. The puppy, a fawn merle pied, is a superb animal, lighter than Eddie Jone's puppy from the same litter and more aggressive. It is good to note that the dog has gone to a first class home. Far too many people change their lurchers as regularly as their socks. If I know where the various puppies are gone, I will never need to outcross again.

My merle bitch from Steel and Merle is beginning to show up in the litter. She is bright, precocious and very pretty. This will be the last litter of lurchers I will breed for some time, I think. I believe she will be broken coated or rough coated, but it is a wise man who can tell a good puppy at this age.

Woolly is jumping very well and he is also beginning to hunt up his rabbits. I feel he will be a better dog than his mother, given half a chance, but time will tell.

My three days of neglect of the dogs has played havoc. Last night, I noticed my Fell terrier puppy was looking very low and I brought her indoors, not a thing I enjoy, as puppy filth and vomit make my bachelor world a tip. I have never seen a puppy vomit so profusely and my vet confirmed my diagnosis of enteritis. The puppy looked desperately ill and threw up milk and any liquid it was given. Standard treatment for this disease is to deny any food and allow frequent sips of water at twenty minute intervals. Add to this an antibiotic injection and you are in with a chance of saving the puppy. The dried toast/arrowroot diet advised by many books is a real killer, such food tends to nourish the bacteria instead of the dog. By nightfall, the puppy had improved beyond belief. Vomiting and diarrhoea had ceased entirely and it was literally begging for food. To have fed it would be courting disaster and it must go hungry for yet another day until the vomiting has ceased for at least 24 hours.

The collie puppies are extraordinary eaters. I caught two rabbits with Fathom this morning and boiled them whole to kill the tapeworms that infest the guts of the rabbit. Within seconds both rabbits had been devoured by the litter. I have kept them short of flesh, I fear.

Merle's first litter from a greyhound bitch: Corporal Hooten's dog Blue and Eddie
Jones' dog Celt.

My Fell terrier is back to normal again and along with the collie puppies, is tearing at the three rabbits I caught this morning. She is very plucky and quick to take offence. This morning, one of the collie puppies, twice her weight, tried to take a leg of cooked rabbit from her. The terrier retaliated with absolute fury, bowling the bleating collie on its back and menacing it like a fiend. What will she be like at 12 months old? She already rags skins, and attacks the effigy of a ferret on my bookcase. Her blood will almost certainly be suitable for bringing into my strain of Jack Russell terrier.

The worming session started today and both Bel-tane's litter and the collie puppies were given a dose of Shaw's Earliworm. I believe this is the best worming medicine available and certainly doesn't harm even three week old puppies. I shall avoid worming the Fell terrier puppy until all signs of enteritis have passed; to worm a sick puppy is insanity, for worming with any chemical or plant essence is bound to knock a puppy about.

The meat shortage is having a deleterious effect on my dogs. After three weeks of meal feeding, I can see the difference. I hope to God to get more flesh this week.

I managed to get a whole pile of sheep's heads this morning and the dogs set on them with a vengeance. No doubt they crave flesh after having gone without it for so long.

One of the collie pups has a rupture between the anus and the vagina. I noticed a prominent swelling when Moses brought them back and it has become worse. I should hate to put her down as she is a sweety, but her tail looks clogged with filth and mess. I think I shall wait and see what happens with this puppy. She certainly seems lively enough and a lively puppy is usually a well puppy.

Mrs Foster of Pershore phoned and said she has homes for three puppies if they are good enough. One person from Belgium has asked for one, but I'm not interested. Not only do I have to keep the puppy for twelve weeks, but it has to be inoculated against rabies and given the usual distemper, hardpad, hepatitis vaccines. Also it's a hell of a fuss sending the puppy abroad. I honestly don't have the time to mess with such things, and it would be hardly worth my while anyway. The price of such puppies is unimportant but I want them off my hands as soon as possible.

Fathom returned with a hen this morning, freshly killed and obviously stolen. I think it was alive until Woolly saw it, and it is fairly certain he will be hard-mouthed, for the hen had its rib cage crushed. I will have to keep the bird and feed it to the babes, both the collies and the lurchers. My God, my morals have reached an all time low ebb because of Fathom. Still, we are really short of meat so I shall not waste the hen.

The collie litter are reasonably well considering their poor start in life. The problem is that the bitch's milk confers a certain degree of immunity to disease for the first milk contains a variety of antibodies that help fight an infection. Sooner or later, the absence of these antibodies is bound to tell and one of the minor diseases will carry off the weakest of the puppies.

The lurcher crop is superb. I've already chosen my bitch and Malcolm has photographed the entire litter for future reference. The difference between a hand-reared litter and a naturally reared one is patently obvious every time I go to feed them. Never ever will I rear a litter of puppies when a bitch has gone down with milk fever.

A very poor night's rat hunting owing to the fact that the place has been poisoned. The haul was good—180 plus—but the sport was poor as many of the rats were doped. Mick Kirby caught his first live rat by hand, an easy sleight of hand even though it looks spectacular for a grown rat cannot climb its own tail and if the tip of the tail is held, it is helpless. A grown male or female for that matter, will attempt to gyrate and grip one's jacket with its teeth when the gyration brings it next to one's clothes. Mick took a young grey by the tail—dangerous, actually, for a babe can often climb up its tail like a mouse.

I bought this cottage for peace, quiet and seclusion but it has not been a sensible purchase. My place is regularly visited by people I do not know, all keen to see the "funny man with the dogs". There is a list of "dread" expressions at the moment among which are (i) Hello sir, bet you don't remember me (an ex-pupil visiting me uninvited) (ii) Can I see your dogs (a particularly annoying type of caller) (iii) Can you tell me where I can buy a genuine saluki/borzoi/deer-hound/collie/greyhound back to a greyhound (an idiot).

August

Friday 1

We will be very short of ferrets this year, I fear. Paul has remated Fudge and her granddaughter to a sandy hob from Melton Mowbray but whether she has conceived is still a bit doubtful. We need a whole litter for Michael Croucher to film and so far no good. The Jacksons of Reading are short of ferrets and the three jills I lent them have not taken, I'm afraid. What an incredibly infertile year for ferrets it has been. Has the capricious weather influenced them or are the cycles of fertility in stoats and stoat kin erratic? Certainly some years produce an abundance of stoats, but I have always thought that this was due to the fact that there was a corresponding increase in the rabbit population and the stoats, presented with large quantities of rabbits, bred accordingly. Perhaps I am wrong however, and there are certain years when fertility in mustelids varies a bit. At this time, the papers are usually full of ads. for ferrets, but this year there has been none. The mustelids are truly the most baffling of mammals.

Saturday 2

Enteritis has struck my collie litter, the result of (a) no maternal immunity (or very little) (b) divine retribution for the theft of the two hens or (c) Parvo virus. I will certainly lose one or two. Rearing this brood has really got on top of me and this, coupled with the cavalcade of idiots who visit my house, is undermining my health. I must cut down on the number of puppies I keep if I am to get things back to normal.

Fathom caught what I hope and pray to be the last of the myxied rabbits this morning. It is surprising how fast they run even when badly infected. What promised to be a hectic winter of hunting rabbits, has now taken on a more sombre note. The land, once filled with tiny drummers, is now a desert. I can no longer train Woolly Bear on the rabbits in my lane and must now journey further afield. The warrens are cobweb filled, proof of the havoc the virus has caused and I will fill them with BHC powder to kill the fleas, vectors of myxamatosis. A sad ending to the rabbits around here. The tinkers made no impact on them, the gunmen didn't even thin them down. My daily catches were small fry, but the virus slew them.

Sunday 3

I am certainly going to lose one or more of the collie pups. They look listless and unhappy. This bug must stop here and not infect the lurcher litter. It's sad, but there is little one can do with a litter that is obviously infected with enteritis, but is this infection simply a symptom of Parvo virus?

Myxomatosis again and the end of the rabbit locally. Fathom caught two this morning and Woolly Bear caught one. Still, it's puppy food, and there is, contrary to popular opinion, no harm in feeding myxied rabbits to dogs, cats or humans. This is the question most commonly asked at Game Fairs, shows, etc. This disease affects only the rabbit and very rarely the hare.

Beige, my lurcher puppy, a collie/greyhound/greyhound hybrid, ran a hare this morning and looked like catching it, until it decided the game was over and quickened the pace. How many single-handed hare killers are there? I doubt if there are many which catch hares regularly, yet everyone boasts of having a dog which takes hares with monotonous regularity.

Monday 4

Once again we put up the hare on the newly cut grass. Haymaking is a bit out of kilter this year—the corn is nearly ready to cut and the hay is only just ready to harvest. Even the wildlife is a bit out of tune; I've found no leverets this month, yet hares usually produce early autumn leverets in July and early August. I've seen only a few hares this year, as well. Could it be the hare is becoming extinct around the district or is it the high rabbit population that is keeping down the hares? Buck rabbits will bite and kick leverets to death. If this is so then, next year maybe, will be the year of the hare as the myxi has wiped out nearly every rabbit in this area.

Personally, I think the heavy poaching by lampers is the cause of the decline, for even poor dogs, providing they have guts enough, can catch hares on the lamp. Searchlight type beams were very common on the land between Catton and Whittington this winter. This is the cause of our hare shortage. It's a pity really, as this used to be a great area to hunt.

Tuesday 5

Pagan escaped and killed and partly ate one of the collie puppies—fortunately the weakest one. This infanticidal streak is unfortunately quite common in my strain. Beltane is a shocker and if her puppies are not weaned fairly quickly, she tires of them and kills them. Pagan will be the same with her own babes, I'm sure. She is wicked with any puppy who comes near her cage, and displays an unpleasant excitement when they are in the run. This peculiar trait has only manifested itself in recent years. Beltane was the first to display these tendencies and I should have taken steps to correct the defect when I saw it in her. Now all my bitches are a little touchy with puppies and it is no longer safe to allow them to run together for more than a moment or so. The excessive maternal instinct of my old strain, an instinct that led to them vomiting food for the pups for months after they were weaned, has given way to the desire to dismantle any weak creature they encounter. Not a good quality, I'm afraid—far from it, in fact.

Wednesday 6

A long hard and not quite in season course for Fathom and a fruitless one at that. The hare rose up as if by magic only twenty yards from her and for a moment, she didn't seem to see it. When she did, she closed with it rapidly and struck at it as it turned into the hedge near Cooper's, bringing it back towards me. Keith should have been here to see this shot. It was a perfect course to photograph, even though she missed it when it passed almost too deftly through the hedge near Cooper's. Fathom has strained all her side in the gigantic effort of trying to catch the hare and limped back to me. If I rest her, she will certainly come right again, but I have worked her quite hard recently and the effort is just starting to take its toll. For the first time in her life she looks thin and not quite right. A heavy fat/meal diet is needed and will soon put back the life into the old girl. She needs to rest now, however. Coursing shots are extraordinarily difficult to get. Keith is having a hell of a time trying to get photographs of a dog actually closing with a hare.

Thursday 7

We missed the ratting for the first time in months. The rain was torrential, the lads failed to turn up and my car was being serviced. All in all, not the most propitious of evenings.

Foxes are very numerous at the moment, and now the grass is cut, they can no longer slink from field to field unnoticed. If the skin prices hold, (though this will certainly offend those who disagree with hunting foxes) I will kill quite a few this winter. I am amazed at how they survived the beating they took last winter, for I am not the only person lamping and hunting them, and, there seem to be dozens of them around.

This area has always been famous for foxes even when the South Staffs. Hunt worked it. Now the hunts are very reluctant to chance working the area because of the roads, and an enormous fox population exists here. I know of fifty-five breeding earths within an eight mile radius of my cottage.

Friday 8

Preparations for Lowther Show are in progress. The Show, one of the best in the North, comes at an unfortunate time when (a) I have a hypocalcaemic bitch on my hands (b) I have a fostered litter that will with the slightest reason go down with enteritis (c) the meat situation is desperate and I am scouring the countryside for dead hens, pigs and what have you. I really need help in times like these and Michael is, frankly, useless.

My dogs have gone fleshless for days and the result is obvious. Omega looks frightful, like a very ribby whippet and Vampire is looking below par. Meal is useful as a stopgap (or a belly filler, as Moses calls it) but in the diet of a carnivore it has only a limited use. Let the dog books say what they will, I have living proof on my premises, and if Omega doesn't improve, the word living is a bit questionable, too! Ten years ago, my dogs stayed alive and well on putrid carcasses of hens and dried desiccated maggoty carcasses at that. Not one lost condition and never did I have a problem. Now feeding a sterilized meal causes the weight to fall of dogs like Omega—though Beltane is as fat as a pig.

Fell terrier at Lowther—a looker and also a worker.

Saturday 9

Lowther Show and after a 5.30 am start, Malcolm and I, accompanied by several ex-pupils, arrived at Lowther. A good show spoiled by incessant rain; several marquees were surrounded by slurry a foot deep and I saw one unfortunate dolly bird lose her knee length boots in slurry. If it had been a good day, the Show would have been excellent.

The standard of the Lakeland/Fell terrier types is a bit questionable and to tell the truth, I was a bit disappointed, I met John Winch at the show and he shared my opinion. Many of the dogs were a far cry from the dogs of the fabulous Harry Hardestey's and sway backs, poor coats and bad ear carriage was all too common. Twenty years ago, one went to the Lakes to get a good Fell terrier. Now many of the best Fell dogs are bred in the Midlands. In fact, the best Fell dogs I have seen this year were at the Cottesmore Hunt Show. It is now big business to breed working type Lakelands and the market for dogs makes many a breeder perpetuate the most unsuitable blood lines. Brightmore has some excellent dogs, I thought. I saw many of his dogs at Lowther.

Sunday 10

Once again the 370 miles round trip to Lowther and home and after two days I am almost too tired to write my diary. The weather is better but the mud still remains, though the hard work of the show organisers has paid off for the straw tipped on the ground has absorbed at least some of the slimy clayey mud.

The lurcher show produced a host of entries, and Colonel Edward Walsh was there. I think his lurcher book must have outsold mine by now and I must admit, it is far more attractively illustrated. In fact, my own books are rather lacking in photographs, a situation I must alter if I am to stay in business as a sporting writer. A bit less writing and more illustrations must be the order of the day.

One of Mick Douglas' dogs was at the show. I recognised the type instantly and my guess was confirmed by the dog's owner, a Durham man who visited Mick to get a puppy. The dog is a shimmering silver fawn, nearly white and very beautiful. It is also an extremely agile fast type of dog by the looks of it. How does Mick breed these exquisite beauties? I don't know, for he keeps a standing stock of beautiful bitches and mates them to any famous hare-catching lurchers available. Anyway, well done, Mick! This puppy was a beauty.

Monday 11

A pig has died on a nearby farm and the meat is mine. Its demise has answered my prayer for we are dreadfully short of flesh. Actually the feeding of a fallen animal is probably illegal as it contravenes a whole load of Public Health Acts, but what the hell! If things got any worse, fleshwise, I'd be grave-robbing and I'm grateful for any beast that is given me. Moses knackered the pig and took 120 odd pounds of meat away. A pig is an enormous beast, at least a fully grown sow is and gives a tremendous amount of meat. Stench excluded, they are excellent for dogs and though a great number of dog books condemn the feeding of pork, a pig is really very good food for dogs. My puppies went berserk for the meat and quickly stripped the head of all the edible flesh. Steel is not particularly keen on pig flesh however, and picked at the meat. Still, she will eat the remaining meat and for two or three days, my dogs will gorge on pork. Omega gained 1 lb in weight on the day I fed this foul smelling beast and Vampire has a lot more vitality. The pig probably died of diabetes as it drank frantically during its last hours, and great thirst is a symptom of porcine diabetes.

Tuesday 12

Fathom took a hare this morning in spite of Woolly. Bear who leaped on her repeatedly during the course. It was a young male hare—at least I think it was. The leveret, for it was little more in spite of the fact it was fully grown, was an early-bred youngster, maybe February or March born. Still, it put up a heck of a fight to escape and Fathom nailed him after he took her through three fields. He is a dark youngster, though most leverets are darker than the adult and it is only in late winter that the yearlings look like mature hares. Fathom was exhausted by the course and walked home head almost touching the floor. In spite of her amazing take-off speed, she is unable to maintain these incredible bursts over any distance. Perhaps Woolly, who is heavier and not quite as fast, will have far more stamina than his mother. If I can get just a bit more staying power in the strain, I feel I will have everything I want, for Fathom has sense, agility and an amazing nose. Still, to breed the ideal lurcher is one hell of a task; and, after all, it must be horses for courses, as the saying goes: Fathom is certainly a super provider-type lurcher where rabbits and game birds are concerned.

Wednesday 13

A curious and interesting day during which I bought four young ferrets and made a TV film, at least part of one. Michael Croucher of BBC 2, arrived at 11.30 am and discussed the day's filming and at 2.30 pm we shot the film. A chap called Mick Mitchell from London arrived with 4 young ferrets and a litter of deformed kit ferrets. They all (the deformed litter) showed a marked peculiarity in their spinal structures and the backbones were deformed and very twisted. I don't think I've seen the like and rather hope I never will again. I think Mick put them down after the show as they were painful to see.

We filmed Emma Taylor, aged 5, with the ferrets—an appealing kid/animal type clip that isn't really my cup of tea and then went on to film breaking the Fell terrier bitch to ferret. A violent and sanguinary scene preceded the filming in which the Fell fell out with the ferret.

Thursday 14

At 9.30 we started filming again—just prop type shots of Woolly Bear and Fathom jumping the gate and hunting the grove. The irony of it all was that Fathom caught a rabbit five minutes after the team went away. We filmed simple filling type shots of Woolly leaping a fence and Fathom jumping on command. Frankly, I shall be glad when we get to the meat of the plot.

My lurcher litter, the bearded collie-greyhound/border collie-greyhound litter, is thinning down nicely. John and Philip took their puppies today and Knowelden takes his tomorrow. With luck, the lot will find permanent homes and to be honest I'd sooner give them to such homes than chance them being traded from post to post by the majority of lurcher owners. Sadly, the lurcher is one of the most swappable dogs in the world and very few do not experience at least five homes before they settle. Mine will go only to friends so that in spite of the fact that they cost £370 to rear they will make me happy if I can see them grow to maturity with their first owners.

Friday 15

Knowelden came for his puppy, bringing with him a painting of a sparrowhawk. He took back with him the powder blue merle puppy out of Steel's litter—a beautiful dog and maybe a broken coated puppy at that. Roger is having the powder blue merle puppy for a pet/hunter for a friend of his. It will be hunted, Roger assures me.

I found the Fell terrier eating a dead and freshly killed magpie today. I have little doubt that she killed it as it came fluttering into the run after a piece of tripe

Nightwing, my fell terrier puppy.

though the demise of the bird could have been caused by Beltane's pups. The Fell is a tigress and a sure bet that she will be a heller to fox. I am fairly convinced that even now she would wallop a rat—but I'd be a fool to try a dog to rat at this tender age. Winter will see her giving the rat population of the poultry farm a hell of a time, though.

Woolly caught and retrieved a tiny myxied rabbit to hand. Providing there is no other dog around to excite him to jealousy, his retrieving is impeccable. He is not good when there is another dog with him as he jealously guards his prey against canine all-comers. Some training will correct this but it's a difficult habit to break.

Saturday 16

Elwyn George has bred a litter of buzzards—very commendable since they indulge in a soaring flight before mating. He has two large healthy eyasses and has reared them on day-old chicks and sundries. In the wild, I've seen buzzards take and kill grass snakes and once I saw one come down with a whack on a black-backed gull feeding alongside the local refuse tip. A buzzard is of little use as a falconry bird as it has such puny feet and a disposition to match the paucity of fighting power. Still, I've seen several kill small rabbits and once trained one who took and held a fully

grown but myxied rabbit. In spite of protection, there is little doubt that the predatory birds are on the extinction trail, and the breeder of predators is doing a great job in keeping the species alive in captivity. I've seen sparrowhawks, kestrels galore, owls of every species and even peregrines bred in aviaries, and as falconry becomes more and more popular this might be the falconer's only hope of obtaining birds for his sport. They thrive well on day-old chicks, but need a vitamin supplement to compensate for their lack of natural food.

Sunday 17

To Wales to my birthplace to film. The filming starts on Wednesday or even Tuesday, weather permitting, with a visit to my village to meet Gwyllim Hardwick—one of the all-time great terrier men, as far as I'm concerned. Gwyllim bred (and still does, I believe) a strain of rough coated unlovely dogs who would commit havoc on any creatures. They are a blend—though blend seems hardly the right word when I consider the type of dog—of Russell/Border/Bedlington and bull terrier with an extra large splash of Sealyham terrier. They lack tongue and many are dead mute, but I have yet to see one that was a coward. San, my old terrier, as good a dog as I've ever owned, was from Gwyllim Hardwick's strain terrier.

Gwyn Williams will arrange the valley meet. I went to his house today to fix it. He has two or three springer pups in hand—understandable, since Kerri, his wife, is Tom Evan's great niece. It always baffled Gwyn why I do not keep springers as I am fairly competent at retriever training. However, I hate guns and the horde of quasi-hunters who tramp my district looking for something to kill. Springers would invite visits from such people and while I find poachers, gypsies and tinkers fascinating (if irritating) I find the average rough shooter a pain in the arse.

Monday 18

A quiet day visiting the place of my birth and childhood with Michael Croucher of BBC 2. The valley is much cleaner than it was during my childhood and the filthy coal-filled brook is now clean, though it is still littered with rubbish. My village looks derelict and the pubs, cinemas, clubs and similar places of entertainment are now closed with 'Reward Offered for Information Concerning Vandalism' posters appearing in the windows. The coal tips are being reclaimed and planted, but there is still an air of decay about the villages. Houses are cheap, very cheap but there is little one can do to make some of them look attractive, so bad is the neglect of the gardens and general appearance of the houses.

Tuesday 19

A good day's preparation. Jim, the camera man and Alastair, the sound man are first rate and very patient with my ignorance of their arts. Morning was spent filming the less salubrious parts of the valley and afternoon was spent shooting a visit to Gwyn's house in Lleust and a trip to Gwyllim Hardwick's house in Blaengarw. Gwyllim has aged greatly in 20 years, but then so have I, and even Phillip Humphries' (Gwyllim's son-in-law) once cherubic face is lined. The crowd at Pwll Carn Terrace still breed, own and work the strain of terrier I knew in my youth and Gwyllim is still the best raconteur in the valley. We filmed three terriers, a mess of ferrets and some lurchers, but my pleasure at seeing Gwyn and Gwyllim greatly exceeded my kick at being filmed. When I see my own even and excellent strain of terrier, I cannot but help thinking with nostalgia of the rough coated, ugly, game little dogs of my childhood and youth. What a lot I seemed to learn from them and what a fabulous team of workers they all were.

Wednesday 20

A badger dig at Carmarthen when I met Alun's friend, Dylan, a first class chap and a good digger. We had a permit to shift a badger to a spot 20 miles away and with camera team, producer and sound recording man, we arrived at 11.0 am at a spot some eleven miles from Carmarthen. Here Dylan had found a small sett that housed a badger that had caused annoyance by rolling flat corn. An easy dig followed—thanks largely to Alan's dog Sandy and also to a terrier locator that he placed in Sandy's collar. It must have saved hours of digging, for we crowned through the earth to a spot directly over the badger which was being lustily held at bay by Alan's dog, Sandy. A grim struggle was prevented by Alan's early tailing of the badger and by Dylan's neat and nimble bagging of the beast. The camera team must have had some excellent shots of us at work and Jim, the camera man seemed delighted with his results. We released the badger at the appointed place and filmed it racing off into the trees. All together, a copy book type dig, which lasted just two and a half hours, and although the dog took a few small bites, he experienced little damage in the confrontation. I think this must be a first class part of the filming. Pray the rest goes as well.

Thursday 21

Home again and a glorious rat hunt, the first for three weeks. The dogs are glowing with health and vitality and the sepsis, the inevitable result of round-the-year ratting, and mange are nearly clear. A savage test for the smallest fox terrier cross who made her debut tonight. Normally, first time hunters, hunting a place where rats abound, will start by killing small greys, immature rats with less size and far less biting power. The tiny fox terrier/Russell cross—I must get round to naming her—actually encountered a large buck who gave her a heck of a bad time particularly as it seized her first and what should have been a simple catch, degenerated into a duel with a rat hanging through the tongue of the dog and the dog endeavouring to kill the rat by battering it to death. Fairly unpleasant, and a bit destructive morale-wise. Over 200 rats were taken—not a huge haul but still a sizeable number. All the fox terrier crosses are working moderately well and although they are a very variable type, the new blood will easily be absorbed in the real McCoy Russell types.

Friday 22

Steel is ready to leave her rapidly dwindling litter. She is irritable and touchy with the remaining five puppies and snaps at them for the slightest possible excuse. Perhaps the constant suckling is upsetting her. Perhaps it is simply a way of ensuring the litter become independent. Whatever the reason, they are perpetually screaming after she has nipped or trounced them for annoying her. The right or natural time for weaning is seemingly not determined by a legal Act of Parliament, but by a biological need. At eight to ten weeks of age, a bitch gets a bit fed up with her whelps and this is the time to part them. Earlier weaning invariably results in the bitch becoming distressed at the premature loss of her litter and the puppies suffering just a little because they are still suckling at the time of separation. Foxes I have bred in captivity show a similar irritability towards their young at this time. The litter are usually left very much to their own devices by the time they are ten weeks of age, for a vixen tends to get away from them all day, returning to take them for fox hunts at night. Foxes kept in confinement (a hell of a punishment for a fox, I have found) often kill their cubs if they are unable to escape from them at weaning time.

Saturday 23

I have stacked straw bales right in the corner of Steel's pen so that she can leap up there to escape the attentions of the pups. The lurcher bitch I shall keep—I shall call her Mara—is a whining little thing who squeals piteously if left alone. She is beautiful, but not as personality orientated as Woolly Bear.

Beltane's litter is not good. The bitch, in addition to having a chocolate coloured nose, is very tiny and sickly and is probably the first warning about inbreeding this line. The bloodline is, as are all bloodlines, fairly riddled with genetic faults that manifest themselves every time I inbreed the dogs. Her head is curiously domed, probably an indication of chronic hydrocephaly (water on the brain). I encountered this genetic fault a dozen or so years ago, but I thought I had bred it out. Little is known about this hideous and fatal deformity, save that it can manifest itself due to close inbreeding. The bitch is one third the size of her litter brothers and has the far away look of a typical hydrocephalic. Dollars to doughnuts, she will not make 10 weeks of age.

Woolly Bear (Fathom × Merle) during his training session. Note the lack of muscle on his hind legs: I am worried about this.

Sunday 24

Woolly put up his first hare this morning and although he set off after it, it was clearly a joke. There was no possible chance of the six-month old puppy ever coming up on the hare. After a few seconds, he discontinued the pursuit and returned to me. One of the most common criticisms of the collie greyhound lurchers, is that they are able to decide which hares are worth pursuing and quite simply, give the rest a miss. Is this such a bad fault, I ask myself? Some lurchers, particularly those with a strong trace of greyhound, will continue to try long after the chips are down and the result is often a "blown" dog, a dog with a torn diaphragm or lungs that are bruised; and I've seen dogs die of a heart attack after an overlong strenuous course. To my mind, the real lurcher is able to decide which hare, rabbit or what have you is worth taking and to give the rest a miss. The "he'll, try for anything dog" may look good on paper but such a dog usually finishes up blown, damaged or dead and as a poaching lurcher is frankly a liability: a dog that will chase any moving quarry, no matter how distant, is unlikely to heed the shouts or whistles of a poacher who wants his dog back and quickly. No, I'll settle for my ugly collie hybrids.

Town and Country Fair, and not a good sales day for books. The morning began unhappily with the death of Beltane's bitch puppy which convulsed into a state of decline, voiding filth and urine at 1.37 am this morning. Most horrible still was the fact that she continued to live until 8.0 am and expired only when I plucked up courage to kill her. I hate sickly puppies, the bleating, the pathetic whining and my sense of uselessness makes me very unhappy, so I spend days getting over the experience.

A curious lurcher appeared at the Town and Country, the result of crossing a Shetland sheepdog male with a whippet bitch. I think I saw the litter advertised in *Exchange and Mart* as "mini lurchers". Not a cross I would like myself, but no sooner do I make a statement like this than I come across an absolute cracker of this breeding. A dog of this breeding, an elegant deerhoundy little mite as frail as an Italian greyhound, but with the reputation of a Nimrod, changed hands for £250 at Lambourn last year. I saw the transaction and while I would have hesitated to pay that sort of money for such a dog—or any trained dog for that matter—the purchaser seemed well pleased with his purchase.

My final choice of collie hybrid and I have chosen two wall-eyed merle puppies, a dog called Richmond and a bitch called Scrimbly. I hope one day to change these frighful names or prevent eight year old children naming my dogs. Both have good coats. Richmond (I really must change that name) is very long coated, almost a bearded collie. When mated to a greyhound, they may well be the parents of the best possible lurcher a ½ collie, ½ greyhound hybrid who will not only be bright, moderately fast, cunning and able, but whose cloddy body shape will be enclosed by and masked by a good thick coat. We shall have to see, I think. Only a fool makes "chickens before hatching" predictions.

The corn is about to be cut and in ordinary circumstances the hunting would begin. However, myxamatosis is still with us and there will be little to hunt. Some partridges have left the fields to feed on the seeding spindle weed in my weedy garden, but even these seem fewer in number. Pheasants are also rare this year and the only common shootable prey seems to be the ever present woodpigeon. These are still very numerous and lure in hundreds of pseudo-hunters (£250 guns and untrained dogs) to shoot the land. I hate these transient countrymen who regard me as a somewhat eloquent Worzel Gummidge and who cripple the game in very crowded land.

There is an offer of a first class coursing greyhound, retired but superbly bred, going free to a good home. However tempting this might be, I shall refuse it. My menagerie is already ridiculously overcrowded with elderly dogs and I excuse myself from putting down by convincing myself that they are breeding stock. My collie bitch, the dam of Richmond and Scrimbly is completely usless as breeding material and in addition to being not suitable for breeding, she is an irritation. Not only is she touchy with some of the puppies, but she is frantic to kill Steel—and I mean kill, for she cannot resist a chance to attack Steel when she is off balance, feeding or even defaecating. This is decidedly unnatural, as dogs usually refrain from attacking other dogs if they are feeding, defaecating or mating. There seems to be an inbuilt restraint mechanism to prevent any dog attacking another during the exercising of their natural functions. The collie seems to lack these restraint mechanisms, however, and because of this is possibly dangerous to the rest of the dogs in the run. A dog whose social behaviour is imperfect or underdeveloped is a bad trouble maker in a pack situation. Fights of the most desperate kind erupt frequently and furiously when one of the dogs lacks what Kipling calls "the law of the pack".

Thursday 28

An excellent night's rat hunting and a really good start for the fox terrier hybrids. All are excellent ratters now. The really small bitch goes like hell in the night. Pagan is off colour but very pregnant and caught very few rats. The amazing Omega is almost whippety thin but in lovely condition. At this weight she performs best, and she took most of the rats this night. Pagan was so weary that she didn't even menace Omega who is normally her mortal enemy. Rollo, Alan's dog, a result of mating the late Hamish to Omega, is an extraordinarily good rat killer for he slips a catch quickly and quietly, and refuses to keep hold of his rat.

Vampire is a different matter, however, for with the approach of old age, he gets slower and slower and is reduced to carrying his now rare kills around the pens. He missed very badly tonight, a catch that he would have regarded as child's play four years ago for he was once incredibly agile. Beltane, however, is amazing for she is as lively and agile as ever and her great nose seems to be unimpaired by the approach of senility. True, she is very mange-scarred and her teeth are quite bad but she is still an incredible athlete and an asset to any rat hunting team. Vampire must be kept at home, I fear, for he seems to have outlived his useful life.

Friday 29

A quite boring day. Beltane "bought" one dreadful bite last night, a bite that nearly severed her tongue. Funnily enough, tongue and mouth bits heal quickly and well, partly because the area is kept well washed with saliva and also because the saliva contains an antiseptic called lysozyme which kills most germs (sounds a bit like a TV commercial). I never treat a mouth wound for this reason and I am fairly certain that next week will find the old girl back on the ratting once again.

Her two pups called Phobos and Deimos, the two Martian moons (my names, I've kept the little girl away from these) will make useful terriers in spite of their brother/sister origins and their premature birth.

Both are totally fearless and very aggressive to the much bigger and heavier collie pups. Phobus ad Deimos—Fear and Destruction, the perfect names for the sons of Vampire and Beltane.

The Fell terrier bitch is due for inoculation soon and I really must start her with stock breaking. She is an absolute heller and may well prove to be an amazing chicken killer as well as a rat killer. A curious thing about rat-killing dogs however, is that very old dogs, dogs not able to keep up with the youngsters, often kill poultry out of sheer frustration. Beltane, aged and sprightly, may be well worth watching for this reason.

Saturday 30

Holkham Country Fair, and I am signing books in the pouring rain and getting "outrageous" and "disgusting" crits on my book *Nathan*. In spite of the fact that this is an historical book and is no way concerned with dog fighting in the present day, the book has caused considerable offence and has been accused for resurrecting the present trend to fight dogs. Some of the BFSS officials (and one in every four of the Country Fair types seem to claim to hold this rank) have approached Doug Cooper about taking the book off the sporting book's list. *Fighting Sports* by Fitzbarnard, a savage, brutal and first-hand account of the

macabre pit sports is tolerated, but mine is not, so it seems. All in all, I am becoming the Public Enemy No. 1 of the field sports, the man they love to hate, a title I seem to enjoy. Doug's friend at the CTF stall says that if I had obtained an army commission, my books might be considered more acceptable, but I think it is me. My views are zany, my style of writing a bit too vivid, my approach to life a bit odd. Anyway, it seems likely that there is a move afoot to prevent *Nathan* being sold on the stalls. Look out world, there's a *really* naughty book on the way!

Eddie Jones came with Merle's puppy, the dog out of the greyhound bitch mated to Merle. What a super puppy, a black and white collie marked animal that is already so attractive as to be an advert for puppies from Merle's breeding—sadly, not all are as attractive. Woolly Bear stood next to him and looked a real dustbin-rummaging cur compared to him. Woolly lacks muscle, lacks class and will never be as fast as this black and white dog of Eddie's. The sister of this puppy, a black and white bitch, died at birth—a pity, as it was spectacularly marked and even as a stillborn had an abnormally long back.

I phoned Dave Harcombe today. He is editor, compiler and distributor of the *Working Terrier Year Book*—an interesting piece of working terrier literature that appears once a year. He is a bit disheartened by the book and doesn't seem too happy to continue with the production of the magazine. It will be a heck of a shame if he doesn't continue to publish this useful booklet. I've had a lot of kicks out of reading it. What is really needed is a book of this type—a magazine concerned with lurcher, terriers and ferrets—a far cry from *The Shooting Times* type article, a magazine more suited to my type of person, one who runs along the slender arête of legality to do his hunting. I do hope Harcombe continues to do this public service. It will be a pity if he doesn't.

Phobos and Deimos aged 8 weeks—they were bad fighters even at this age.

Eddie Jones and Celt with his first hare. This is probably the best puppy I have ever bred.

September

Monday 1

A taxing accidental run for Woolly this morning when the hare on the edge of Brough's Earths suddenly exploded from the grass. The result was inevitable: a very winded puppy and a hare racing into the distance. The puppy is too lightly muscled for a hard run at rabbit and a hare is far too much for him.

I am judging Lambourn this year because Mrs Soames is unable to attend. How curious it will be for a man who delights in appearing the disdainful recluse to mingle with the aristocracy of the lurcher world. I must confess that had not the BBC 2 team been filming there, I should have refused the offer of judging for I am not very show orientated and the vision of me in the ring alongside well-bred young bucks looks incongruous even in my mind's eye. I shall never judge again as long as I live and while I feel at home with Moses judging alongside me, Michael Lynes leaves me a bit in awe. Lynes is an artist, a master at capturing the fleeing beast and the pursuing greyhound, and I have long admired his work. My ragged attire and my solitary nature will no doubt brand me as an even greater eccentric than ever. At times like this, I really need Moses with his simple, earthy wisdom alongside me, for, for all his lack of formal education, he has an aplomb I cannot match. He is judging the BFSS show at Shughborough that day, so I am truly alone.

Tuesday 2

A gloomy day and a hell of a forestaste of things to come. At dawn, Woolly chanced on a rabbit and we took it back for the puppies—much to Woolly's disgust I must add. When I gutted the creature and offered it to the puppies, Richmond seemed a bit off colour and a mite reluctant to gobble down the carcass with the other savages. By night time, he had a far-away look and I took him to the vet. On the way down he became very limp and floppy and lay down to receive his antibiotic shot. His gums were white and his faeces loose, but I've seen enteritis before and Wright, the new vet, gave me odds of 6–4 on rapid recovery. On returning home, Richmond perked up a little though he seemed reluctant to settle down in one spot. Within an hour, however, he looked frightful and I raced him back to the vet again, but he was dead on arrival there. Is this the dreaded and long awaited parvo virus—the killer of baby puppies? It could be, but I have my doubts. The speed of poor little Richmond's death made me think it was, but the faeces, while they were liquid, lacked the usual bloody flux associated with parvo virus. I am quite shameless about the fact that I really loved Richmond and I will certainly miss him. It is an ill-fated litter, that is for sure. Now I must wait to see what happens.

Wednesday 3

Hugh Davies of Davies and Jones, our local vet, is not of the opinion that the cause of Richmond's death was parvo virus, for the infection lacked the classic symptoms of parvo virus. Scientists now believe that the fading puppies of yesteryear, a condition attributed to Rubarth's infection, were the result of parvo virus outbreaks. Samples of Richmond's faeces will be taken and set to Edinburgh for analysis and electron

Parvo victim number one—this puppy died of convulsions.

miscroscopic examination, but by the time parvo virus is confirmed, the disease will have worked its way through the dog population of my kennels. Yet another puppy has gone down with something—once again one of the collie puppies, yet there is not the slightest indication of the disease in the other puppies. Logically, if this is parvo virus, the other puppies should also be ailing, but this is not so. None of my dogs have immunity to this disease so there can be no maternal immunity confered on the puppies from any of the bitches. Perhaps, at the first sign of the disease I am too quick to label my infection as parvo virus.

A matter of two weeks ago, Bill Colclough came to borrow Fathom. Bill is, as many Midlanders are, out of work or rather on short time and used Fathom to supplement his income. Bill will lamp her and get all he can by daytime, rabbit catching. I miss Fathom, but with Bill on short time the chances are he will give her a lot more work than I can now that I have started school again. Furthermore, I am able to give more time to training Woolly Bear. I've missed rabbits with Woolly that Fathom would have easily taken, but unless I train Woolly now, he'll never become very useful.

Thursday 4

A hard and not a particularly successful hunt with less than a hundred rats to our credit. John Marshall and Paul Coffey alone turned up and two are not nearly enough to block and cope with a pack of ten terriers. Frankly, I need to train a team of enthusiastic young-sters—lads of twelve or fourteen—if I am to cope with hunting an even larger pack. A larger pack of terriers particularly of Vampire's breeding are hard to curb and harder to prevent fighting, though to be fair, there is no fighting during a hunt even though at times the run is a bloodbath.

Tonight, just prior to the rat hunt, I saw a par-ticularly savage battle taking place. Vampire is old now and as with old dogs of his kind, he becomes fractious. He thrashed Rollo, Alan's dog to sub-mission as soon as they went in the run and hammered the border terrier dog as soon as he'd finished with Rollo. He then proceeded to terrorise the bitches who, except for Beltane, cringed to submission; but, ex-hilarated by his success perhaps, he made the fatal or nearly fatal error of attacking Merle. Near fatal is just about right, for Merle weighs nearly sixty pounds and is as skilled a fighter as Vampire, who at twelve

pounds stands little chance against such an adversary. One of the most commonly repeated fallacies of my childhood were tales of how dogs of Alsatian size were brought low by tiny Sealyham-type dogs who got underneath the big dog and wreaked havoc on the belly of the giant. Stories of this type were repeated so often (and so eloquently) that many lads believed that a good little 'un was more than a match for a good big 'un. Stuff and nonsense, I'm afraid. A few pounds of muscle, let alone forty-odd pounds will be enough to tilt a battle in favour of the big 'un. Charlie Lloyd, the ace of dog fighting, who made (and spent) more money from dog fighting than anyone and whose expertise was beyond question, once faced a coward-ice accusation when he refused to let Paddy, a rip-roaring bull terrier go against a half-bred mastiff-type dog twelve pounds heavier. Tim Corrington, who refereed many matches in Tulsa and Sonora, once advised a dog fighter to withdraw his dog against a pit bull only four pounds heavier. Good big 'uns really slaughter good little 'uns and Merle nearly saw off Vampire.

Friday 5

What an incredibly tough dog Vampire is. I really do sell him short, I fear. Last night, after the Merle v Vampire battle, Vampire ratted with the best of them, yet this morning found his jaw swollen, twisted and severed. In my ignorance, I had ratted the poor devil with a broken jaw. The irony of this is that Paul Coffey had remarked that the poor old devil was on top form tonight and I know for a fact tht he saw off at least a dozen rats.

Yet another collie puppy went to the wall this morning and his cadaver looked little more than a furry skeleton. Whatever the cause of his demise, the death is quite sickening and all too sudden. Every symptom points to parvo virus—hell, it was just a name in January, now it is my thought in waking and

sleeping—but I am still not convinced it is the cause of the deaths. The terrier puppies look hale and hearty, but the collie litter is now down to two. No way will I experience this nightmare again. I shall place the pathetic cadaver in the pens of the pregnant bitches so that they too will be infected and though they will obviously be a bit off colour and even quite ill, they will passive immunity on to the puppies via the placenta (for dogs can receive antibodies this way) and via the colostrum. Pagan is very pregnant and is in the ideal condition to receive this hideous and macabre form of immunisation that will undoubtedly be frowned on by both the genteel and the Public Health. But I am determined to stamp out the virus.

Saturday 6

Mara is down with this hellish viral infection and looks decidedly ill. I am now fairly certain that this Satan bug is not parvo but an equally deadly bacterial infection, possibly an E. coli bug of the sort that slays hens and pigs. I injected all the suspect puppies with Ampicillin. Richmond, poor devil, received similar treatment, but too late, I fear. It is now all to do with fate, but with luck I shall not lose Mara. A few minutes ago, she passed stools with blood stains and is displaying classic parvo symptoms yet I am certain I am right—the bug is a simple E.coli bug and not parvo. I cannot explain why I believe this to be so, but I hope to God I am right. I will certainly know by this time next week. Question—am I morally right to judge Lambourn tomorrow? I have dry cleaned all my clothes and I shall bathe and disinfect myself at dawn,

but am I right to judge such a show, possibly carrying such a virus?

Bill Colclough returned Fathom tonight, a bit thin but in good condition. I lent him Beige as a substitute. If he has patience all will be well. If not, it will be a disaster. Since Fathom went away, Woolly Bear has come on in leaps and bounds. One of the most common errors in dog training is to concentrate on the training of one dog to the neglect of the up and coming puppies, and when the veteran becomes too old to be of any use, there is nothing to take its place. Having Fathom returned does rather tempt me to do this, I must admit, but Woolly must be properly entered this winter.

P.S. My ferrets are not ill and parvo kills them like wildfire. I am now certain I am correct.

Sunday 7

Lambourn Lurcher Show, where I judged—not well and not wisely before the TV cameras. Thanks to Michael Croucher, producer and advisor, all went well—that is except for one lout, twelve lurchers on leash, who shouted "You couldn't judge a dead dog"—not sporting, not a good loser, but one who will go down to posterity because the TV van were recording at the time. I am regarded as a renegade by the official coursing associations, but this man, a dog dealer, is a bastion of the coursing leagues.

As a show, Lambourn must be just about the tops

and my co-judge Michael Lynes an artist of some considerable note is a man hot on conformation and a better judge than I am. The show run admirably by Mrs Philippa Upton, a bit of a charmer, was a success, although it did convince me I was socially inadequate, for I felt a little out of place among people obviously one class above my own associates and, let's be truthful, myself. Few of them are more articulate than I am, but they possess a strange aplomb that sparks off my inferiority complex.

Only two merle lurchers were at the show and both

were smooth and classless. If Mara lives, and praise God, she may, a new strain of ultra-bright, ultra-glamourous lurchers may appear, but the question is "Will Mara live?"

With Eddie's dog Merle x greyhound and a black puppy out of Terry Ahearne's collie/greyhound x greyhound, things look quite good. Now the hunting instinct is in question, I suppose, though Steel is excellent and her sister Shehan, a glamorous bitch now quartered on my premises, is not only outstanding as a single-handed hare killer, but she is bright and has an excellent nose. As far as shape goes, she is outstanding and I saw nothing at Lambourn to touch her. I think I may be on the right track and barring illness, accident,

theft and a dreadful saluki misalliance with one of my bitches, things look good.

Moses judged the BFSS Country fair at Shugborough today—in the hopes of being away from me, he said! As a judge, he is obviously moving into the top bracket—a year ago, taking second billing to Moses was a joke, now it is very much a reality, I'm afraid.

My colleagues have decided to call the black Fell puppy Nightwing—an appropriate name as she is to be mated to Vampire. Since her enteritis bout, she has come on in leaps and bounds and is now ready for inoculation for the big four. This time next year, she will be ready for fox or bigger stuff.

Monday 8

Another collie puppy is a bit off, the last bitch, a pale wall-eyed merle puppy. I took her in and kept her in the kitchen with Mara, much against my rule as I

dislike the stench of dog in my house. I injected her with Ampycillin and by nightfall, she looked much better. I am certain the result of the injection brought

Jacquie Fallon's border terriers—all excellent workers.

about the improvement so there is no doubt that the infection is caused by a bacterium which rather rules out Parvo virus). Still, they all need careful watching, and with four bitches in whelp, careful is the operative word. Not since the distemper outbreak of 1973 has such panic swept over me.

A still born calf was dropped tonight. Providing they are stillborn through anoxia or some accident of birth, then most calves are first rate food, but with my present dog problem, an outbreak of brucellosis (contagious abortion) could see me off. The dogs improve dramatically on a whole carcass diet and most forsake the red muscle meat and tear out the bowels of the beasts. Wild animals invariably eviscerate a prey before dining and usually eat portions of the entrails before they start on the red meat. Stoats are an exception to this rule, as most mustelids gobble through the brain before they start on the meat proper.

Yet again another border bitch is in season—a curse, as they are nearly always phantom pregnancy prone. Maybe Jackie and I should breed from them, using Jackie's dog Bugsy; not a Kennel Club specimen but a worker, and what is more a holder of a genuine MFH certificate, for he served a complete year at the Meynell Hunt and emerged with flying colours.

If borders are to be resuscitated, it must be by breeding away from the aristocratic multi-champion studded lines; show champions must be viewed with suspicion and dogs that are capable of work must be used. There is no doubt that, in spite of what breeders say, the border terrier is not the working breed it used to be when I first started working terriers. I trained some crackers from the Deerstone strain but these terriers of today are a different kettle of fish. I need to breed from these bitches to stop the phantom pregnancies but I steadfastly refuse to use useless, untried dogs on these very second rate bitches. Hence, it's Jackie's dog and Jackie to dispose of the puppies, I hope.

Tuesday 9

A mixed evening and a trip to Halifax to fetch the car.

I bought Shehan this evening, Steel's illustrious and beautiful sister, a vision of loveliness and reputedly one of the famous hare-killing lurchers of the Midlands. Like Steel, she is out of a blue greyhound bitch called Cilla and a working trial bearded collie dog from Pershore. I bred this bitch and had the stupidity to give the animal to one of the typical lurcher buying and selling meddlers who abound in the Midlands. She stayed with this messer of canine psychology for two weeks until she was nine weeks old, in fact, before she was passed on yet again to the present owner. Here she stayed for two years until a marriage break-up forced her present owner to sell her. Fortunately, I had first choice to buy her back and I practically snatched his hand off to buy her. No one but a fool would refuse such a dog.

Another dog down with what our team now call the Satan bug. Nightwing is the latest victim. It is bound to run right through the whole puppy batch, but how many will it see off? So far, it only seems to slay those who are a bit under the weather, and the Ampycillin shot certainly seems to clear up the problem. The symptoms are certainly not indicative of the deadly parvo virus and I believe if I had had the knowledge I now possess, poor little Richmond would not be dead. One of the collie hybrids is also very low, but I do not see it as the killing bug I once believed it to be. The temperature of the puppies soars, indicative of a viral infection, and Mara's temperature nearly topped 106° F. Mara is on her feet and looks fine, but relapse in such diseases is very common. My own mental state is suffering badly as a result of viewing the carnage caused by this disease. I am very depressed at the constant sight of illness. What is even more disturbing is that my rat hunting team must bring leptospirosis, hepatitis and God knows what back to my premises, but with the puppies in this state of constant ill-health, any form of inoculation is a bit out of the question. All the puppies are approaching inoculation age but they are just going to have to wait. If a puppy is inoculated in this condition, death seems reasonably likely.

Question—Is the disease firmly established in my buildings or have I a sweetie known as a "carrier" among my dogs? My dog dealer at Lambourn boasted he knew everything about dogs. I envy him his knowledge or the peace of mind of his ignorance.

Fathom is back on form but it is impossible to take her out. A band of tinkers, seven caravan loads, have settled at the end of my lane and to show Fathom or worse still, Shehan would be courting disaster. Dog breeding in a tinker area is thwart with danger. The sight of a useful running dog draws them like a magnet and they follow a distinct course of action to obtain a dog. Firstly, small children aged 8 or 9 appear and ask if the dog is for sale. Next, the adults appear with the same request. On refusal, they return with an offer of money and the next night the dog is gone. Tinkers rarely steal dogs while they are camped nearby, but invariably hit a place a few days after they have left. Police prosecution or even arrest is unlikely: they simply pull in a tinker, the itinerant gives his name as James Brown, the most common alias of all tinkers, and hey presto, they have moved again. At the moment, the site looks like a scene from a Boat People documentary and the ditches are full of lightly buried human faeces. My green and pleasant land! What a hideous joke!

The Fell is displaying some slight interest in food. Tiny morsels of minced meat are taken, but sparingly. This disease, if noted quickly and acted upon more quickly, is beatable, of that I am sure. Poor old Richmond, I can't help thinking about him. I am certain I could have saved him if I had not wrongly diagnosed the disease as parvo virus. It now has all the symptoms of a fairly dangerous coli bug. Anyway, I'll wait for a vet's report before I make any more spot diagnoses, but I will endeavour to starve out the bug by keeping the pups only on an electrolyte solution.

I will soon have a fair crop of terrier bitch puppies, all alike, all even and all excellent rat hunters. Pagan may be carrying a useful bitch puppy and maybe there will be a Vampire-type puppy in the litter. I may even mate Omega to her own son to breed the type of puppy I want; but she is woefully overbred now and another litter is not likely to help. One of the fox terrier puppies is in whelp to Vampire and I might even consider mating the other one to Rollo, Alan's dog. I dislike mating untried puppies during their first seasons, but I do need replacement dogs and I can see no other way. My seasoned bitches are nearly senile and I'm afraid I must perpetuate the line using veteran males and untried females. I've nearly allowed this useful bloodline to become extinct and I am now reaping the benefits of my folly. What I really need is an outstandingly classy, utterly game brood bitch quite simply for stock. I could then maybe, sterilise my working bitches and keep them only for work. I should then have everything I want—a day dream, I'm afraid.

Thursday 11

And so I enter into my 43rd birthday and I have little to show for my time on this earth. I have parvo virus. It is now confirmed. Glasgow tests are positive. An elderly team of terriers well past it, apart from Omega and Pagan, a few good lurchers and a brood bitch. Moneywise, things are better than last year (well, a little better), but not much, and my usable capital is invested in massive doses of antibiotics.

Steve Jones' bitch whelped two weeks ago and a black and tan bitch, identical in marking to Pagan, has appeared in the litter. The breeding is far superior to Pagan's, though the proof of the pudding is in the eating, not in the genetic make up. Though they are similarly bred, there is not enough really hard stuff in Pagan for my liking and this new puppy is bred from an excellent family of head thumpers. The sire of both Pagan and the new puppy is Nigel Hinchcliffe's Jaeger, a super dog as has ever been bred but the pedigree of the dam is interesting.

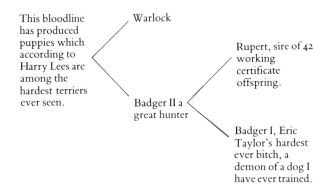

This bloodline has produced puppies which according to Harry Lees are among the hardest terriers ever seen.

Warlock

Badger II a great hunter

Rupert, sire of 42 working certificate offspring.

Badger I, Eric Taylor's hardest ever bitch, a demon of a dog I have ever trained.

Pagan, heavily pregnant, performed very badly tonight missing several kills because of her bloated shape. I have allowed her massive contact with the suspect parvo puppies, encouraging her to drink from their water dishes eat alongside them and also to clean their very wet anuses, a bit macabre perhaps, but also very necessary to endeavour to get Pagan to contract the infection and to cause her to give some maternal immunity to the puppies. Omega once again excelled herself tonight. When in a whippety condition, she is incredibly fast and dextrous. Vampire ratted again tonight and with his chipped jaw, the result of last week's encounter with Merle, he proved worse than useless. He now carries rats around in his mouth, even rats he has not killed and spends the night simply defending his carcasses. Senility happens to us all.

Friday 12

I do not intend to lose either the Fell or the collie puppy to this hellish infection and much as I am told that they will both die by all and sundry, professional and amateur, I shall will them to live. At the vet's tonight, I was driven to a frenzy of temper by the comments of a silly old woman. In the waiting room was an anxious, upset young woman with a parvo puppy, being advised by a silly old knowall who said, "Just give it a few drops of brandy in milk, love, be right in no time." How many such idiot comments have sent a thousand animals screaming to an agonising death. How many ludicrous old wives' tales have butchered a host of unfortunate beasts and even people. Alcohol for any small animal still suckling must be as lethal as cyanide, yet I still get "The puppy wouldn't suckle so we gave him a few drops of brandy"—guess what? It died, what a surprise! I often feel one should need a licence to own an animal, a licence obtainable only by an examination, a test concerned with the needs of the beast. It would certainly do away with loads of silly sod comments—or would it? Few Acts regarding animal welfare are still observed. Awful atrocities are often preperated on animals which are about to be slaughtered at abbattoirs and the Dog Breeders Act of 1973, an Act that was designed to be a measure to curb the misery of the many puppies and adults alike has now become a joke; few authorities enforce it and ghastly hellholes still escape detection because the laws of the land are strung together by idiots. The law is a ass, Mr Bumble said Dickens, and he would hardly rejoice to see his statements made true by the spate of insane, ill-constructed, ill-phrased lunatic laws, all of which start out as good intentions and become a mockery because the legislators leave huge legal loopholes through which one can drive a horse and dray.

Saturday 13

I paid the owner of Shehaan £10 as a deposit and he promised to deliver her today. So far he has not and it is 12 midnight as I write this. What an idiot, I am, a trusting blind fool who credits everyone with the same intentions I seem to have. If the law is an ass, so am I. I don't even know his address. Perhaps he will turn up tomorrow and make me feel wretched about my suspicions, but I doubt it. I allowed him to kennel her at my premises for a few weeks free of charge, I must add, and he came four times a day then. Today, with my £10 in his hands, he has not been up once—or have I missed him when I was out? Tomorrow will prove my case, one way or another. If he comes, I will be surprised. Twice this year someone from that area of Lichfield (there are unpleasant areas even in posh little cities like Lichfield) has ripped me off—once with my taperecorder, another with a load of money to buy a bag of dog meal and now I think I am at flim flam expert number three. He asked for all the money in advance. Thank God, I had some little wisdom to refuse this request. If this diary gets off the ground, gets finished and maybe even published, I shall use the book as a source of revenue to pay off my bad debts, debts created by my own credulous nature. It is all the more curious that I get taken each and every time. The dog meal episode was brought about by my giving £14 to a woman with a host of sticky kids who had left her purse at home and lived in fear of her husband's wrath if she returned without the dog food. I gave her the money, she took my address but I never saw her again. Bri, my boy, you are a BF 3.

As expected, my £10 deposit has vanished and no dog has appeared. Will I never cease to be an idiot? Each time I get taken for a ride, I vow never to be taken again, yet a few weeks has but to pass to find me once again in trouble for my credulity.

Paul Taylor has found me an adult male wolf to mate to my bitches. The trouble is, I've given the collie away. After her milk fever, she was taken in by Richard Jones, my vet and he diagnosed a heart illness as well. Now for the 64,000 dollar question.

1. Heart illness is rare in collies as most are tested to bursting point.
2. The collie bitch was tiny and I attributed the small size to the fact that she had been ill as a puppy.
3. The illness was one of the gut and not only did she have dysentery but there was a considerable amount of blood in the faeces.
4. She became emaciated and dehydrated and remained poor for months.

Was this illness (some 2 years ago) parvo virus. If she had reared her puppies would they have had an immunity to this disease? It is of enormous importance to know this before the faeces samples analysis comes back for so little is known of parvo and apart from the fact that I have two dogs very ill with the disease, the rest seem hale and hearty (for now that is). Heart illness and cardiac arrest often follow parvo virus infections.

My cottage—the rats use the wild clematis to climb into the roof.

Vampire's puppies, Phobus and Deimos (Vampire × Beltane) are little hellers and a savage fight broke out this morning involving the two tiny puppies. They will surely kill themselves one day, for they have all the ferocity of Vampire and let's hope they have all the wisdom of Beltane. If they survive the parvo bug, they will be giant assets to the ratting team.

The corn is being cut behind my house and hosts of small creatures are invading my premises. Rats have taken up residence in the roof once again and field mice are all too common in the kitchen. Each year, the cutting of the corn sees the same problems and each year, I am reduced to putting poison in the roof to kill the rats which are invading the house. There are problems being next to a cornfield, but the advantages far outweigh the disadvantages.

An offer of a returned male puppy, sired by Vampire out of a bitch of doubtful breeding. The owners cannot control it—a common statement, I'm afraid. In my years of dog training I have had very few bitch puppies offered back, but uncontrollable dogs are a dime a dozen. Personally, I can never understand how anyone can allow a dog to get out of hand like this. The dog may well be simply bored or may possibly regard the owners as rival members of a pack. Whatever the cause, it is obvious that people who allow a dog to be master of them should never be allowed to own a dog.

The new Deer Act is a killer. Bob just brought *Shooting Times* over and there is an article by Peter Carne on the new deer poaching Act that may be the new deterrent to end all deterrents. Fines of £500 per deer or 6 months in jail seems to be reminiscent of the Forest Laws of the 13th century and confiscation of vehicles, dogs and poaching equipment, nets etc. Thus, a person with six deer might cop up to three years in jail and £3,000 fine. Will this deter—I wonder?

When capital punishment was the standard punishment for premeditated homicide, murderers still chanced their necks and killed people. The psychology of poaching, or of any crime for that matter, is interesting. Is anything a deterrent? Kellow Chesney, in his book *Victorian Underworld* stated that eighty per cent of all executed murderers in Bristol Jail had seen a public hanging.

A hard run for Fathom this morning but a catch at the end of it. We have run this particular hare for a month now and not once has Fathom looked like catching it. Yesterday, the barley was cut, however, and the sport became a little one sided as Fathom hunted up the hare and ran it towards the field that once had held barley. Fathom is neither fast nor is she a stayer, but she is certainly able to predict, the quality that divides the true lurcher from a greyhound, for a lurcher is not simply a rough coated sight hound but a thinking, anticipating hunter. Anyway, the hare, a middle sized adult doe, headed for the field that once held barley with Fathom not particularly hot in pursuit. At the edge of the field, the doe stopped almost as if she expected the barley to be still standing and then wonder of wonders, she headed back along the track directly towards Fathom, swerving to avoid collision with the bitch. Fathom is not fast but she is very dextrous and took the doe in a flying tackle. No way would she have taken the beast in a fair course. Stories that hares are stronger and more difficult to course after Christmas are not without foundation. The cut of corn or hay must have a devastatingly disconcerting effect on a hare used to using such cover and the first days after the corn is cut often sees the death of many hares, I am sure. Certainly we take quite a few during these confusing days after the harvest of the barley.

A typical S. Welsh Valley type terrier with obvious Sealyham ancestry. My old dog San was from such a family.

Thursday 18

Like a twisted version of John Peel's legend "We canna hunt this Thursday" as we have to bury puppies. I think the last has gone. Before God, I hope I am correct anyway, for my team cannot take this constant viral hammering.

A curious day and yet not an unprofitable day trainingwise. My lurcher puppy Mara, has started learning the jumping process and is very good at scrambling over 2 ft screens. The jumping action is quite easy to teach to a babe, but very difficult to teach an adult. I've seen many dogs, adult 3 year old lurchers, stand whining at a 2 ft obstacle and refusing even to hop over the damn structure. Such a dog shows that it's training has been attempted by a crass amateur. The jumping process taught either by running the dog at an obstacle and shouting the "Up" command or simply by calling a puppy over a barrier, is easily taught and quite essential for training a hare-hunting dog, for unless one is hunting the Fens or Salisbury Plain, it is impossible to catch hares regularly with a dog that will not jump. Woolly is not up to the enormous leaps brought off by his illustrious grandfather, but within a year, eight and nine foot hurdles will present no obstacle to him. He is still very lightly muscled, however.

Friday 19

A request from a man called John Everard to rat his pig farm—why he doesn't get the Ministry in, baffles me. It is far more efficient to poison and gas rather than to ferret. A curious name, Everard, particularly curious for a pig keeper for Everard, a corruption of Eberhard, means literally, brave as a boar. Pigs are vastly under-rated beasts of the chase and the title of the most dangerous quarry in the world must go to the wild boar. I've hunted boar and have the scars to show it. Shakespeare (here I go again) knew him well for they still roamed in the Forest of Arden during Shakespeare's youth. The bit I like is from *Venus and Adonis*.

"And where he strikes, his crooked tushes slay"

What a foe the boar would have proven to the hunter of old. Now, with his telescopic sights, high velocity rifles and a multitude of bullet types, the boar becomes just another foe, but arrows were easily deflected by the quarter inch "rind" and a spear thrust would need a strong man to drive it home. I hope to hunt the pig in January and have the greatest respect for it. Anyone wishing to read an accurate if bloody account of a boar hunt would do well to read the fourteenth century poem Sir *Gawain and the Green Knight*.

Saturday 20

Sadness of sadnesses, once more I am forced by circumstances to dig and kill yet another badger. I really dislike hunting this poor old devil. Not only is he a fighter, but he is also one of the most amiable middle-sized mammals in Britain. Yet a dozen times a year I am called out to shift or destroy the poor old devils. What harm they are supposed to cause, I do not know, but all sorts of felonies are attributed to them. They are supposed to roll ripe corn—no great damage if one harvests with a combine. They are reputed to harbour brucellosis; so incidentally, is man. Some say they slay fowl. I've rarely found this to be the case and I've never known one touch a lamb. Motor cars kill them regularly, they are gassed and dug by all, yet they still survive. Anyway, to work at dawn with Beltane and Merle and after an aching 14 hour day, we dug a boar and sow. Both were killed, I confess, painlessly and quickly, I must admit, but I always feel bad slaying such creatures. Merle is utterly unafraid of anything; fox and badger, are grist to his mill. He tries for them, misses a hold now and again, learns the trade of taking particular quarry and becomes adept.

Sunday 21

Yet once more, the dreadful ferret sequence from *It'll be all right on the night* has been shown—a thirty second clip actually which shows very pompous yours truly being interviewed about my book *Modern Ferreting*. During the interview, a young jill of mine latched on to Richard Whiteley's finger and held on like grim death. Whiteley panicked a bit and I did little to help by being a very pompous twit about the whole business. To be fair, Richard Whiteley took the whole business in his stride and did a series of other interviews that day. Originally, the catastrophe took place in Leeds and went out on a programme called *Calendar Tuesday* but most parts of the world seem to have seen my disaster movie. One friend saw the programme in Germany with dubbed voices trying to blend in with my blasé pompous attitude. Boy, oh boy, when I fall on my bum, do I fall on my bum?

Pagan will whelp some time this week and looks as though she is carrying what Moses calls 'a belly full", six or maybe eight I would estimate. Actually, I'm not very keen on the litter as I've seen one from a full sister mated to Vampire and it has dreadfully bent legs. Pagan has been mated to Rollo, however, and may produce something quite special. Anyway, we'll wait and see, milk fever, parvo virus, the works in fact, could be more important than simply bent legs.

Monday 22

Bill Brockley, the Etwall terrier breeder, phoned and asked if I wanted to sell my border terrier bitches as broods. I do actually, for as hunters, they are very substandard. I hate parting with adult dogs but then I have little time for these bitches. Both are destructive, slow to learn and such famous escapists that there is scarcely a kennel intact in my run. I really do need new kennels; my present batch look a hell of a mess. I shall use an entirely new design for the next batch and with any luck, I shall be able to burn the old kennels by Christmas. I hope to take my terrier pack to thirty once again this year, so there is a grim time ahead entering this number of puppies. An early morning walk around the block will do much to help teach the pack team work, but the roads get more crowded by morning. My quiet and peaceful lane has become a race track some days, and if I am to exercise the pack, it could be a risky business to say the least. But it will be good to be back in the swing again. What I do need is a first whip to help me keep the team in order; but who on earth will get up at 4.30 am to exercise a team of terriers? I will, but no one in his right mind will join me. Still, with new kennels, the border terriers well and truly sold and gone—who knows what can happen? I feel positively jubilant about the border terriers actually going.

Tuesday 23

Pagan whelped tonight, eight puppies I think, for at the time of writing this, she is very protective towards them. Correction, I've just looked. She has seven— one tan male puppy, one black and white male puppy, two tan and white, one dog, one bitch, three black and white or tricolour puppies, one dog, two bitches. The division of the litter should be easy. Trevor, one of our most loyal rat hunters, is having the tan dog, the two "Vampire" puppies are mine. Paul Coffey wants a black and white bitch puppy and Peter Evans, a fifteen year old from Cambridge, has spoken for the black and tan puppy. This leaves me with one black and white bitch and one black and white dog. Alan Thomas will certainly have the bitch and the dog puppy will easily find a place among the team. That's if they live, and believe me, under present circumstances that is a big "if."

David Hancock phoned tonight to ask if I wanted to learn photography from the word "go". It would be priceless, as I see so many worthwhile things to photograph, but I have neither camera nor skill. If I can learn the trade, I can do my own photography for my books, an enormous task I fear for I am very "undextrous" at learning any skill. At the risk of a pun concerning photography, I am very much in the dark. Still, I need to buy a camera and start work with David tomorrow. A camera will cost about £150, David says—quite a price, actually.

Wednesday 24

My first tentative steps in photography are about to be taken. David Hancock of Blake Street, Sutton Coldfield, will be my guide and mentor and tonight we spent in dark rooms in his house, and with luck and a hell of a lot of experience before this time next year I will know just a little about photography. Up until now, I have relied on Keith Ruston for my photographs and I've had no complaints. Keith's work is superb but he is not with me every day of my life— though he damn nigh was at one time. David Hancocks is a competition photographer specialising in animal photography and also in minute detail in photographs. I am not practical, but I hope with a great deal of experience to become good enough to do my own photographs.

Pagan's puppies look small and rather weedy and curiously there seems to be a marked disparity in size twixt the Jack Russell types and the coloured terriers. The black and tan and the tan are much smaller than the others. Question—Is there some genetic reason for this or is it by the merest chance? I think the latter. Pagan seems quite exhausted with her wards and I think she must rat tomorrow to perk up her spirits. She seems very down in the dumps but this is quite normal with a bitch who has just whelped her first litter. Let's hope the strain was not in vain and parvo doesn't carry off the litter.

In spite of her incredible antiquity, Beltane caught a mink his morning on the banks of the River Thame, a river that has the dubious distinction of being Britain's most polluted stream. At first, I thought she was on the losing end of struggle with a large rat, but the stench of mustelids soon convinced me of the nature of her quarry. In fact, the battle took nearly a minute to finish. I dislike protracted battles for I hope I am a hunter and hunters detest baiting of any sort, but the sight of my veteran going lickety spit at the creature, gave me a huge kick. She is as game as ever, and well worth inbreeding to. On the subject of inbreeding, the future looks a bit more rosy with Pagan producing a Vampire marked dog puppy. With luck, mated to his grandmother, Omega, the strain could be revived with no loss of nose or type.

Thursday 25

A hard night's work with only a hundred or so rats to show for our troubles. Pagan worked like a demon but she is exhausted by her efforts. Perhaps ratting her in her post-natal depression state was not such a great idea, though she would have bitten through a wall to have come with us. She caught a fair proportion of the total but her condition seemed wretched late that night: tail down, coat poor.

Vampire is now simply a stud dog, I fear, for he has taken to carrying a rat around all night instead of killing the brute and leaving it. Six years ago he was good—no, good is not enough, he was great—but now he is a doddering old man who tries to show he is still up to it. With good luck he will live to a ripe old age and stud to his heart's content but tonight convinced me that he is finished as a mainstay of the team. Mick's dog Toby is coming on a treat, hunting almost as well as Beltane and killing with the best of them. He is agile, energetic and has a wonderful nose, all in all the epitome of what a good terrier should be. Hybrid vigour personified, Tony Powell, a biologist friend of mine called him. Will this wonderful temperament be passed on to the next generation is the question now? Will Pagan's puppies be as useful? Madge Hastings, the owner of a puppy from the sister of Pagan mated to Vampire, is fairly happy with her dog, though I doubt if the dog will ever be tested properly.

A dead pig and a blessing at that. Hunt Kennels refuse pigs and most dog books tell that the fatty meat is bad for a dog. Personally, I think this is a load of nonsense. My own dogs thrive on dead pigs and Paul Taylor reared a sensational litter of lurchers on pig meat. Furthermore, the high fat content allows the carcass to stay fresh for several days and this in itself is a treasure in these days of dog meat shortage. I am perhaps more than fortunate that I live in the heart of some of the best pig breeding country for to keep my pack of dogs would cost the earth if I lived in a town. I feed anything and everything, dead hens, dead pigs, dead sheep, calves and sometimes even foals and my team thrive on them, particularly on dead hens. This is all the more important as we are discussing increasing the team.

Friday 26

A strange sort of day starting with Woolly catching a myxied rabbit and finishing with a constructive discussion with the ratting team on the future of the pack. Woolly is now catching quite well, but he just cannot seem to be able to "put it together" to work with Fathom. If she hunts seriously, he jumps on her or annoys her in some way. She savages him, tries to avoid him yet he continues to annoy her and hampers her when she is hunting. I must take him out alone and re-enter him in a different manner. In spite of his lack of muscle, he is quite fast and well able to jump. He really needs a lot of individual attention minus Fathom, I think. If I continue to hunt them together, I feel he will never be very useful. He must be worked with ferrets this winter, taught some sense, some hunting technique and above all allowed to muscle up, by this time next year he will be useful, I'm sure. At this moment in time, he is capricious, juvenile and a poor doer weight wise.

The new terrier pack is to be discussed. I need new puppies and badly at that. The team is good but senile. Vampire's two puppies, Phobos and Deimos, are ideal blood stock as well as superb potential hunters. Paul Coffey will have the two puppies from Pagan (God permitting they live) and these and my own puppy mated to either Vampire or his sons, Phobos and Deimos, will give me just a bit of breathing space. Providing all things pan out properly and parvo doesn't slay the present puppies, I think 1982 will see a pack of young lusty terriers eager, willing and more than able to do a job. Furthermore, if Paul honours his agreement with me and mates back to the real old bloodline I may never have to breed any more damned puppies.

Pagan looks wretched and has very bad diarrhoea. I must be out of my mind to work her in such dire straits. Not only is she looking quite poor but she is from a bloodline that is fairly rich in milk fever bitches. This is a bit worrying as she has seven puppies to rear and this will drain a bitch quite badly. My den, where Pagan is rearing the litter, will soon be a filthy mess. I will have to clean up the place and fumigate it when Pagan leaves it.

Saturday 27

A super rat hunt using Fudge, Roger and Mick. Since the corn behind the house has been cut, we have been invaded by rats. They "dig" in my vegetable plot, invade my house, gnaw the rafters year after year. Harvest time is a hell for rats and not a cottage around the cornfield escapes their ravages. I shall have to poison, but we usually have a considerable sport with them before the poisoning. Some invariably invade the hedgerow around the potato patch and today Mick surprised one and drove it into a rotten tree stump. We flushed him with Fudge and enjoyed a terrific hunt before the rat vanished into cover. In spite of the fact I take 200 odd rats in a good week, I envy Jack Ivester Lloyd's Bagley Rat Hounds and their few eventful kills. In lots of ways he enjoys more sport than I do—he is certainly able to relate his hunts better than I am. Anyway, two days of hunting them and then we poison.

This year I shall use a posion called RATAK, a proprietary brand of chemical called Difenacoum, a poison that acts like Warfarin, but slays more quickly. I've used this chemical before under another pro- prietary name and found that in addition to being an anti-coagulant, it reduces the rat's body temperature until the rat eats his way towards a source of heat. One burrowed through my floor and died next to my immersion heater, which was fairly nasty to say the least. Three days should see an end to the rats in the cottage roof and not before time. The sound of them gnawing and racing around the ceilings seems to pall as a conversation piece after a time.

Michael Croucher phoned about filming "lamping" with Fathom. Fathom is a good lamper, for a few runs at least, for she has little weight to hold stamina. Her daughter, aged 7 months, is catching well but Fathom will have to perform in front of very high powered lamp lights. Will this lamplight be strong enough to blind the rabbit or will it also blind Fathom? These extra bright lights will prove a bit of a task for Fathom, I fear. I'd also like shots of Woolly missing badly on the lamp as any puppy will. It will at least reduce the chance of people imagining all forms of rabbit hunting are easy. Still, there's many a slip 'twixt cup and lip, or to be precise between now and 20th October, when we film.

Sunday 28

New kennels and a boy, do I need them! My old kennels are foul, dirty and mange ridden—also if I manage to beat the parvo virus, I shall need more space. Mick Kirby and I will build them out of pallets and 3′×2′ wood. This time, I will mix the creosote with benzene hexachloride as a mange remedy or prophylactic measure. Also, I shall build these taller to make them easier for cleaning. I shall run on thirty terriers, mostly males, as I hope I shall not have to breed many puppies to replenish the pack from time to time.

I shall breed no more lurchers for years to come, for I feel I have more than enough. Mara will be trained and entered and in five or six years I shall breed from her. I do not intend to join the breed of person who keeps strings of lurchers, all untrained and the majority unentered. Furthermore, I am kidding myself if I say that I need a lurcher other than Fathom and Merle. Fathom will take most game that doesn't bite and Merle, although slower, will face anything. Woolly is a bit superfluous and Mara is merely bitch I bred to fulfil a genetic dream. With Eddie's dog at standby, the future is fairly certain lurcherwise. Oh, that my terrier team was as certain!

The ferret population is rock bottom—Fudge and two others—and I nearly lost Fudge yesterday. There's a thing to panic any man, a ferret on the loose in a district with free range poultry. Curiously, Fudge is six years old and still keen on hunting rat. This is not because she is exceptional but merely because she has been lucky in not meeting a doe with a nest of two day old kits. Such a beast would be the end of Fudge's ratting career, I'm sure. Her great-grandmother met her Waterloo in her first season when a doe with a freshly drawn nest slashed her badly on her first ratting trip, which made her useless for ratting although she eventually became a great rabbiter. Sooner or later, Fudge will come up against such a doe and take a very bad beating and subsequently quite the game. Until that day comes, she will be priceless, for she tears into rats like a tigress.

Monday 29

A morning run and a live rabbit retrieved to hand by Fathom in spite of Woolly's attentions. He is becoming more and not less annoying as time goes by and sooner or later Fathom will stop retrieving if Woolly is about. A pity really, but it is a *Catch 22* situation. If she continues to go out with Woolly, he may improve, if not he will certainly remain the nearly useless brute. Fathom looks a bit off colour lately, either a slight parvo infection or maybe even the onset of a phantom pregnancy, the next few days will determine which. If she has a phantom pregnancy and it seems likely as Woolly tries quite fruitlessly to mount her throughout her season and this is often enough to trigger off some hormonal reaction. In spite of not looking right, she runs well, picks up well, but something is amiss with her. Her appetite is capricious and she sometimes goes two or three days without an interest in food, after which she is frantic to eat. By Friday, if things are unchanged I will certainly worm her or take her to the vet.

The terrier pack run by a committee and financed by subscription, seems a reasonable idea. Control of a pack of terriers is difficult, far more difficult than the control of a group of hounds which are naturally pack animals. I pride myself on the control of my team, but

Tuesday 30

I've only just realised how long I've bred this strain of terrier and I feel decidedly old when I think about it.

When I look at this pedigree a host of memories come flooding back: Jade who bred litters of 12 and 14 and every one a worker; Spidey, a bitch from Joan Begbies' illustrious Seale Cottage strain; Rupert, sire of 42 working certificate offspring, a dog who never bred a poor nosed puppy yet a spiteful, bad tempered dog in kennels; Smalley, a demon dog 10″ tall and rough

With luck and a lot of help, this week will see our new kennels finished. Mick Kirby is a carpenter by trade and works with speed and efficiency. The kennels will be built in a block of six with wooden walls dividing the compartments. Must watch the kennelling of dogs, however, for two bitter enemies like Pagan and Omega will bite through walls to get to fight each other. I once used wooden partitions of this type and had hell's delight when my stud dog Rupert bit through the walls to kill a rival stud. Constant checks are needed to ensure the dividing walls of such a kennel are intact.

this morning they went berserk after a healthy rabbit, ran it to ground and refused to come out. Calling one terrier from an earth is child's play but calling out several is a nightmare. Pagan, who has a litter, stayed three hours to ground. Subsequently, I was late for school. Lucas, in his book *Hunt and Working Terriers* mentions a certain Mr Cowley who owned a most obedient team of terriers who would stand in certain marked out squares and kill only rats who came into that square. I envy this Mr Cowley. My own dogs slaughter rats in a free-for-all, but then I do more rat hunting than Mr Cowley, so I must make allowances.

I must phone John Winch about the law governing the running of a subscription pack. Where there is a membership fee, there must obviously be laws to govern the use of that money. Fox hunting packs, beagle packs and such like must be acquainted with these laws and advice from Winch, the president of the Fell and Moorland, is really needed. I need help regarding kennels and new land on which I can hunt. Perhaps if I advertise in *Exchange and Mart* or *Shooting Times* enough people with land will invite me there to hunt. Otherwise, it is just the old Thursday night hunt and whatever else I can scrounge.

coated who looked like a toy dog, yet she would fight anything on two legs or four; Laddie, a tall, poor-coloured, thin-coated elegant dog brought in from the Chiddingfold and Leconfield Hunt as an outcross when cleft palates and hydrocephaly appeared in my strain and when I inbred to him, bad mouths took the place of the other defects. What other problems will I meet in the years to come? What troubles await me when I try to inbreed the litter that is in Pagan's nest

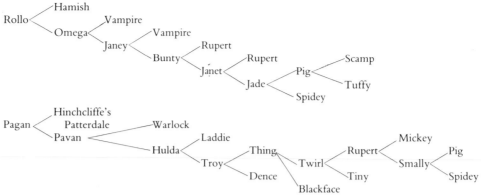

```
                  ┌─ Hamish
        ┌─ Rollo ─┤
        │         └─ Omega ─┬─ Vampire
        │                   └─ Janey ─┬─ Vampire
        │                             └─ Bunty ─┬─ Rupert
        │                                       └─ Janet ─┬─ Rupert
        │                                                 └─ Jade ─┬─ Pig ─┬─ Scamp
        │                                                          │       └─ Tuffy
        │                                                          └─ Spidey
        │
        │         ┌─ Hinchcliffe's
        └─ Pagan ─┤   Patterdale
                  └─ Pavan ─┬─ Warlock
                            └─ Hulda ─┬─ Laddie
                                      └─ Troy ─┬─ Thing ─┬─ Twirl ─┬─ Rupert ─┬─ Mickey
                                               │         │         │          └─ Smally ─┬─ Pig
                                               │         │         └─ Tiny              └─ Spidey
                                               └─ Dence └─ Blackface
```

box? Hulda's sister had no incisor teeth when her second teeth came through and curiously they never grew. I gave her away, praying no one would breed from her and fortunately no one ever has. I must certainly keep an eye on poor bone as some very fragile puppies are appearing when I inbreed to Vampire's strain. With luck, Hinchcliffe's dogs are able to counteract this defect, but it is still worth watching.

My garden is swarming with rats. I go out at night and hear them scurrying in the deep undergrowth. I would estimate that my acre and a quarter of land must hold over a hundred of the brutes. Soon, the cast seeds of corn will be eaten and the fallen apples blitzed by frost and the majority will leave the district via the streams that cross Barlow's land. Until then, it is a pure hell. The dogs are constantly barking and my ceiling resounds with the patter of tiny feet. Poison is being wolfed down yet still the rats seem to get into the roof.

Rusty—a Warlock son, 1981.

October

What ill luck I am having! The Gods seem adamant that I must lose my best ferret, Fudge. Today, I found a young hob wandering in the fields and when I returned to the house I realised he was mine, but Fudge and the young jills have vanished into the air. Theft or escapes? I just don't know. Let's hope it is the former, for a ferret at large is too frightening to contemplate. The ducks at the end of the lane are goners for certain if Fudge is loose.

Woolly took off after a hare again this morning, watched by Fathom who realised the slip was too long, and just didn't try. Woolly will learn in time, but it really does take time for a coursing dog to become a real lurcher able to assess, hunt up and anticipate. I'm not unhappy about his determination regarding a course, but he simply had no chance of catching this hare. He coursed it for maybe a mile, always twenty yards behind the hare who didn't really seem to mind the chase. A pity. Woolly so needed the confidence a lucky catch would have brought.

One of Pagan's puppies, the tan one, Trevor's puppy, just doesn't look right. It is only half the size of the others although it is still suckling. Question—is a fading puppy the result of this parvo virus that is beginning to obsess me? Is parvo the cause of fading puppies—Rubarth's infection was blamed for this but now even vets question the cause of the trouble. Will I lose the puppy or more to the point, the entire litter? They look healthy enough but it's early days yet, I fear. I can only hope Pagan's eating of the diseased puppy will have given the litter some immunity and a sporting chance of survival. I am reminded of the days when over a hundred terrier puppies bit the dust as a result of a distemper outbreak.

The Fell terrier and her fellow sufferer, my beardie/border collie merle puppy are doing fine, and are well over the plague. Will Richard Jones, my vet's, prediction of a heart attack killing the pair, be correct? God, I wish I was over this bloody plague. It has ruined my year and done wicked damage to my strain of dog. Still, some have fared worse, I believe—at least I've had two puppies survive the disease; some breeders have lost every puppy.

Mara is scratching madly and so are the collie puppies. Are they lousy—Moses has lice in his kennels—or is it due to the barley awns drifting in from the cut fields? A dip in benzene hexachloride will cure the first, but I've seen barley awns deeply embedded in the bodies of dogs and causing bad sepsis particularly between the toes. I shall dip the whole brood this weekend—adults as well. Lice can drive a dog mad. I know all about lice. *I've* had them.

A night spent searching for ferrets by lamplight is hardly conducive to a day's hunting and this morning the lurchers remained unexercised. They will lose little from a day off though Woolly needs every bit of experience he can glean if he is to get out of his silliness. He spends most of his time annoying Fathom and irritating me, and I have doubts that he will be as useful as I had first thought. In any case I would not have been as welcome on the land I normally hunt today, for the Meynell Hunt met at the end of my lane this morning. I received a few rather vicious vulpicide jests as I passed, jests more in fun than to hurt I hope, but the area is thick with foxes and there are plenty for everyone. I catch sixty-odd foxes a year from this district and they are still numerous, so numerous that keeping hens can prove a problem.

My remaining ferret, a young polecat hob, is pig-mouthed or undershot—not a particularly serious defect when rabbit hunting is concerned, but a genetic fault that should not be perpetuated. I must fetch Fudge's daughters back from the Jacksons of Reading. The bloodline of these ferrets is good and while I believe that all ferrets will hunt and work well if given a chance, my own are tame and I have had this line for twenty years now and so I am loathe to part with it. One jill, a rather unprepossessing grizzle polecat had excellent potential and may well replace her illustrious mother. Still, I am continuing to search for Fudge, for there is a chance I may find her. If I fail, some luckless chicken owner will certainly do the finding for me.

P.S.

Luck is with me. Early this afternoon, David Green who is working at my place, picked up a ferret that had hidden under my dog pens. It was Fudge. I cursed the rat population in my hedge, but it caused Fudge to hang around the buildings. Her side has an ugly gash ½″ long, the result of a rat bite, I'd say, but she is still the best rabbiting ferret I've ever owned, even if she jibs at rats from now on.

Friday 3

A freezing morning and two rabbit catches for Fathom—I would have had three but Woolly behaved very badly again.

Trevor's puppy is still desperately holding on to life though it is very small and dehydrated. It is in quite a bad way yet it is still quite lively. Heat lamps are priceless pieces of equipment when one is rearing puppies and they must save dozens of whelps. I use a German made porcelain heat lamp that gives heat without light—a fairly expensive piece of equipment but it has saved no end of puppies. I'm not particularly fond of the survival of the fittest doctrine practiced by some of the breeders—useful as well as sickly puppies go to the wall if this notion is followed to its logical conclusion. I've seen whole litters of Spartanly reared puppies die in midwinter. Furthermore, sick and damaged animals will often recover if placed under a heat lamp for animals off their feet with shock will frequently pick up if kept in warmth.

Royal Shakespeare Theatre and *As you like It*. I confess I am a Shakespeare buff but the bard may have been quite at home living the life I have. His plays are full of quotes on hunting. *As You Like It* quote:

> "As the falcon the bells
> So hath man his desires."

Philip Glasier named his book *As the Falcon the Bells*

from this quote.

Arden is no longer a forest but I've taken a huge number of foxes from this area. Three years ago I killed fifty-two foxes within spitting distance of the town. In Shakespeare's day, boars and deer abounded in the district and Shakespeare himself was hauled up for poaching deer. (With the new deer Act in the offing, such an conviction would have assured him of a quiet place to finish his plays.) Deer are no longer plentiful in the district where the bard hunted. Enough of my passion for the plays, however, for Roger reads this diary almost daily and warns against my passion for Shakespeare.

Mara's training is in swing. She begins lead training today—an odious task and one I'd sooner give to one of the lads, but an essential part of training nevertheless. Mara has however, an irritating whining nature that annoys most people. If she is not the constant centre of attention, she whines piteously and begs attention. Her jumping is proceeding well and she retrieves reasonably well after a fashion, though certainly not as well as her father, Merle. She is not particularly bright either but it is early days as yet. Eddie's merle/greyhound dog is more with it and far more eager to please than Mara, but again Eddie has put a lot of work into this dog, and lurchers are made, not just born.

Saturday 4

Trevor's puppy has disappeared and no trace of it can be found. The answer is quite simple, Pagan has eaten it. Wild dogs invariably keep their lairs clean by devouring the waste, birth trappings, faeces and cadavers and either vomiting the filth away from the lair or simply digesting it. No doubt Pagan simply began by licking the dying puppy to revive it and when she drew blood she continued licking and finally ate the carcass. Lorenz watched a panther frantically cleaning a sickly cub and wagered by dawn the cub would be eaten. In fact, any excessive display of motherly love in animals is suspect and will often herald a tragedy. Beltane carries feeble puppies around in her mouth preventing me from looking at them but next day the puppy has usually vanished. To impute human sentiments to animals is not only unscientific, it is quite often dangerous.

Not another bantam, Fathom! The morning exercise (I turn her loose behind the house) was broken by Fathom coming like hell in the night across the fields with a hen in her mouth. I really must get to know more about the breeds of bantams. I get so many of them these days. I spent four mornings walking her through poultry and was convinced the Kanniechor image was broken. Back to square one, I fear. She is back to chicken stealing again; and by returning hen in jaws, she has made Woolly think hens are fair and legal game.

Photographed Eddie's dog Celt today. The first photograph I've ever taken and I'm a hell of a way behind Keith Ruston as far as technique goes. There is obviously a great deal more to photography than meets the eye.

David Hancock, my photography mentor, describes the camera, a Pentax, as an idiot's camera as the camera apparently does it all for you. I find it very complicated. It will certainly take years to get up to the standard required for illustrating a book, although David says it will take less than a week. I have little mechanical aptitude, however.

A colony of rabbits at the bottom of the lane has somehow escaped the ravages of myxomatosis and seems to be thriving. Fathom ran and caught one this morning, retrieving it alive to hand. It is expedient not to catch rabbits in this colony, so I turned it loose again much to Fathom's amazement. I found a silver-fox-coloured rabbit feeding among them this evening which brings back memories. Twelve years ago, a silver-fox rabbit escaped and for a while silver-fox type rabbits were quite common but myxomatosis slew them all seven years ago, or so I thought. Two of the silver-fox bred rabbits have clearly survived.

Sunday 5

Now that the parvo scare seems to have passed, I need to get the puppies inoculated for the deadly evils distemper, hard pad, leptospirosis and hepatitis. There is still a chance that the effects of parvo infection might slay through heart attack but that's a chance I will have to take. An outbreak of another disease will knock my kennels for six. Expensive as inoculation is, I cannot afford not to have my dogs inoculated.

Harold Hodson Walker phoned. His friend is breeding a strain of French rabbit called *Géant de Buscat*, an enormous strain of rabbit that can weigh 22lbs and one that is entering the commercial rabbit market in this country. One of these attacked a Yorkshire terrier and damn nigh killed the poor devil, and most will put a cat to flight. One of these brutes could undoubtedly do a man damage, though Harold tells me they are the most phlegmatic of beasts—a good job too, for two rabbits of this size could rule the world. Whether or not the release of such giants in my district would increase the size of the wild rabbits is doubtful. Wild provender would hardly keep a beast of 22 lbs through the winter, although during late summer such an animal might survive on ripening corn. For a generation or two perhaps, such hybrid stock might survive but it would inevitably revert to the average wild size 2½–3 lbs. Such a size has stood the test of time and has proved the ideal size to survive on the limited pro-

vender of the temperate zone and able to resist the temperate zone predators. Near Muckley Corner, where Roger and Mick hunt, one of the local farmers turned loose a few New Zealand White rabbits, huge 10 lb and 12 lbs brutes but they were soon absorbed by the native wild stock and though white rabbits do sometimes appear in the fields (I've run them with the lamp and Fathom) they are no bigger than the native brown agouti rabbits. Most books on rabbit warren management and rabbit hunting advocate releasing tame stock to swell the rabbit population and increase the size of the stock, but such eugenics would have little permanent effect. A better way would be to cull out the small wild rabbits and keep only the up to size progeny. This way, the size of the wild rabbits would be maintained if not increased.

We finished the new kennels today, tarring the roof and floors so that the kennel is waterproof. We caulked any gaps between the boards with bitumen as a shipbuilder might do, and, with luck, we have a substantial and very cheap kennel 6×16 ft; the beams 3"×2" cost us £12 and the rest of the timber came free. Add maybe £16 for sundries and we have a very cheap reliable type of kennel that will last six or seven years and easily house 10 or 12 terriers. Thanks again to Mick Kirby for his technical expertise.

Mick with our new kennels—a 12 foot unit we built for £16.

Monday 6

I ran a badger with the terriers this morning. What an unruly lot they are! A few days ago (I think) I wrote about Jocelyn Lucas' book *Hunt and Working Terriers* and mentioned how a Mr Cowley had absolute control over his terriers. Sadly, I have no such canine charisma. Beltane scented the badger and ran it nose down for about four hundred yards and bolted it from a patch of dying thistles. The badger ran for some minutes harassed by the terriers and finally vanished towards Whittington village. All the terriers returned this morning except Vampire who probably followed the beast to ground. Anyway, I thought I had lost him for he is foolhardy enough to believe he can kill a badger but late this afternoon I returned from work to find Vampire waiting in the porch with just a tiny strip of chest fur slightly mangled. Strange that, for I had kept him off badger because of his reckless disposition.

What caused a badger to be abroad at daybreak? Four suggestions come to mind.

1. It was a boar driven out from the sett by a rival male possibly his own size.
2. The sett had been earth-stopped by the hunt that came through here last week.
3. The badger sett is flooded by the heavy rains this weekend—a bit unlikely as I've known heavier rains which did not shift the badgers.
4. The badger is quite simply a captured that some folk had tamed and turned loose.

Add a P.S. to this. It could be a freshly caught boar that someone has released after tiring of baiting it. This area is already overstocked with badgers and a new one, particularly a male, would certainly be attacked by the native boar badgers. Badger fights are very savage, particularly territorial battles that occur when territory overlaps or when an alien badger is turned loose in badger country.

What is even more interesting—though I will never know the answer—is what happened to the badger at the end of the run? Where did he go and what has happened to him? Also, how did Vampire come out of the skirmish unscathed?

Tuesday 7

The morning run with Woolly and Fathom and nothing to show for it apart from the fact that Mara, Steel's puppy has very bad diarrhoea. She has passed a pink gelatinous jelly for two or three days now and is losing weight fairly rapidly. Parvo virus or simply enteritis? I injected her with 5 mls of Amphipen and dosed her with broth containing a kaolin based antibiotic and by 6.0 pm she seemed a bit better. I just cannot afford a parvo virus flare up with Pagan's litter just out of the protection through maternal antibodies phase. I must get them off the premises as quickly as possible. The two I am keeping will have to take their chances, I'm afraid; there just doesn't seem to be any other way of looking at it.

Omega is close to season and we film a rat hunt in eleven days. It will be a tragedy if she is in condition to mate when we film as she is the most professional rat killer I have ever owned. Her speed is absolutely fantastic and her striking ability has to be seen to be believed—and when she is filmed it will be seen. She has featured in hundreds of still shots but now she will be filmed. Her killing speed easily matches that of the formidable Billy, the world record holder in the against-the-clock contests. We shall not film in our usual ratting place as the lights disturb the poultry, but I have another place in mind and it will be an easy spot to film. Whether or not it will be the spectacular spot our usual place is, is open to doubt.

The tan and white bitch puppy from Pagan—the one I want to keep—looks fairly wretched. It always seems to be the way. Immediately a puppy I wish to keep is born, something seems to happen to it. Dollars to doughnuts, something will go amiss with this bitch. The rest look fine but the tan and white bitch is certainly dehydrated for if I take a fold of skin on the back of the bitch and pull it away from the body, it is slow to regain its former position. Tomorrow will probably find her stiff as a board in the nest box. If this bitch dies two courses of action remain open to me.
1. To mate Paul's black and white puppies to either Vampire or one of Vampire's puppies.
2. To mate Pagan to Rollo once more and get my tan and white brood from the second litter.

The death of the puppy is a bit sickening, but it is a temporary setback.

Wednesday 8

Michael Croucher phoned about the filming. Michael suggests we set up a rat colony and film some of the social characteristics of rats—difficult task for many reasons.

Firstly, rats tipped on to a particular area are reluctant to remain there even if food is plentiful. Most will leave and find a ready made hole in which they can find sanctuary. I tried this experiment a few years ago but with little success.

Secondly, few people would welcome a thriving rat colony on their premises; indeed I can think of no one offhand who would. I could breed them quite easily on my acre and a quarter of land (I already have what can be described as a standing stock that has moved in from the surrounding fields, but even these are a huge unpleasant nuisance). Dogs bark all night as a result of hearing the activities of the rodent nucleus and my ceiling resounds to the patter of tiny feet. To increase this nucleus would be murder; and life would be a living hell.

Thirdly, and this point is often overlooked, not only is it illegal to harbour rats on one's premises but to keep rats in captivity involves a bit of a legal tangle. A Home Office licence is required and they have the power to refuse such a licence. The laws regarding the keeping and breeding of vermin are curious. Obviously, they should not be allowed to escape and clearly when the experiment is over they must be humanely destroyed but there are a great many other regulations which are difficult to enforce or to operate.

Lastly, how long would I be able to keep captive rats, in close captivity in a barrel or a corn bin, before I started the colony? Obviously, the rats are well able to survive captivity—the notorious London rat pits proved this and Jimmy Shaw, the old Corinthian boasted to Mayhew that he always kept a standing stock of 2,000 rats on his premises. I have no doubt I should find little trouble in keeping captive rats in barrels. However, the matter requires much thought and planning—Michael Croucher's job fortunately, as I feel only capable of menial tasks in this filming of the TV documentary.

An evening of live catching of rats by hand—we perform this bizarre activity twice a year and for no reason other than from the hell of it. It is not difficult—in fact, nearly all our team can live catch. A bit crazy? Well, hunting is a pastime and an entertainment and we refuse to treat it as serious. We catch maybe one in every fifty we see and tonight we caught thirty-nine. They cascaded off the trays as soon as we threw the lights and I failed (quite dismally, I'm afraid) to photograph any of them. What a photographer Keith Ruston must be! Some of his shots are quite remarkable.

David Green trapped (alive) a rat that had been scurrying in my roof. Trapped rats behave very strangely and while they hiss and spit at hands that come near the cage trap, but within minutes of being captured they feed on the meal given them. I dislike catch-alive traps as they give me the unpleasant task of disposing of any trapped rats—an odious task, ill fitted to the ways of a hunter, but one that has to be observed as no way can I justify turning captured rats loose. Our own rats are considerably thicker furred than the poultry house rats as they have to withstand the hardships of living out in the fields. They are also fairly free from mange, a constant companion of the poultry house rats we normally hunt. David Green breeds rats and is convinced he can get a wild one as tame as the rats sold in pet shops. Not my scene, I'm afraid, as rats are creatures to hunt in my book, not creatures to keep as pets.

The puppy from Pagan, the tan bitch designed to keep my bloodline intact, is dead. I found its dehydrated corpse under the straw this morning. After a puppy is about a week old, few bitches will eat it even after it has died through fading; but puppies that die shortly after birth are invariably eaten. It's a pity this puppy has died as my strain is desperately short of good breeding bitches. Still, Paul's two tricolours are still alive and able to perpetuate the blood.

David Green with live rat in trap, I was idiot enough to get this one out of the trap with my hands—in front of the T.V. cameras.

Yet another rat in David Green's trap and still the patter of tiny feet continues in my bedroom ceiling. After the corn is cut, rats abound around my house and use the wild clematis that covers the front of my cottage. I am considering cutting down this picturesque tangle and sorting out the rat problem once and for all.

The Fell terrier and the collie hybrid are back to normal and probably no longer infectious. Thus the problem of keeping such a pair in isolation is no longer quite so vital. So little is known about how long an ill dog can transmit this virus. Still, they are over it and if they do not die of an untimely parvo-induced heart attack, as many seem to do, they can become useful members of the team.

Just recently I have taken to feeding dog meal as a substitute for tripe and while the dogs look well on this mixed diet, I am a little in doubt as to its value. This morning we experienced the first frost of the year, frosts that caused the scampering in the ceiling to become deafening and before leaving for school I found sparrows pecking at the dog faeces on my compost heap. At first, I thought that the mess must be insect ridden and the birds were simply feeding on the grubs that infest compost heaps but closer examination revealed that the cause of the sparrows' interest was undigested corn in the faeces. The bowels of a dog are a bit inefficient, very inefficient in fact, and maggots find considerable provender in the stools of meat-fed dogs but the amount of undigested grain in the stools shows just how wasteful meal feeding can be—cheap but not good for dogs, I'm afraid.

Broken coated Patterdale type—note the curious ear carriage. Buck's bitch Topsy carried this ear carriage.

Spent the day filming the terriers of my valley—a curious unlovely breed but very game. They resemble lightly built Sealyhams of the type used by John Tucker Edwardes (not the show type of today which are all bone and no guts). Some of the dogs are prick-eared but most are extremely even. I photographed three generations of terrier in Pontrhyl near Bridgend and they were like peas in a pod. Few of the family are now worked, which is a bit sad but those who are are still formidable. Tough terriers like this really need hard work and should not be kept as pets. Just as "Satan makes work for idle hands" so does he find "work" as a sort for the idle terrier that is bred from working stock. Dogs of this type, denied the right to practice the work that instinct decrees they should have, become "hellers." Still, there are people who quite happily keep these dogs as pets and though they often become cat killers and stock worriers, they are still sold as pets, and any breeder might find a ready market for fluffy terriers.

Went to see Gwyn Williams today but he was out "beating" and picking up in Bridgend. Gwyn breeds springer spaniels, and the valley, denuded as it is of game, affords little chance to train springers. Still, the dogs that win well at trials are often bred and trained in such gameless areas. Gwyn is constantly asking me to take up spaniel training, but it is not to my liking. I loathe guns and the people they attract, folk who disturb the solitude of my countryside.

My negatives (photographic) look promising and not too bad for a crass amateur who has never taken a photograph in his entire life. Still, I have a good camera—a Pentax and an even better lens (also a Pentax)—a pity such a piece of machinery is in the hands of such an amateur. However, who knows how proficient I may become—even approaching a passable standard, perhaps. I learn such skills slowly: I once had a mechanical aptitude test reading of 7.5 (near idiot) but once I have acquired a skill, it sticks.

Returned from Wales very tired with pains in my chest—I believe these pains are simply muscle tension. If I sleep they usually go away. Still, they have no time to go away for we are live catching again this evening. I would really like to put an end to this insane pastime as it will sooner or later end in death, I'm sure. Forty-six were taken alive in two hours of easy catching. I'm too old for this sport, and my reflexes cannot compare with the younger members of the team.

Omega is near season and with luck she will be able to continue her illustrious bloodline, but not this time, I think. She has been woefully overbred already and is getting to look a bit baggy. When she comes in use there is a dog in Sutton Coldfield, the result of mating her half sister to a dog bred by Bill Brockley that may be worth using. It will be a very handy outcross if it

pays off—not too far out to lose the essential killing instinct of the strain, but far enough out not to breed in troubles like fine bone and bad mouths. Bitches from this bloodline might be welcome in the strain for suitable mates to Phoibus and Deimos, although at one time I did consider putting her back to her son Rollo. I just don't want winter puppies; not only are they expensive to rear, but they involve a great deal of time. A summer mating usually produces better puppies.

A very cold night, one almost certain to put the foxes back below ground, for at this time of the year they are living out in the kale, having forsaken the corn for the cabbage. Funnily enough, the cold spell invariably brings in a great number of foxes to the fields near the house.

As I expected, the foxes are back to earth. This morning at first light Beltane ran into an earth, a simply straight through drain and flushed one. Fortunately, it bolted easily and I say fortunately because Vampire, Omega and Pagan followed behind

her. Whenever a terrier goes to ground and another is straight behind it, all hell breaks loose. Last year Eddie Chapman lost Sinbad, one of the most important studs in the Jack Russell Club of Great Britain, in just such an accident. Eddie was exercising his 30 terriers when Sinbad went to ground in a badger sett and the rest of the terriers followed him into the earth. Eddie dug to the sound of the baying but before he could get Sinbad out, the badger had killed him. The end of an excellent dog—a great tragedy.

I started to get Pagan's puppies to eat solid food tonight, and while they did show some interest in the minced meat, they ate very little. This is probably because Pagan still has a lot of milk and as yet she is still able to maintain the puppies on this milk. A bitch who dries up quickly invariably has hungry puppies who will feed on solids quite easily. Meat, not milk, is usually the best starting food, particularly scraped meat, meat devoid of fibre or bone. Similarly, a dead hen, fresh killed and fatty, will usually trigger off the interest in semi-solid food. In two days time I will try

again and I shall be fairly certain of good results this time. Last year, I saw a litter go to six weeks without eating solid food and they went on to become rather runty puppies. At about three weeks of age puppies will usually start to eat flesh and by four weeks they are usually feeding very well.

Mara has taken to carrying things around in her mouth. She comes in the house each night and regularly carries my socks out of the bedroom and to hand. Now is the time to start her retrieving, for she has given me the first signs that she is ready. I have great hopes for this bitch and I shall test her to the full this winter. She looks every inch the perfect lurcher, rough coated, bearded and not too greyhoundy, in appearance. If she works as well as she looks, I think I shall be more than satisfied.

Tuesday 14

As I expected, the foxes are all to ground now that the first icy winter days are here. I netted the Copeland drain and put Beltane through, bolting a large cub and entangling it in the net. The skin is worthless at this time of the year, so I turned loose the cub. There will be plenty of cubs before the end of the year, of that I am sure. Skins are only worthwhile in late November to early January, and pelts taken before this time are often pockmarked with blue black patches that indicate the animal is still moulting.

I must watch Pagan for the first signs of milk fever. She is not lactating very heavily and she is fed well but it is always better to be safe than sorry. At the first sign of a stagger or a tottery walk she must be injected with calcium boroglutinate. It is difficult to tell which animals are prone to milk fever in midwinter as they are usually fed and examined in semi-darkness—which is another reason for not breeding in midwinter. Still, I need the new stock to carry on the bloodline.

The remaining ferrets look first class. Their diet of rats has certainly worked wonders, not only is such food cheap, and readily available, but it is a first class diet for ferret and although there is always the danger of mange when rats are fed (for rats are frequently mange carriers), I still feed the rats to them sorting out and rejecting the obviously scabrous brutes. My ferrets literally glow with health now. I hunt Fudge infrequently now that the lads are trapping live rats in the fields behind the house, as ferreted rats in a state of nervousness are reluctant to feed and thus refuse to enter the catch-alive traps.

I really must spend more time with Richard Jones,

my collie hybrid, as his intelligence needs exploiting. There is no danger that he has not been socialised for he was reared with humans, hand reared by Moses and his wife. He is, however, untrained and while he shows a keenness to please and an enthusiasm for retrieving, this parvo bug has prevented much training. A collie of this breeding could be the all-purpose dog, able to hunt, guard herd and perform amazing feats of retrieving. I shall use him to produce broken-coated lurchers of high intelligence and stamina. But he needs training to get the best out of him.

Richard Jones, my attempt at breeding a Smithfield Collie, sleeping out in snow.

Wednesday 15

Woolly is catching quite well and is fairly reasonable on the lead. He refuses to retrieve to hand when Fathom is out with him, but this is not such a serious fault, for he is very eager to fetch and carry when he is hunted alone. Collie blooded lurchers are very enthusiastic retrievers as a whole and their desire to please makes them admirable candidates for training as provender hunters. I hate dogs that simply catch and stand over their kills instead of fetching them in.

My lamp is just about finished, partly due to the terrific hammering it had last winter and also to the fact that I have neglected it. The original came from C.T.F. and an excellent piece of equipment it has proved to be. I took 78 foxes using this lamp and a host of sundry quarry besides. I have also used this lamp in the most appalling conditions, heavy frost, bad weather and in the indescribable filth of a maggot factory, yet the lamp has been with me through shot, shell and corrosion. I need a completely new lamp for the battery has been seen off by misuse and the beam smashed on January 19th, the night Merle cracked his ribs on the frozen slush. I shall send to C.T.F. for another complete lamping unit. No complaints—I've had terrific service out of the lamp.

A casual midnight rat hunt to keep up the interest in the team. We caught by hand ten rats, a pathetic haul but I don't want the place disturbed until the 20th October when we hunt the place properly and film the hunting. TV work is very tiring and the preparation and worry that precedes the performance is very disturbing. At one time, I thought I'd like a Phil Drabble type show of my own, but I don't think I'm up to it. Croucher is a superb producer, however, and has smoothed the way for me, so I have not experienced the full force of preparing for such a show!

Thursday 16

Fathom must be taught to perform in front of a brightly lit light and run rabbits in that blinding beam. She has three days to learn the skill and God help us if she fails. Hedges, ditches, gate posts, walls all become dangerous when a dog is running blind. Len Witton, a fellow lamper (he owns Fathom's half sister) is an electrician and he may possibly help. Personally, I think our lamping trip is likely to end in failure as I have no idea of TV equipment and the TV technicians and producers have no idea of the way a lamping lurcher works.

The dogs are geed up with no where to go. Fights are all too common often through the merest provocation. Both Vampire and Beltane are fractious and difficult to control. A hard night's ratting will calm them all down and bring some sense of unity back to the team. Omega and her son Rollo are so bored that I turned them loose in the run that night and found a dog squirrel near one of the fruit trees this morning. Omega has a tiny nose bite, so I gather it was Omega who caught and killed the squirrel. Squirrels abound along the lane where my cottage is situated and cause constant barking when they invade the fruit trees in the run. Vampire tears his mouth on the bars of his cage when they flash between the trees.

Two of Pagan's puppies, a tricolour bitch and dog, are very dehydrated—an ominous sign in puppies—and are unlikely to survive. I injected about 4 mls of Amphipen and gave some saline solution subcutaneously but I have little hope for them recovering. If any survive, I shall regard it as a bonus although the three remaining puppies look healthy enough—now.

The parvo survivors, the Fell terrier Nightwing and the collie hybrid bitch look fine, but now there are suggestions that they might be carriers. I have little doubt that the Fell terrier brought the disease to the premises but if the suggestion of Ray Onslow, a scientist friend, is correct, the Fell might be a biological time bomb capable of reinfecting all and sundry like the lady in the Bilston cholera infection.

Friday 17

Next year looks fairly bleak breeding bitch wise even if we beat the parvo bug. The broods are ancient and the young stuff as yet untried. Tonight, Granville Maddocks, the MFH and MH of the Atherstone and the Warwickshire beagles offered to master our pack of terriers next year, if I hunt them but at this rate it will look like an OAP outing. To field a bobbery pack of Russells (all shapes and sizes), Fells, and borders

138

would be easy and frankly a good way to start, if we fielded a few beagles with them to encourage pack instinct and encourage nose work among the youngsters, but they would look fairly awful. Furthermore, the fielding of a bobbery pack would be a certain way of almost inviting the inevitable clown who would ask, "Can I bring my Aunt's alsatian/labrador. He's a great rabbiter?" and in next to no time chaos, with everyone bringing along a handy cur or so. Terrier packs need careful attention and care; for most, unlike hounds, view an onlooker's dog as quarry rather than casual spectators. Hounds tend to ignore the hordes of dogs that usually accompany any field.

I shall advertise for a lad to help in my kennels as the once a week visit from my two cleaning lads is simply not enough. I intend to do the morning exercise myself as not only is a child unable to cope with the problems of handling a team of high-spirited terriers but the simple fact is, I need the exercise. I am, so most medical journals assure me, approaching the coronary age and I need exercise like nothing else. A few months ago, I contemplated taking another degree but a sedentary life is not for me and to be honest, I'm a bit old for learning the clap trap dealt out as education.

The borders have at last entered to quarry—they are now killing rats, not well, but at least they are trying. David Green, who is helping me at the moment, had them catching today. Will they now catch up with the Jack Russells or will they fade out into mediocrity? The latter, I fear. Little is being done to maintain the hunting instinct in the breed, in spite of protestations of many breeders. Workers are only bred from dogs known to work. Going to ground, staying, courage, nose, are lost forever if things go wrong.

Saturday 18

As I approach the rat hunt before film cameras, I do so with some trepidation. So much can go wrong, as unlike a fox or badger dig, a rat hunt can be over in minutes or worse still, seconds. Also, my dogs all resemble each other, so how can a camera man, a chap who doesn't know my dogs, capture the speed of Omega on film when he can't pick out Omega from the other dogs. I am a born show-off, I admit, but I should really like the world to see my incredible bitch in action.

Suggestions as to how I can increase my parvo-troubled terrier pack are coming in fast and furious, but to get a level terrier pack of 30 trained and stock-broken terriers is no mean task. I need to keep my present strain of terrier and not dilute it too much. Suggestions of how to breed the new pack are as follows:-

1. To advertise Vampire at stud in *Exchange and Mart* and accept Fell bitches and top grade Jack Russells for mating, taking a puppy in lieu of fee. A Fell/Vampire bitch puppy would be tan or black and tan and this mated to Rollo could produce about half the litter of Russells of Vampire's type and marking. Likewise, a Russell litter bred from a good bitch of good type and guts, might do to produce one or two puppies straight from the first generation.

Personally, I like the Fell terrier mating best as although it will take another generation at least to breed the goods, at least the blind pluck of my present strain will be maintained or even bettered. Where

Patterdale puppy, supposedly the last of the pure strain kept by Cyril Bray.

would I find breeding term homes for a batch of Fell/Russell bitches though—homes which would work the crossbreds thoroughly and not jib at mating the pups to Rollo and letting me have Vampire type puppies in exchange! A problem.

P.S. Caught 46 rats tonight—a poor show.

Sunday 19

The day passed somewhat slowly, primarily because my mind is totally preoccupied with the TV performance tomorrow night.

I was filmed taking a rat out of a catch-alive trap with my hands—I make no excuse about my exhibitionism for I am a shameless extrovert where rats and cameras are concerned. So much for the showman image. Anyway, the rat is still alive and my hands are intact. The rat, a middle-aged doe, was the most ferocious I have ever seen and attacked the bars with great fury when I approached it; altogether the show went off very well.

The highlight of the day (says Plummer the impresario) was however, the filmed visit of Martin Knowelden (my book illustrator) and Rupert Brown. Martin and I have just completed a book called *A Dog I Knew* (no, I didn't like the title, either). The book, which consists of eight essays, is magnificently illustrated and is one of those huge limited edition, coffee table books which sells at £150–£180 (no, I can't afford one either). The line drawings are quite remarkable but the bronzes cast by the Bellini lost wax method are the *pièce de résistance* as far as I am concerned. One, which consists of two long coated lurchers chasing a fleeing hare, is the best example of "sculpture" since Michelangelo. Knowelden also produced a wax model of a dog slaying a rat—certain to enchant me, if no one else.

Knowelden produces only one of his models and refuses to duplicate. Still, his one-off jobs are magnificent, cheap at half the price, Moses says, expensive though for they sell at up to £1,500 each. Speaking of Moses, he seems booked up as a judge next year. He's certainly more popular than I am—some you win, some you lose.

Fathom killed her first rat this morning. I'm surprised she had it in her. She is so soft-mouthed that she has yet to kill even a small bird, yet the rat was very dead when she fished it out of the straw, a quick sharp squeak and then silence. Can dogs actually sense which quarry will give them any trouble? Fathom is terrified of ferrets and has never seen a rat. What odd instinct told her the rat could hurt her?

Monday 20

Monday night and the rat hunt. We had baited our shed with corn until the rats poured in to feed each night. Twelve pounds of meal per night had been taken so we knew that there were a few rats creeping into the shed to feed. The sheds were wired at mid-day and just before 9 o'clock rat exits and entrances blocked. Omega, Vampire, Beltane and Rollo were dropped in and the carnage began. 83 rats were killed in about 12 minutes. It was like shooting fish in the barrel, actually, as there was no way the rats could escape. Not particularly sporting, but a planned TV sequence is not supposed to be particularly sporting.

Mick Kirby rat netted some holes around my run and we filmed them being ferreted. A grey slipped, slithered through the nets and escaped—an incredible photograph and Jim Saunders, the cameraman, caught the whole thing on film. The rat nets, skilful pieces of construction, were made by Paul Jackson of Reading who was filmed net making only yesterday. All our nets were made by the Jacksons who are perhaps, Britain's best net makers. Not exactly an advert for Paul's rat nets, perhaps, but to take a young grey is certainly the most difficult of tasks.

Jackie Fallon lost her two border terriers last night. They escaped and vanished into a field thick with rabbit warrens. At 10.20 pm Jackie phoned and nine of us set out to seek the two borders. A useless task, as it happened as it was pitch black and misty—darkness and mist, a fearful combination. We searched for two hours but we could hear nothing and see even less. Anyway, after two hours and a bad wetting with the thin drizzle, we packed up and went home, leaving a rather tearful Jackie swearing that she would never again keep terriers or any dog that hunted.

Tuesday 21

Six am and Jackie phoned to say the two borders had come home, muddy and exhausted but undamaged. I was up and ready to search for the dogs. Merle would have been used to find the pair as he is very skilful at finding trapped dogs below ground. He will usually stand directly above the trapped terrier and gaze fascinated at the bare soil. Dogs, particularly sight-hound blooded dogs, are exceptionally good at detecting the slightest sound. I've seen lurchers and collies detect slight sounds well below the range of a terrier detector kit. I don't usually get terriers trapped, as I am coward enough (or experienced enough) to stay well off deep earths. Merle is well able to hear the baying in shallow earths and bowl the bolting foxes—I've killed several using this method, bolting them with Beltane and killing them with Merle, but I am a bit reluctant to rely on a dog as a canine detector kit. Derek Pasmore of Cumberland however, owns such a canine detector kit, a mongrel border collie that not only finds trapped terriers with regularity, but also helped find a trapped potholer in one of the old mine workings in Yorkshire.

On the subject of trapped terriers, a curious case came to my notice today. Stone, our local pig/poultry farmer, lives in one of those eighteenth century farm buildings with walled gardens. The wall that encloses the garden is filled with passages, for such walls had fireplaces built into them so that fires could be made, the walls heated and grapes, peaches, nectarines could be grown against the walls and ripened in the gentle heat. Badgers have lived in these fireplaces ever since the chimneys ceased to be used. Stone's Jack Russell, a bitch in whelp to Vampire, ran into the wall yesterday and seemed to be jammed in the flues. He listened to the barking for a day and came to fetch me. There must be nearly a mile of passageways in this wall, all sections are connected, an impossible place to dig. Anyway, she emerged slightly bitten this evening— end of story.

Alan Thomas' Gypsy. I used this strain for out crossing with my own.

Charlie Perfect phoned tonight and solved my problem of getting new bloodstock. He has agreed to get Alan Thomas's Patterdale bitch and mate her to Vampire. He will keep the hybrid puppies and mate them to Rollo. I shall keep the Vampire puppies, Charlie will sell the coloured puppies and Alan will have the Hamish marked pups. All in all, a sensible, profitable evening phone call—and a good start for the new pack.

Wednesday 22

A day's coursing to remember and in front of TV cameras as well. Martin Knowelden arranged to meet at Six Mile Bottom between Cambridge and Newmarket and what a place for hares it proved to be! We filmed one rather chaotic course where a dog belonging to a friend of Martin's broke loose and created the chaos, but the remaining courses were nothing short of superb. Knowelden's dog, the result of

mating Moses' bitch Steel to my own stud dog Grip, is about 12 months of age and nothing short of superb. His effortless bounds eat up the distance and his frail shape is deceptive, for he is a powerhouse of stamina. He also retrieved a hare right up to the camera, a hell of a feat when one considers the paraphernalia that accompanies the typical TV crew.

Fathom did not accept the noise, bustle, etc. as

readily however, and although she caught well (one rabbit, two hares before the camera team), she steadfastly refused to retrieve her prey to hand—which, incidentally, made me look more than a little foolish. Still, wasn't it W. C. Fields who said "Never work with animals and children," though for a somewhat different reason, I believe. Her picking up ability is incredible and there are few of my dogs who can hold a candle to her. Of course, there is little one can do to guarantee the dog will make a bid for the selected rabbit, as the TV team realised today. We ferreted a bank and two rabbits bolted; one, a tiny drummer, hopped out and hopped back through the nets, while the other, a large adult, bolted straight for the cameras. Fathom, of course, made her bid for the one that hopped in and out of the nets and the other simply raced away to another hole. Infuriating, but that's the way it goes. Consolation prize (I suppose) is that her coursing ability and picking up and kills are also beyond question.

The highlight of the day however, was the run by Eddie Jones' Celt (Merle/greyhound) a babe of six months, far too young to course but he put up a valiant try across ploughed fields and through hedges. The hare escaped, of course; only fantasy dogs catch fully grown strong hares when they are just six months old and Celt is only just over six months. Still, Eddie was delighted with his puppy.

The attempt at filming the lamping sequence failed miserably in spite of the valiant attempts of Jim Saunders, the cameraman and Michael Croucher. The reasons for the failure are obvious.

1. The lamper needs to be illuminated.
2. So does the dog who is blinded by the beam.
3. It is impossible to film a fleeing rabbit in a beam.
4. A sound, light and cameraman must accompany the lamper.

Michael Croucher before the start of the badger dig.

John Green's deerhound × greyhound lurcher—a powerhouse of a dog.

Thursday 23

Home before dawn or just about, and after a session of filming, I am exhausted. Dogs suffer a great deal as a result of little or no attention and the last few days have been the busiest of my life. Not only do the dogs look decidedly off peak condition, but there has been considerable weight loss. The pups have suffered most and the saplings look a bit seedy as well. It's times like this when my team of dogs looks overstocked. The prospect of increasing the team to produce a subscription pack of 30 is now just a bit terrifying. Frankly, I can do with the help, not just 20 minutes a week such as I'm getting now, but daily help.

The chances of redundancy in my teaching job are fairly good. What else I shall do to make a living, I just don't know. Like most teachers, I can do little else but cope with kids. The prospects of making a living as a dog breeder don't appeal either. I don't like people very much and the thought of producing an endless stream of puppies depresses me a little.

The border terrier bitch, the one who has started work, is now in season. She is lightly fleshed, in good fettle, just inoculated (or rather re-inoculated) so she is just right for breeding. Jackie Fallon's dog, although not bred in the purple, is ideal. Not only is he practically unrelated to the bitch, but he is a cracking little worker with an excellent nose, superb hunting instinct, a real stayer to ground and dead game. Against him, his face furnishings are lacking, but there is far too much interest in cosmetics in the breed at the moment. I like this dog and to hell with what the Kennel Club standard says. I shall mate her to improve a rapidly fading breed—fading in working ability, that is.

Dog fighting is in the news again, so it seems. A group of dog fighters in Devon have been picked up together with a BBC camera team staging what they claim to be "a mock" dog fight. The outcome will be fascinating—a direct violation of the 1835 Act, an Act that abolished all baiting sports except for the rat pits which became illegal in 1911, the last prosecution was in 1912 in Leicester. On the subject of rat pits, tonight's rat hunt is "off." My dogs were badly slashed up in the Monday session and to the two Durham lads I met in the Penrith Show who told me rats don't hurt dogs, all I can say is "come and see". Vampire and Beltane are terribly bitten and badly swollen about the face. Mercifully, Omega is totally unmarked again.

Friday 24

Last night I phoned Winch, and at long last began my research on the Fell terriers and arranged a weekend interviewing Maurice Bell and Frank Buck. Bell, Master of the Wensleydale foxhounds, is one of the great authorities on Lakeland and Fell terriers, a position he shares with Frank Buck. Bell is reputed to have some of the very toughest Lakeland/Fell terriers in existence and Winch says that the Wensleydale Show produces some of the very best of these dogs. Lowther Show was certainly a big disappointment as far as Lakeland went, but it seems a little strange that North Yorkshire should now be the centre of the Lakeland terrier world. I shall spend 31st October, and 1st November with Bell and Buck and I can think of no more enjoyable way of starting my book than hunting a full day with the Wensleydale foxhounds.

A dead calf was dropped with me today. Illegal perhaps, but priceless. I simply slash the abdomen slightly and put it in the run. The dogs disembowel the beast first and eat the red meat later. The reason—well, firms like Vetzyme believe that the dog starts on the bowels to obtain certain vitamins that are found only in the viscera and perhaps they are right. My own personal belief is that dogs begin on the guts first simply because it is an easy area to start a feast and wild dogs needed to eat quickly and so they bolted the soft bowels first. Certainly, dogs fed exclusively on bowels don't look particularly good, whereas dogs fed only on red meat rarely show vitamin deficiency. Yet I've never met a dog that didn't wolf down the bowels of an animal.

The puppies from Pagan need worming, for they are very pot-bellied. I'm a bit doubtful about worming puppies after parvo virus however, for the virus is bound to leave a somewhat inflamed gut (blood in the dung is one of the symptoms of parvo virus) and the worming medicine is bound to

Maurice Bell hunting Hawes—an icy day.

aggravate the condition a little. Will the worms cause more problems than the worming medicine? Piperazine citrate or another piperazine salt, the main component of most roundworm medicine, causes little trouble gutwise, but even a slight irritation might bring about diarrhoea and consequently dehydration. Still, tomorrow I will worm them and chance the consequences—after all, I've already lost over half the litter and the bitches I really want are already dead.

The ferrets have not been affected by the recent parvo bug, which is a bit curious, to say the least. Feline infectious enteritis, which is similar to the dreaded parvo bug, is a great killer of ferrets. A book on ferret diseases is on the cards, I think. Welstead, or one of his friends should consider this suggestion.

A pompous lout from South Wales—and boy, can some of my fellow countrymen be absolute pains—called uninvited to mate his fawn greyhound bitch to Merle. I was already a bit irritable and was about to tell him to get the hell out of here, when an idea hit me. I told him he could use Merle and the fee would be £1 an hour. He gave me a look that said "silly sod" and laughed at my stupidity, but he did not understand Merle's awful gaucherie at mating. I left him to it and hours later he was still desperately trying to get the exhausted stud to mate. He left without paying and stole a catch-alive rat trap. I hate uninvited people just turning up. Most are simply nuisances anyway, out for a day, looking at dogs and annoying people, while some are absolute thieves.

Saturday 25

Merle caught a fox this morning—by mistake as it happened—and killed it after what was probably a savage battle. He ran loose last night through my sloppiness at shutting him up and went hunting by himself. Dawn, and I found him lying next to the steaming carcass of a fox, a young male with a poor coat. Where he caught it, is still a bit of a mystery but his coat is matted with pond mud, so my bet is that at first light, he must have come on the fox in the middle of Barlow's field and run it to the pond earth, near the farm, killing it perhaps in the foetid mud that lies in banks around the edges of the pool. Merle is bitten quite badly around the face and also in the muscles of his hind legs. A waste of a good skin, for not only was the pelt stained and damaged, but the moult marks make the pelt quite useless.

I ordered a copy of Dan Russell's *Working Terriers* this morning. The book is a good one in spite of Dan Russell's protestations that it is not. Dan Russell's real name is Gerald Jones, he is secretary of the Exmoor Hunt and one of the authorities on the working terrier. He knew Arthur Heineman quite well and has a great affection for this oddly anachronistic man. Will some up-and-coming terrier man at some future date say as much for me? I doubt it. My solitary dis-position, my temper and my paranoia are not exactly conducive to praise from the world at large or even from my close friends. If Eddie Jones survives me, perhaps he might say a word or two in my favour, for Eddie too, is a solitary.

Phoned Knowelden this afternoon to arrange for a hunt or rather, a coursing meet in Cambridge—a private one, for we had too many hangers on at the last meet on Wednesday. Eddie, Martin, John, who owns the land, and myself and that should be enough. Fathom is too whippety for the country in spite of her terrific will to course and her picking-up ability. Over heavy ploughed land, she would suffer greatly, I think. Maybe Woolly is the ideal shape for the country. He is heavier, has tougher feet, stronger bone and great stride—the trouble is, he is an absolute fool at this age. Early days yet, however.

Bill Colclough called and says Beige, my ¾ bred collie puppy, is nearly ready for her first course. She is whippetlike and quite fragile, not my ideal choice for the ideal lurcher. Terry's puppy, a litter sister looks a much better prospect. She is a strong, powerful bitch, heavily muscled and chunky—an excellent prospect for hare coursing and game enough for the bigger quarry that is now forbidden.

Sunday 26

A visit from Guy Page and fiancée with a black and white lurcher, bred from my collie bitch Blue mated to a top-class blue and white greyhound dog. The litter, bred by Paul Taylor of Melton Mowbray, pro-duced some whippety dogs and bitches. Paul Jackson, the net maker, owns one very slender bitch, but some of the litter were very heavy. It is, however, a mistake to equate a whippety shape with great speed. Some of the fastest dogs I have ever seen, and some of the best hare killers as well, have been quite heavily built, for muscle, at least running muscle, tends to make a dog an athlete and whippety dogs, while they may look every inch the streamlined, athletic type of dog, are often not muscled enough for the hard course neces-sary for hare catching. My personal opinion is that this dog is probably the ideal shape for lengthy and hard courses. This is a dog that, should he stay the pace and become a useful hare courser, I will mate to Mara or Mara's offspring. This dog, coupled with the progeny of Eddie Jones' dog and the children of Richard Jones (actually a half-brother of Guy Page's dog, for they are both out of the collie bitch Blue) will be the foundation blood for my strain of lurcher. Speed is easily obtained in lurchers—simply infuse the strain with pure greyhound (or horror of horrors, saluki blood) but brains, stamina, courage and that indefinable something are hard to bring into the strain and very easy to lose. Guy says that most people say the dog is the wrong shape for a lurcher, but modern dog keepers are conditioned by the lurcher shows to expect greyhoundy dogs when they see a lurcher. I let Page's dog exercise with Fathom and compared their speeds. He is easily as fast as Fathom and his muscle power indicates a far greater stamina. This is the type of dog that with exercise, practise and some training, will make a super hare-catching dog.

I must inoculate the puppy crop for distemper, hardpad, leptospirosis and hepatitis. They will need no inoculation for parvo for they have had the dubious distinction of being in contact with the real McCoy, not a weakened virus or a similar type of virus to create immunity to the real infection. The survivors must have massive resistance to parvo virus, a resistance they will probably pass on to their offspring—at least the bitch puppies will, through the first milk or colostrium—at least that's how it should work. In all probability, my dogs will probably need several generations before they are immune to this insidious and lethal infection. This is the last entry concerning this disease, for, God willing we are past the worst. So far, not one adult dog or older puppy has become ill through the bug and I am inclined to think all the supposed cases of adult dogs dying through parvo are false, and that these adults have died through other diseases.

Monday 27

Missed a fox with Fathom and Woolly this morning, and I can't help thinking that they tried very hard. Fathom is a changed animal since the New Year. She was a crass coward afraid of even a rat before she bred her litter. I had always thought that the tale that a bitch improved after she had bred a litter, was an old wives' tale. Perhaps it is not. Perhaps Fathom has grown keener since her litter, or perhaps she was simply not ready to course fox this time last year. Anyway, she will have her chance, for she will go out after fox with Merle this winter. There is no reason why she should not take fox; her mother was a top class fox-killing lurcher during her prime and I've seen many lurchers much smaller than Fathom take fox quite well. Last year, she was very apathetic about coursing fox and chased them for fun, turning them, jumping over them and racing back to me. Today, she ran the fox like a fiend and I am certain she would have killed it had it not bolted into a hole on land on which I had no permission. There will be other times, Fathom, other foxes, other places without boltholes.

The puppies in Pagan's litter—the survivors that is—are just beginning to teeth. My dog puppy, the one marked exactly like Warlock which I considered actually calling Warlock, is not quite right in the mouth, although it's just a little early to tell yet. I've yet

to produce an undershot puppy in my strain, but there are two unknown factors in this litter.

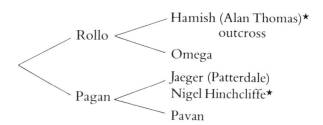

Hamish has bred an undershot or so, and even Rollo has a level even bite, but an undershot mouth can only appear in a litter if *both* parents carry the factor. Many stud dogs have a bad reputation for throwing undershot puppies but they can only throw such puppies if the bitch also carries the factor. Both dog and bitch may have a perfect mouth, but if they carry the undershot factor, roughly one quarter of the litter will have bad mouths. Still, baby mouths often correct themselves at eight weeks of age and these puppies are scarcely five weeks old. It would be a pity if this male was "bad in the mouth". I had hopes of him being a stud dog and even mating him to the ageing Beltane and to his grandmother, Omega.

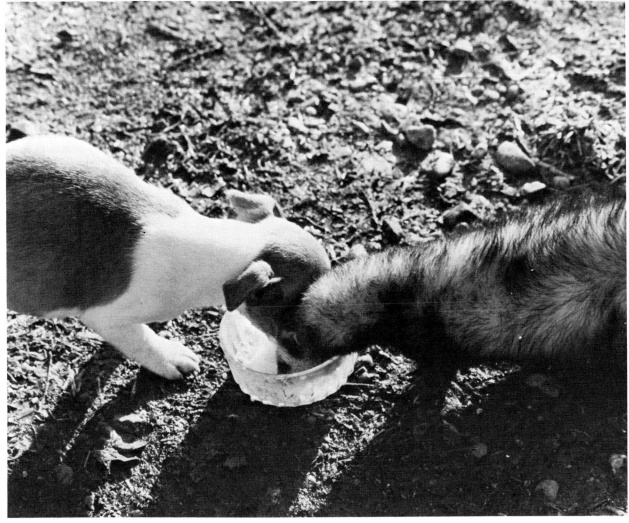

Pagan's dog puppy meets Fudge.

Tuesday 28

A dawn hunt as usual and not a sign of a fox. We took a rabbit with Fathom and witnessed a bad miss by Woolly Bear. It looked an easy run, thirty yards from the hedge. He ran it, reached down for it, a perfect sitter I thought, but at the last moment it jerked, flung him off balance and he returned to me lame, having bruised one of the toes of his front leg as he braked. I intend to run him in Six Mile Bottom in three or four weeks. He is light on muscle at the moment but he eats well, fattens quickly, and with luck he will be on form for this first-ever real course. He is too young for a real run, of course, but such are the hares in Six Mile Bottom that I will run one hard with Fathom and slip Woolly on the tired, turned hare. Even then, there is

doubt about him catching it. He was born in February, which makes him scarcely nine months old—far too young to make a real showing. This time next year will be time enough to test his mettle. Mara will get her first test a year from now. She is much classier than Woolly and her square head makes her look less collie like than Woolly. Shape wise (so far) she is outstanding and if she has go to match her looks, I have a winner. But there is much that must come together to make the ideal lurcher.

I bought six bags of meal today—of a different type to my usual meal with a higher protein level. Meal is a poor substitute for meat and I'd sooner feed raw tripe than meal. As soon as the tripe situation gets better—if

147

it ever does—I shall stop feeding meal. Until then, it's meal, I'm afraid. Witch looks dreadful on her meatless diet. Her ribs look fleshless, her coat worse than poor. Some dogs obviously do very badly on meal. Some years ago, rather than feed meal, I fed rotten and dried hen cadavers and the dogs maintained condition. Now I add eggs, oil, etc. and I can't get good coats without considerable amounts of tripe and raw flesh.

I think Pagan's puppies' mouths will come out all right in a few weeks. They look considerably better than they did yesterday. I shall certainly keep the dog, and after watching Miriam Stoppard's heart disease programme, I will increase my exercise ratio by taking out the pack each morning in addition to simply exercising my lurchers. Heart illness must be fairly low amongst lurcher keepers, for the dogs keep a person lean because lurchers need much exercise. Terrier keepers, however, must be constantly in a state of stress, so not so good heartwise.

Wednesday 29

Twice a day feeding for Woolly and Fathom between now and the end of the year, which, coupled with exercise, should bring about a great muscle increase in two rather whippety dogs. It is an idea I saw in an article called "Pumping Iron", an account of the training method of one Arnold Schwarnecker, a highly fleshed person who is reputedly the world's most muscular man. High protein plus supplementary feeding and daily weighing should muscle up the puppy if not the bitch. At least, that's what the article implies. Well, it certainly works on people. This should allow Woolly and Fathom to look the part, if not act the part. Personally, I've doubts. Superb muscles do not always enable a dog to become a great athlete. Anyway, here we go. Day 1. Fathom 40 lbs 4 ozs, Woolly 39 lbs 8 ozs. I've increased the amount of food by 8 oz and feed ¼ oz. of muscle building supplement a day. I shall weigh them each day and compare the relative performances at hare.

I arrived home to find an unpleasant, sickly sweet smell in my immersion heater cupboard—a smell of rat, for come winter, the apple fall, the cutting of the corn rats burrow through the floor to get near to the warmth of the immersion heater. Sick and very nasty, but recently I used a poison called Difenacoum which lowers the rats body temperature so I must expect rodents to burrow through to get to the radiators, etc. The rat problem is now quite serious and Vampire, Beltane and Omega bark incessantly at the sound of rats moving around the run. The thought of a live rat moving in my house is sickening and I must disinfect everything tomorrow. The floor must be recemented though tales of rats eating through ferro concrete to get to food and warmth are common. I shall increase the poison tonight and use a Warfarin based chemical. Ten days from now should see the end of the rat problem.

An annoying visitor of the sort I've had before, but do not wish for again. A chap from Redditch arrived uninvited to ask if I'd sell Mara. She is now a lovely creature and I can appreciate his interest in her. When I refused his £10 (cheek) he replaced the money saying "When this goes back in my pocket, it will stay there." He was like something out of a 1940 American gangster movie. This sort of person, the type who thinks any dog is for sale, makes my blood boil. Do these idiots believe I spend ten years breeding a dog to sell it at a caprice to a chap who will pass it on at its first problem? It does not speak highly for the typical lurcher man, who buys and sells dogs and who treats dogs as currency, swopping them for bantams, pigeons, and anything else he fancies.

Thursday 30

The rat in the immersion heater cupboard is now Public Enemy No. 1 as far as I am concerned. I saw him this morning and the thought of a rat living in the house filled me with nausea. I poured bleach down the hole in the floor in the hopes it will keep the brute at bay until I can poison him. The danger is of this hole becoming a regular passageway and even if I kill this rat there will be others. Nasty, repulsive, in fact. I like rats in their place—and their place is certainly not in my house.

The puppies look good, at least the three survivors do. One is promised to Peter Evans of Cambridge (the dog puppy marked like a Manchester terrier, a large headed, straight legged dog). The black and white bitch should be collected by Paul Coffey on Sunday, while the Warlock marked puppy a straight legged, bull-headed babe with lots of spirit, will be kept by me. What a grand litter they would have been if they had lived! I will certainly mate Rollo to Pagan again. The improvement in bone and head size is remarkable and providing I use frequent Fell crosses, I cannot see any future problems. I may not be able to field a pack to hunt with Granville Maddocks this year, but next year I shall certainly have a neat team of yearlings.

Mara ran a moorhen this morning and ran it with an almost insane frenzy. She will make an excellent coursing bitch if this is an indication of things to come. She had little chance of catching the bird, but the sight of Mara exerting herself to the full in pursuit of the bird was fascinating. She is fifty per cent sight hound and the instinct to chase is very strong in her. The puppy is muscling quite well and if she has the speed, she will certainly have the stamina to stay well. The most amazingly heavy dogs often make superb hare killers and my bet is Mara is as near as dammit is to swearing, to being my ideal lurcher. She has looks, build, coat and strong retrieving instinct. If she grows apace she will be the ultimate in lurchers. Still, there's many a slip between cup and maturity. I've seen beautiful puppies grow into monstrous dogs and really unsightly puppies grow into beautiful animals.

Friday 31

The tinkers are back, and their children have been in the lane and invaded my dog run yet once again, causing fury in my dogs and sadly the inevitable. I turned my back for a few moments and Witch, the sister of Vampire was over and killed in moments, horribly disembowelled—a hell of a death. Witch was a stock bitch and one I could ill afford to lose. Causes of such a six way fight? Several.

1. The irritation of having tinker children playing in my run. This caused a death only four years ago.
2. I have two bitches in season and my stud dogs are decidedly irritable—usually fights of this nature result in the death of a male terrier. Witch was unlucky, I suppose.
3. There has been little hunting this last few weeks and boredom is usually the cause of hellish fights. I often wonder how people with sixty terriers cope with these battles.

I was reluctant to leave David Green in charge of my dogs to journey north to begin my research on the Fell terrier. First port of call, the very hospitable Maurice Bell, Master, huntsman, and secretary of the recently formed Wensleydale Fox Hounds, a Fell pack based at Hawes, a small town between Sedburgh and Northallerton along the A 684. Wild, cold country and a road so winding that I nearly drove the car off the road twixt Sedburgh and Hawes. Maurice started his pack from a few trailhounds (broken of aniseed) and some entered fox hounds from Scotland. Hunting just eleven hounds, he caught 18 foxes his first year. Terrier wise, he keeps a nice strain of Lakeland bred from some of his old stuff, bred down from a very hard pair of terriers: Frank Buck's dog, Twist, and a granddaughter of Hardesty's Turk—a superb dog who features in most of the top-class terriers of the Fells. Winch's, Tyson's and Bell's dogs are all descended from this dog. It is in this country that I shall find the outcross blood I need to revive my flagging strain of Jack Russell terrier.

The land around the fells is bleak and cold, the earths dangerous and the work hard, so the testing of a terrier is hard. By judicious use of these Fell terriers and by careful placing of the offspring I can easily create a sensational strain of Jack Russell terrier, not a whit inferior for its mixed ancestry.

149

November

9.30 am and kick off with the newly formed Wensley-dale Fox Hounds at Hawes. We hunted a forested slope and my God, what a slope (a 1 in 2 slope). Scenting conditions were bad; the wind nearly blew me off my feet on the top of the fell around Hawes. Still, we put up a fox, ran him some four and half miles across stream and fell, hollow and rock and put him to ground in a very difficult earth, an earth so difficult that even Bell's terriers failed to shift him!

This evening we visited Frank Buck, one of the all time great terrier men; past it a bit, I'm afraid, but still a hive of fascinating stories. Buck breeds and has bred a strain of black Fell terrier, very hard, very game and extremely typey. Some of his stock are superb, good fronts, tight coats and fabulous heads, the epitome of good Fell terriers. Buck tells me his stock are bred down from blue Fell terriers kept by his father with occasional dashes of Lakeland/Fell blood from Cockermouth and the Lakes. Some of his tales are fascinating for Buck is a great raconteur. These tales really need capturing for posterity; pray God I am up to it.

Maurice Bell's terriers, a mixture of Fell blood from Tyson, Hardestey and Buck are a hard bitten band, some of which are descended from his dog Britt, a do or die sort of terrier reputed by the hunters of Wharfedale to be as hard as flint. In his heyday, this dog slew many foxes also butchered and hacked his way into many others. So hard did he become, that he developed a catch-hold technique of grabbing the jaw of the fox and crushing it with a bite. He became old and senile eventually, his injuries accentuated by a kick from a horse. His stock is still excellent, and well worth considering for outcross blood. I enjoyed my

Frank Buck with Chew and Tigg, two of his fell terriers.

stay with the Bells. Their hospitality was incredible. Winch described Maurice Bell as the last of the Fell men, and the passing of this interesting breed of man is to be regretted.

Research is needed into some of the terms used in the Fells. I found the conversations between Maurice Bell and Frank Buck fascinating, but sometimes bewildering. Shake holes, grykes and gills all threw me for a while. Shake holes are deeply eroded holes in limestone, which are sometimes bottomless pits. Foxes use these earths often in the Fells, leaping on to ledges ten feet below the surface of the earth, chancing death perhaps, but somehow realising that such a place is sanctuary from all but the most tenacious terriers. Grykes are eroded crevices in granite and are found in profusion in and around Shap. Grykes can often be death traps for terriers for some can go for hundreds of yards and are quite impossible to dig. Gills are steep sided streams that cut deep V-shaped crevices in the hills. Many have earths along their sides; some of these earths are even half-filled with water. Bell came out with a superb piece of advice about earths filled or half-filled with water. Bell will enter a terrier in an earth which has water running out of it, but never into an earth into which water is running. Some streams run for miles underground and emerge in the next valley. It is a hell of a district to hunt and I do not envy him. Such a land must claim the lives of hundreds of terriers.

Janet Evans and sons came for their puppy today. The dog will certainly have a good home and the lad will definitely try it at rat, rabbit and possibly fox. Not a bad spot to place a puppy that I may one day require for breeding. Many terrier keepers are the same "buying and selling" idiots that are found in the lurcher fraternity. This puppy will certainly have a permanent home.

I used 12 lbs of rat bait around the house and it vanished overnight. Even assuming the birds ate some, there must be an amazing horde of rats feeding around my house. I shall continue to bait for two or three more days and wait for results. Must keep the dogs up though, for the cadavers, if eaten, can cause death. Wednesday or Thursday I should see the dead and dying rats around the cottage or worse still, in the house—a ghastly thought. I'm not happy about this position; I bought a bag on Friday and baited heavily, but the rat population seems to be as strong as ever.

A bad fell earth on Penn Hill.

Mara chased, caught and let go again a dying rat, obviously poisoned and daft enough to be out in the field after dawn. She ran the rat, picked it up and tried to retrieve it to hand, but it must have bitten her for she dropped the beast as if it was red hot. I doubt if it will stop her picking up, though. All in all, I am well pleased with her progress.

Rats again, and my unwelcome friends seem to be thriving on the rat poison I am putting down. Twenty-eight pounds has now been eaten and not a single cadaver has appeared. Furthermore, the patter of tiny feet in my ceiling has grown louder. At night, it is nearly impossible to sleep with the territorial battles and lovemaking taking place above me. If things don't quieten down in the next few days, I shall resort to Warfarin and maybe even ferret the ceiling. The brutes must be doing considerable damage to the rafters and electric wiring above my head. Sooner or later, a fire or roof fall will bring the House of Plummer to an end. Nor is it a comforting thought to know they have gobbled up 28 lbs of food.

The puppies are now partially inoculated; they've had the first distemper shots (coupled with a leptospirosis jab). I get the vaccine from my vets and split the ampoule so that one dose distemper vaccine is enough for three or four terriers. Mara and Richard Jones share one vaccine. On the whole it reduces the staggering costs of keeping my dogs.

Joan Hancocks brought her greyhound bitch to mate to Merle. Greyhounds are difficult to mate at the best of times as many have tiny vaginal orifices and often take quite a lot of effort to mate. Joan's bitch has had one litter and should therefore, be a fairly easy bitch to mate. It was not so, however, for the bitch was positively paranoid about being served. Tomorrow we will try again and perhaps the bitch will be easier to mate.

¾ bred Collie greyhound out of my blue greyhound bitch Cilla.

Feeding time and now that we have tripe aplenty, the weight and condition of the dogs is improving dramatically. Meal by itself is of little use to the team. They will live entirely on tripe and still keep weight and condition but without flesh they look terrible. Maurice Bell has offers of dead sheep which he refuses as hounds fatten very quickly on mutton. I would jump at such offers. Sheep carcasses swell badly but even the putrid green meat is much relished by terriers. Maurice also avoids using pig meat, partly because of its fatty nature and also because it is difficult to get. Any meat, even in a state of putrescence is preferable to none.

The tinkers seem to have dug in for the winter and the Public Health people are doing nothing to shift them. The lane looks like a pig sty, rubbish, filth, human excreta litters the site. Rats are breeding rapidly there at the moment and feeding on the lavatory waste. Really, the law should be amended to deal with such people. The land looks like a quagmire and is littered with mess and rubbish. Each year, they visit the lane and each year they cause absolute chaos. Early this morning, one of the tinkers killed a man with his untaxed, uninsured, bald tyred vehicle and there was hell to play when the police arrested the woman who was driving (without a licence, of course). The story is that the band attempted to storm the police station, but such tales are often exaggerated. It's a racing certainty she will get bail and like in the very best fairy tales "she was never seen again." There is no law in Huddlesford, I'm afraid and the tinkers do as they please.

Omega looks pregnant, damn her. She is a peculiar bitch who never shows colour when in season and mates clandestinely. The sire of the litter—if litter there is to be—is her son Rollo, but what will I do to rear them in this freezing weather? I hate winter puppies. They cost the earth to rear, rarely do well and attract the Christmas puppy thieves like flies. I need good bitches—and desperately at that—but she has conceived every season: far too many puppies for a bitch this age.

An icy dawn, cold and frosty, and Woolly, Fathom and Merle looked very miserable at the morning exercise period. Woolly is carrying a lot of muscle since the twice a day feeding and even Fathom is gaining weight though it may be due to feeding according to the ideas I had concerned with body building. Let's hope performance increases with muscle. The pair get five miles each morning which improves them greatly but does not do all that much for me. I am tired and feel exhausted—the TV and book writing added to talks and travelling is not doing me much good.

Bill Colclough brought back Beige tonight. She looks in superb shape, hard, lean and keen. I hope she performs well in Cambridge, for I shall course Six Mile Bottom next month. Shape wise she is superb, though a little lightly built. Perhaps the new muscle building diet will help, but I doubt it. She has a saluki look about her and such dogs never fatten. It is a pity he has brought her back at this time, for I need the space more than the bitch at this time.

A day of lurchers, I'm afraid. Pete Bishop, Head of Science in my present school, sent a friend over to get a lurcher puppy from Harold Hodson Walker. The puppy, bred from my blue greyhound bitch Cilla, mated to Terry Ahearne's dog (a collie greyhound mating) is a blue bitch, 12 weeks of age and very attractive. It retrieved as soon as they bought her and seems very eager to please. I do hope it is kept and not traded like so many lurchers in the Midlands. By rights, I should have copied up my Fell terrier notes tonight; I'll certainly have little chance tomorrow for we are rat hunting yet again.

Vampire's puppies are getting to be a nuisance. They cause fight after fight in the run and sooner or later death seems on the cards. If I enter them to rats now I may get some peace, for puppies often calm down after they have known work. They are decidedly touchy about ferrets and will take some breaking to make them useful.

I start using my ferrets tomorrow—the undergrowth has been killed by sharp frosts and my ferrets look particularly well. I think I shall certainly use Fudge for the TV filming. She is a picture at the moment and keen as mustard.

Paul Coffey no longer wants Pagan's tricolour puppy, well doesn't want is a bit of an "untruth." He has joined the others in the dole queue and is unable to afford to rear the puppies. So I am stuck with a tri-colour bitch that is a black and white replica of my own strain, marking wise, size and shape. I am not sorry Paul is unable to use the puppy for I should like to keep it and, while it will be out of place in my tan and white team, mated to either Phoibus or Deimos, Vampire and Beltane's somewhat potty sons, she will breed tan and white puppies for I believe both are incapable of breeding black and white puppies—a wild guess perhaps, but one I believe to be true. Vampire carries black and white so mating him to the

black and white babe would breed 50% black and white and 50% tan and white.

Where do country type story writers get the idea of itinerant families, gypsies, tinkers, what have you, having the early morning poacher image, rising before dawn and out in the dew before light appeared? I took Fathom, Woolly, Beige and Mara past their caravans this morning at daybreak and the drunken snores were so loud that Mara appeared nervous as we approached the camp. Tinkers poach quite openly, for there is no way one can get convicted with the bail laws as they are. When arrested, they up sticks and go, breaking bail and avoiding the area where they were arrested for a year or so. When they return, they give

Rollo, Omega's son, killing a rat at a curious angle. His dam is an expert at those odd "snatch" bites.

their name as James Brown and deny any knowledge of their crimes. It is a crazy world that allows such disregard for the law. I have yet to see a tinker or a gypsy up at dawn with a lurcher on the slip.

Fudge's cage mate is going tonight. I'm giving it to Mick Kirby, a bit of a gift horse actually, for the young hob has an undershot mouth. I brought him in for the filming and now he is a bit superfluous. Fudge will see me through a season, I'm sure, and I don't really need other ferrets. I ran her through the rat warrens in my hedge this morning just to break Beige

to the sight of ferrets at work, and Fudge bolted several very dopey rats. I think the poison is at last beginning to work. Certainly, enough has been eaten to kill a multitude.

The tinkers left today, bound for Norfolk, I believe, leaving a pile of filth, faeces and waste. Rats are feeding everywhere and it might be better if we hunted this place tonight instead of the usual rat-hunting pitch. Certainly, we'd get a good haul.

P.S. Caught 78 rats tonight—not bad between 8.37 pm and 9.12 pm.

Friday 7

Mick, David Green and I ferreted the tinker site this morning—they left last night—and we caught 42 large adults—rats, not tinkers I must add. Tapper, the councillor in Whittington, knew of our intentions and asked in the press. The haul of rats looks fairly impressive outlined as it is against the scrap yard of waste in the lane.

Mara is retrieving quite well at the moment and her skill at finding hidden objects is quite good. Nose wise, she is more than eager to hunt rabbits, but her training programme is well behind that of Merle's. What are the reasons?
1. Hybrid vigour comes through first crosses and is a bit adrift by the second cross. Merle is a first cross and maybe there is such a thing as hybrid intelligence as well. Mara is a second cross and perhaps lacks something of the first generation hunters.
2. Merle was a serious puppy, easy to train, quick to pick up training and very eager to please. Mara is frivolous and quick to bark at strange objects.
3. Merle was given an intensive training session for the book and I have spent much less time with Mara. If a person is to train a lurcher properly, he must put in all the time he can with it.

Pagan looks quite poor even rearing two puppies and God knows how she would look if she had had to rear the seven. Last night, she performed magnificently but towards the end of the evening, she looked desperately tired. I gave her a whole dead hen bone, feather, the lot, but she seemed too exhausted to eat it for she licked the blood from the head and left the meat. David Green opened the bird up and she began to eat and by nightfall she looked much better—an advert for whole carcass feeding, in fact.

Beige is quite lean but superbly fit, and she looks like she could run forever. In a month, I shall run her at Six Mile Bottom on hare. I have little doubt she will do quite well on hare but her nervous disposition makes her unsuitable for the ideal lurcher. Her sister, Terry Ahearne's bitch, is bold, aggressive and is a far better hunter but she lacks Beige's enormous effortless, stylish lope. In third gear she is more than able to come up on a hare. As a competitive sporting, coursing lurcher, she will serve me well, I am sure, but Fathom leaves her standing as a provider of game. Rabbits are scarce since myxomatosis and unless she learns to be a bit more nimble, she will be little use to me in this area, which is short on hares.

Saturday 8

Peter Beddows brought his bitch, the sister of Woolly Bear. She is a stocky, powerful animal, well muscled and chunky. A lamper's dream, but Pete has neglected to teach her retrieving. A tragedy actually, for such a dog, properly trained, could keep a man in meat. An untrained lamping dog, one not trained to retrieve, is like a hole in the head. She makes Woolly look very unsightly, however, which is not particularly difficult as even I make Woolly look unsightly.

I had the galley proofs for my new book *Lepus* this morning. Looks good, but you never can tell with a novel. It may well come down on its bottom. Richard Barber, my publisher, has set it's publication date for February 1981. Lepus is based on my own experiences and I believe it to be very accurate. It began as an idea when I saw a leveret being born early in 1979 It must have been by the merest chance as I know of few other people who have witnessed this phenomenon. I had

155

been sitting on Cope's gate bewailing as usual my unhappy lot in the teaching profession, when a doe hare ran almost to the gate and without further ado, began labour. She passed the leveret easily and quickly and began to carry it around the field in an aimless manner. I think Cope's collie must have disturbed the doe for, though I remained stock still and undetected, the doe seemed very restless and uncertain about what to do with the leveret she was carrying. I took to thinking what a harassed beast the hare was, pursued by all and sundry, having no place to hide. *Lepus*, Latin for hare, was born out of this idea.

Foxes have been causing trouble at Shenstone only four miles away. I had a phone call this morning concerning poultry damage. It is obviously fox; I went there to check. Usually such damage, which is always attributed to foxes, is the work of bored dogs. The phone will be red hot with calls to catch foxes before December is out, for the cold weather and the absence of rabbits will give the foxes Dutch courage. Three weeks from now and I will take to hunting them seriously for not only will people welcome me on their land, but the pelts will be worth taking. Things look a bit bleak economically at the moment in Britain, but there seems to be a ready market in fox pelts. Some I will obviously have to dig, but others I can hunt with Merle using lamp and salting the land with rotten tripe.

Parvo clear; at least I think it is. The next litter may well prove me wrong, however. My fox terrier/Russell bitch is next to whelp, Vampire is the sire so they will probably be good workers and useful lookers as well. What will survive is another matter, though. The cold spell might help to clear up the virus, however. There is far too little known about viral behaviour.

Sunday 9

A hard, fast and furious running battle with a strong adult fox which outfought Merle in the dells behind the cottage. We chanced on him at noon, and what he was doing above ground at noon is anyone's guess. Merle picked up out of coursing range and went in on him hard, fast and without quarter. I saw him throw up the fox twice and the running battle continued for ten minutes. I was certain he'd catch him for there seemed to be no way he could escape. Yet he did, and Merle returned breathless, quite badly bitten around the face and a bit dispirited. Anyone who boasts that they own a lurcher that can run and catch any fox would do well to see such a run. There'll be other days though, and the winter has just begun.

I need to develop some of the film I have taken. I took two or three shots of coursing but I doubt if they will come out properly. I am well behind Ruston or Malcolm Green, I'm afraid and though I am well placed to get photographs—for I hunt daily—my skill is very low, I'm afraid. Some of the photographs look good enough to include in a book, I think, but I am uncertain how they will reproduce in print.

My fox terrier/Russell bitch will whelp tomorrow or Tuesday. She looks and feels pregnant and I can detect one puppy moving in the womb. Personally, I'm not too happy with this cross. Not one of the puppies has the—for want of a better word—"zip" of the mother and while they hunt after a fashion, I have seen and bred much better. She is in whelp to Vampire so I expect the puppy to be straight-legged and of good type, even if it is of doubtful use as a hunter. The long, elegant head of the bitch appealed to me at once, but I am no longer besotted with good looks. If the line hunts exceptionally well, I shall keep it. If it fails, no matter how attractive it looks, it will be given away. The Russell is doomed to "pet" status anyway and I might as well be one of the last bastions of working Jack Russell terriers.

Monday 10

A lengthy run for Beige at hare on the only legal piece of coursing land I have. She is incredibly fast and turned the hare contemptuously a dozen or more times, but she is not capable of picking up a strong, active hare yet for she cannot unravel the looping, jinking run. After much practice, she will however, and I am confident Beige will go out to become a first class hare killer. Hares are easy now—well, as easy as hares can be—but after Christmas when the hares are fully formed and strong and nature has weeded out the weakest, the hare is a terrific athlete and it is one heck of a dog, run singly, which can bring a hare down. Beige is just such a dog, I think and I am fairly confident she will become a classy hare killer by this time next year. She has speed aplenty, her greyhound ancestry has ensured this and from her collie grandfather, she has inherited an awesome stamina.

The fox terrier/Russell bitch whelped today, a single puppy, huge and well formed and quite dead, for in parturition, it had suffocated. The puppy, a tricolour, was a bitch and boy, do I need good quality stock bitches. Still, there will be other terriers and the death of huge single puppies at first whelpings is far from uncommon. Next time perhaps, a bigger litter, an easier whelping and some live puppies. It is far easier for a bitch to whelp five medium sized puppies than one large one.

The mouths on Pagan's surviving pair look fair, but not perfect, I must be more than careful about inbreeding to this line. True, the bone is superb and the heads almost bull terrierish. I have certainly corrected these weaknesses in my own strain. No dog with a bad mouth should be used for breeding, however, and the border terrier went through a very sticky patch because of negligence concerning the use of crooked-mouthed stud dogs. The same problem will undoubtedly ruin my own strain if I am not careful. Overshot mouths lack strength of bite and the teeth of undershot dogs are often torn out in battle with foxes and badgers. A correct mouth is a must for a working terrier. Once in a strain, however, a bad mouth is a heller to breed out.

Tuesday 11

The ground was frozen hard this morning and so, apart from a few fruitless runs at rabbit, we did nothing. A lurcher damages itself quite easily on icy ground. Feet and dew claws suffer badly after a hard run on hare or fox. Merle knocked up two toes after one hellish run on frosty ground. A sharp dash after rabbit may have the same effect, but I need to exercise the dogs and an occasional rabbit is bound to pop up.

The Sunday Times has quoted some pieces of the Jack Russell terrier book—out of context, of course—concerned with badger baiting. As usual, the book is misunderstood and the author of the article in *The Sunday Times* has confused badger baiting with badger digging. Badger baiting—the pitting of dogs against a captive badger—has been illegal since 1835. Badger digging, however, the capturing of wild badgers by means of digging out badgers with spades and dogs, is not illegal providing one has permission to take the badger.

I've cleared the rats at long last and the mice are no longer around either. The rumblings in the roof ceased last night as well so with luck, we are free of the rats, unless the tinker site survivors invade the premises. Rat poisoned in summer smell quite badly when they die but rats killed in winter simply mummify to dry paper like cadavers. The ceiling must be full of mummified rats.

The ferrets look really good, thick furred and healthy. I have fed them exclusively on rats for several weeks and the whole rat diet has proved beneficial. I shall use Fudge to wipe out the stragglers on the tinker site this weekend as there are still a large number foraging amongst the filth. She is now very dextrous at rat killing and she still rushes in and attacks any rat. Not bad for a six year old jill! She is a devil at rabbits, however, and knows how to kill rabbits very quickly. Jills or hobs who are very dextrous at rabbit killing are usually over the top at bolting rabbits, for few rabbits bolt when a ferret who is hell bent on killing is used to drive them out. When a ferret becomes a skilful killer, he or she is not much use for the task of ferreting.

Wednesday 12

Hard frozen soil prevented hunting this morning, though I must admit that I did take Merle out lamping before dawn. The ground was so hard that to have run him on fox would have courted disaster. At 3.40 am I had seen five foxes appear in the beam but decided not to try for one. Merle is very frustrated and looked decidedly downcast when I fed him this morning.

I weighed Woolly. He weighed in at 44 lbs 3 ozs, a decided increase in weight thanks to the article "Pumping Iron." Now to see if this extra muscle will carry him forward at greater speed. I now feed, in addition to the meat and meal diet, a protein supplement and now the tinkers are gone, Fathom, Woolly and Beige have almost total liberty. They certainly look good and Woolly, in spite of his collie shape, is quite fast. To build up a show animal, this diet is obviously ideal, expensive but excellent, but will it produce a better athlete? Two of our P.E. teachers say "no" and that this extra muscle is just show, flesh that in no way helps performance. The dogs look really good, however. Beige's weight and muscle conformation are increasing daily and though she lacks the bulging muscle of Terry Ahearne's dog, she will level out as a huge, muscular whippet.

I had the offer of a greyhound male tonight, a strong powerful black of two years old, sired by One and Only out of a Patricia's Hope bitch, impeccably bred and only slightly damaged. He would be ideal as a breeding male but the chances are he would be reluctant to mate, and anyway, the ownership of such a dog could only be justified if the dog had at least sixty bitches a year to him. Terry Ahearne came up with a moneymaking idea concerning five greyhound bitches which are all too easy to obtain now that the winter season and unemployment are here. Terry suggested getting in greyhound bitches, mating them to either Merle or next year to Richard Jones, my bearded collie/border collie hybrid. Mated bitches carrying a normal number of puppies could sell for up to £200—an excellent moneymaking scheme for someone, but not for me. I dislike the time-wasters and clowns who will invade the place immediately a bitch like this is advertised for sale. There are people who spend half their time wandering around kennels, wasting time and not buying. Some ads in the *Exchange and Mart* actually state "no time wasters" and I know just how such advertisers feel. The dog world is literally full of the lunatic element; madmen abound.

Thursday 13

Hard frost and no running at dawn or lamping by night, but this won't last according to the weather forecast. As soon as the weather breaks, I must catch and kill a fox that has already slain several fowl for Albert who lives at the end of my lane. On Tuesday, the fox took one young goose and a bantam. I had my heart in my mouth about the bantam as I thought Fathom had started up again. However, when I looked around Cope's field next to my cottage, I found the remains of a fox kill, the typical deplumed carcass remains and the delicate surgery on the bones of the goose. Foxes are quite finicky eaters, vying with the cat as precision feeders.

I shall ferret Clelland's embankment at dawn tomorrow. Fudge is in superb condition and I need the rabbit meat for my terrier puppies. Clelland's warrens are not deep and a before-work hunt shouldn't prove too much of a problem. Famous last words. The last time I planned a before-school hunt, we finished up digging until noon. Predictions of this nature are bound to produce disasters. Still, I shall ferret the bank as it is getting quite rare to be asked to get rid of rabbits. I often get asked to kill foxes, but rarely rabbits.

A woman in a panic called last night. Her Afghan hound slipped its leash and vanished in spite of, or maybe because of, her cries for help. I can't understand why people keep such dogs. They must get little pleasure in owning such an untrainable beast. This breed is by nature intractable and even Afghan hunters get trouble with them. When show breeding and the sacrifice of brain for show quality takes over, things get really bad. I know of some breeders who have some control over these beautiful but hairy wards, but most simply accept the fact that the breed is nearly impossible to discipline. Personally, I should prefer a stuffed Afghan hound to a live one, for the stuffed animal is certainly more controllable.

Rat hunting fast but poor. The rats are not feeding in the same numbers as usual and we barely scraped 40 rats. The sport was, however, good and very fast. Omega was superb and very quick, but for the first time in ages, she received a very bad facial bite. The rat hung on the face as she tried to kill it under the poultry pen but she had no space to shake it to death and the struggle took over a minute. The wound is quite something.

Friday 14

Interviewed Brian Nuttall of Holmes Chapel, Cheshire with a view to collecting data from him for my forthcoming book *Fell terriers*. A quite unassuming chap, a far cry from supposed dog experts who frequent the shows today. Nuttall had some seven terriers of fell type, all of which were worked regularly and one of which had the most powerful head I have ever seen on a Fell terrier. I was envious of the ownership of his bitch, a good black bitch, dam of Peter Phelan's Poker.

Nuttall is from a long line of terrier men, and he obtained his first terriers from his grandfather. Nuttall says his first dogs were of Fell type with decided Bedlington terrier influence. These dogs were game and fearless, but his grandfather took Fell terriers to Northumberland to mate them to pit fighting dogs of the bull terrier type (not Staffords but an unregistered type of fighting dog now probably extinct). From this came the Nuttall strain fortified with dogs from Frank Buck and the inevitable Cyril Bray. A potent mix, to say the least, and Nuttall boasted—but boasted is not the correct word—that he had never bred a quitter.

As a boy, Nuttall had hunted fox, rat, and so on and later became a keeper at Wildboar Clough, Derbyshire. After this, he held a full time terrier man's job at the Cheshire Hunt, a post he held for four seasons. He left this to go concreting, but he still works as part time terrier man for the Border Counties Otter hounds. A knowledgeable, interesting chap who understood and practiced eugenics (stock improvement by genetics), an odd subject for a terrier man to understand. He will be a reliable asset when I write up my book, for not only is he intelligent and truthful, but he has a book full of records—priceless data.

I ferreted Clelland's embankment this morning. I took four rabbits and bolted a load of rats which skipped through the nets; not an auspicious start for my year of ferreting.

Saturday 15

A quiet Saturday, or so I planned for I had anticipated copying up my notes concerning my interview with Brian Nuttall while it was still fresh in my mind. Fate had other things in store for me, however.

At dawn, I turned Woolly, Fathom, Beige and Mara loose for exercise, noting the weights of the three adults and feeding them. Woolly, Beige and Mara played in the fields around the house, but Fathom disappeared. At first, I had misgivings about the new batch of tinkers at Fradley having picked her up, but at 11.40 she appeared with a cock pheasant in her mouth. It transpired it was a golden pheasant, a small, tiny-bodied male that must have come from a breeder's pen. I phoned Arch Thomas, a breeder of such exotica, and asked who bred these pheasants, but there is not a single known breeder for miles around. Where on earth did she catch this lovely bird? I turned it loose and it flew off somewhat aimlessly. I thought she had stopped this madness. Seemingly, she has not, so I must keep her up.

The phone rang at 12.20 just as I had finished the first draft of my interview with Nuttall and yet another farmer asked for me to kill a fox that is causing him trouble. Beltane checked all the earths around his farm but there was not a fox at home. People always seem to think that if a terrier fails to find, the dog is of no use, but foxes occupy a huge area and inhabit many earths in the course of a winter. An acre or so of land around here has several earths ranging from enormous badger setts to small, seemingly fox proof, rabbit earths. Thus I was forced to hunt through the night with lamp and lurcher. I killed two. John Cope skinned both, but the pelts are not ready for use as they have thick blue moult marks along the loins. Foxes moult head to tail and the blue moult lines slide down the back as moult continues.

Sunday 16

Stiff and tired and glad Cope has to skin the foxes. I am getting too old for a hard night's hunting—it really is a sport for a younger man. I lay in bed until eight o'clock, too sore to move and it was only Woolly's incessant barking that caused me to rise.

Steve Jones' puppy (a Warlock daughter/Hinchcliffe's Patterdale) came yesterday. It is well reared but docked ridiculously short, the ruination of many a good animal. Not only does a short dock spoil the appearance of a dog, giving it a Doberman or Rottweiler look, but the dog, not carrying enough "stern", is impossible to drag out of an earth using the tail grip. Yet so many people spoil dogs by short docking. Anyway, I shall use her for breeding as much as for work and mating her to Vampire will certainly produce good workers, of that I am certain. Bent legs may become a problem though, for Vampire has thrown a few when mated to Pagan's sister. Really, Russell blood throughout the country could benefit from an infusion of Patterdale/Fell blood before the Russell degenerates into the spiteful farm and house pet. Working strains of Russell, 100% working strains, are more than rare these days, as the number of people going over to Fell type terriers indicates. Nuttall said he knew of several good working Russells but these are usually "one off jobs" without working pedigree or knowledge of background.

Monday 17

Wrote up the Maurice Bell interview. I am now convinced my book must be an opinion-type book similar to the book by Jocelyn Lucas—an opinion-cum-anecdote type book would suit me and my readers, and would be a permanent record of breeders' views.

Old hat history concerning people like Peel and Piper Allen may have some use, but not much, I fear. A man may lie during his lifetime, and after his death his lies multiply, Nuttall said last Friday: a wise man indeed. Furthermore, every damned book has such data, and I intend my book to be an original. Hardesty and the Lakeland men must be my next port of call. A slightly different type of dog is bred by these people which resembles a small Irish terrier. Indeed, Winch, an authority on the breed, and one who should really be writing the book, believes that Irish terriers played a big part in the makeup of the working Lakeland. Certainly, old photographs of Lakelands show a scraggy cur-like dog, a far cry from today's working or show Lakelands.

Bell is one of the diehard brigade of Fell men, men who refuse to cross in the showable type of Lakeland to improve their native stock. His dogs are good lookers but too rugged to succeed in the southern hunt shows. Furthermore, the craze down south is to produce huge show Fell terriers. The excuse given is that big dogs are needed in the Fells. Bell who hunts some of the really bad country around Hawes, proves this a lie, for his terriers are never bigger than 13½ inches at the shoulder.

I lectured tonight in Bromsgrove Public School to a batch of 16+ lads and curiously, two girls. They fielded eighteen for my talk, a compliment actually, as a nationally famous poet only attracted two boys. Such is the power of *rattus norvegicus*.

A poor day's hunting with nothing flushed, nothing run. The tinkers have caused chaos locally and I have grave doubts if the land will recover from these frequent onslaughts by illtrained, unruly dogs.

Tuesday 18

The puppy from Steve Jones is settling in nicely and in spite of its ridiculous tail, it is very attractive indeed. The dog puppy from this litter, a bright tan, went to Swadlincote, only twelve miles from here and is well worth watching.

The morning has been spent unwisely, for in teaching Beige to jump, she has knocked up a toe. A knocked-up toe must be a bit of a disadvantage as a foot is designed to have all the toes functional, yet in spite of this, there are few great coursing dogs who do not sport a toe or so out of alignment. Still, I feel bad about the damage—it wasn't done during a course or even a particularly bad jump.

I see an advert for a Staffordshire Bull terrier/greyhound litter for sale in our local newspaper. It must be a fair risk to buy such a pup as a hare-coursing dog though most tend to favour the greyhound rather than the Staffordshire Bull in shape. There is a bull terrier whippet hybrid in Burton and it resembles a huge, bulbous headed whippet. Few have intelligence. The idea that such a hybrid has fire or guts inherited from its Stafford parent is a bit in question as well. Many greyhounds are spunkier than the modern show bull terrier and I know for a fact that many dog fighters (and make no mistake, there are plenty) still mate heavy-headed Patterdale type smooth Fell terriers to their pure show Staffords to give the pit dogs fire. Spunk is practically bred out in the majority of Staffords.

A hard journey south to lecture or read to South Wales (Newport Wildfowling Club). The poster was billed *The Rat Hunter* and the sight of posters advertising my show gave me a hell of a kick, I must admit. The reading was a success, I think, and I met Marni from BBC 2 who was continuity girl to Michael Croucher during our first filming.

Wednesday 19

I really must learn to give a talk properly. I must give a reading and stop at that—no questions with a yob audience and there are always one or two in every audience. The questions degenerate to a shouting match of "our terriers are better than yours and other crazy comments. The talk turns from being an interesting one into a boring slanging match. Nineteen year old belligerents can wreck a lecture tour, let alone a talk. I now vow

1. Not to lecture to clubs where there will be an open bar; the noise and belligerence is distressing.
2. Not to lecture to an audience where children are present. Some of my stories are not suitable.
3. Not to let the audience ask questions after a show, or to keep the questions off the personal level. Ridiculous questions and persistent nuisances ruin an otherwise good lecture.

I shall not breed another litter of lurcher puppies for the next few years. Not only have I no use for lurchers, but the once booming market for lurchers has now obviously died. Bob McIver, who bred a litter of lurchers by mating the powerful collie greyhound dog of Terry Ahearne's to a good coursing greyhound, has had great difficulty selling the pups. They would be great coursing prospects yet they are still unsold. Two years ago, such puppies would be literally snapped up. Now they are unwanted. I can assume from this the lurcher craze is at an end. Still, good lurchers can still be sold, I suppose, particularly the long coated ones, although one should not equate the length of the coat with the worth of a lurcher. Dealers can pick up puppies very cheaply these days.

Thursday 20

Not a good morning, I'm afraid. Merle is overweight, Fathom is near season and sluggish, Beige has a toe out so at seven-fifteen when a hare got up on the golf course it was Woolly who gave chase. Funnily enough, he put up a hell of a course at the hare, turning it a dozen times without catching it. I am still convinced that given the right breaks, he will make an excellent hare killer. He is much faster than Fathom—so am I for that matter—and certainly tries far harder. When he is older and more experienced however, he may not "try" at difficult rabbits and hares. Still, what makes a good lurcher other than the ability to be able to predict the rabbits he can catch and those that are scarcely worth the trying? A greyhound is usually a bonehead and will run anything that moves. A true lurcher can tell whether it is quarry that is within range. Fathom, for all her lack of speed and casual attitude, is a good lurcher, and any gypsy could live off such a dog. Indeed, I may have to if I am made redundant in the New Year. A badger appeared on the way home—it was 7.47 and it ambled off into the mists. Merle was running free and saw the badger but didn't even bother to try. Had I told him to go, he would have coursed it and taken it with ease. So much for the day's coursing.

A good, no, a great, night's rat hunting in spite of the poor numbers. Trevor failed to turn up with his lorry so we transported the dogs in the van. Subsequently, bad feeling developed between the studs, bad feeling that eventually developed into a fight during the last few minutes of the hunt. Rollo fought a spiteful though not particularly savage battle with one of the fox terrier crosses. Typewise, they are quite good long backed but still reasonable, but the crosses lack the edge on the pure bred Russells (though God knows, my strain are anything but pure). My Patterdale crosses are better than my pure bred Russells and much quicker than pure bred Patterdales. I have thought of fielding an entire F1 (Patterdale/Russell) team. They would certainly be easy to breed, and easy to make homogenous, for the first cross puppies exactly resemble each other. We took 100+ rats last night, mostly large adults, and there were quite a few diminutive greys that escaped. Hanzek says four litters a year for a healthy wild rat—ridiculous! In places like this poultry farm, a rat can breed (and I believe *will* breed) fourteen or so litters in the course of its brief life.

161

The wounds on the dogs are quite bad and the faces on the young stock are badly swollen. The older dogs are immune to the staphyloccus injected by rat bites. Two years ago, I lost two dogs (left with me to train) with rat bites—a Fell terrier and a champion border terrier, Gaelic Coffee. They were bitten on a Friday and by the following Thursday, both had died. The dangers of rat bites are often underestimated. My fox terrier/Russell hybrid bitch has her mouth so badly swollen that she cannot eat. In a year or so, they will be so used to the filth of rat bites, that they will take any rips without so much as a septic wound. There is no doubt dogs get immune to massive staphylococcus infections.

I shall start dawn exercise with the terrier pack now that the tinkers have left. Daily exercise for the pack might help to hold the team together and stop the fighting. Problem—a fight in mid-road with a whole team of dogs (15 or more) exercised and controlled by only one man, is sure to end in a death. My dogs do not understand the whip, a method that controls hounds, so the first few days of pack exercise could be downright difficult. I'll need help the first few days, as there is very bad feeling between some of the stud dogs. Until this bad feeling ceases, pack exercise will be very hard for just me to handle.

The ferreting of the banks near the railway starts tomorrow. Not difficult, I'm sure, but the roots of hawthorn make a lie up a hell of a problem, and no matter how careful the ferret is, observing silence, taking great care, a lie up is always on the cards. Funnily enough, in spite of the icy weather, I bolted two tiny drummers with Woolly only this morning as I allowed him to run in the grove opposite the house. This bodes a bit ill for ferreting tomorrow. Still, I've just got to do the banks or I'll lose the land I hunt—I pay nothing for my hunting and it is a struggle to keep the land. I must be at everybody's beck and call, killing foxes, ferreting rabbits, killing rats at a moment's notice to keep in with the landowners. Tomorrow dawn, bad weather or good, I must ferret these banks.

I watched a kestrel take a magpie this morning as I travelled to work (late, I confess). If I had not seen this with my own eyes, I wouldn't have believed it. Kestrels do not normally take anything bigger than a mouse, so an attack on a magpie is a bit bewildering. Also, the fact that the kestrel held and killed the magpie is all the more surprising. I've trained kestrels and I've never even managed to take live quarry with them. Tales of them taking starlings are numerous but I've always doubted them—until now, that is.

Saturday 22

This morning I received an interesting letter plus a well made rat net from a youth from Stoke. Actually, since 1978, the date of the publication of *Rat Hunting Man*, several firms are selling rat catching nets. Paul Jackson of Reading, turns off some of the very best I have ever seen, and he makes them to order. I've used rat nets just recently, but personally I find Moses' nylon stocking attached to a tin more satisfactory and certainly a lot cheaper. Netting rats is certainly not as easy as people imagine. Rats slink out of their lairs when ferreted unlike a rabbit that crashes out and gets entangled.

I broke Pagan's puppies—I must name them this week—to ferret today, a ridiculously easy task as they are scarcely eight weeks old and find the ferret a great source of interest rather than a creature to butcher. Within minutes they drank from a dish with the ferret. I used Fudge, of course; she knows and understands puppies and a young hob or jill would have become very nervy or aggressive when presented with two excitable puppies. Some ferrets try to kill the puppies, latching to the neck like a ferret would with a rabbit. Fudge, however, ignores them unless they behave badly. I tried to photograph their antics but with little success. Ruston is certainly one hell of a photographer. I will never get to his standard, I'm sure, no matter how I practice.

Phillip brought the merle litter brother of Mara to show me. Like most first crosses, he is a chunky, classless dog, classless but useful. Phil says he is having trouble with getting the dog to chase. He is a baby yet, and many lurchers, particularly dogs with a small amount of sight hound, are slow to chase but when they get to know what is required of them, they are really superb. The dog, called Wellington (and my names are daft?) was born on 30th June which makes him less than 5 months old—a bit young to write off, to say the least. A dog is still growing at that age and his training should consist of obedience work, not entering.

Sunday 23

The gun men are back, killing and maiming whatever moves. I really hate the brood that swarm across the lane, six or seven times a year, while reams appear in *Shooting Times* on the sportsman's attitude to hunting, and shooting men are supposed to epitomise good sportsmanship. Stuff and nonsense! Blackbirds, thrushes, jays and squirrels litter the landscape after a "vermin control hunt".

Yet another lunatic phone call asking if I want to run my lurchers against his—a total stranger. Am I an institution or something, that someone who is bored, restless or belligerent can simply phone up at a moment's notice? Anytime, day or night, I seem to be on call. I've had 2 am phone calls asking for an address of a person who bred Bedlington/greyhound hybrids. I shall get my phone number changed—I've had enough.

Guy Page appeared with his dog. It has started work and taken three rabbits in two days, no mean achievement though most of the show breeders boast an enormous haul by this age. Rabbits really take some catching. The dog is a lamper's dream, fast, powerful, agile and full of stamina. He will certainly make a cracking rabbit dog if not a hare dog, although I've seen heavy dogs pulverise hares over long arduous courses. Guy is delighted and Paul Taylor, who bred this dog, will be even more delighted.

Jackie Fallon phoned at midnight. Her bitch Rosie is in the process of whelping a litter to her stud dog Bugsy; a grand worker, whom I've used myself. To cut a long story short, Jackie's bitch began parturition and Jackie panicked. Normally, birth is a fairly easy process in a healthy bitch, but the first litter can be a fairly lengthy parturition. Few bitches come amiss when left to their own devices, but some do come unstuck. Anyway, by 4 am the bitch had finished and cleaned up the litter. I don't get angry or upset when would-be dog breeders phone—being over-careful is better than being undercaring and callous about a bitch in trouble.

Monday 24

Both my border bitches are in whelp to Bugsy; one is a week pregnant, and the other is three weeks pregnant. Jackie will sell these, I hope. Personally, I am not really interested in the puppies and I only hope Beltane doesn't come into season until these puppies are off the premises. At least they will earn their keep which is more than they have done to date. In spite of the sales bumph, very few border terriers are worked anyway, so this lot (much against my will) will probably go as pets.

Beltane will go to Rollo in the next few weeks—that's if she ever comes in season again. Omega, however, will be mated to one of Nuttall's or Hinchcliffe's Patterdales. A good strong boned puppy is what I want from her, but not yet, I suppose; but a mild damp winter seems to bring bitches into season ahead of time. Light plays an important part in determining when bitches come into season—or at least it is supposed to. The book *Innocent Killers* (Van Lawick and Goodall) gives an indication that light must be the most important factor.

Andrew Cocks (Countryman's Library) phones. We are contemplating doing a *Working Terrier Year Book* type of book concerning terriers, lurchers and ferrets. I phoned David Harcombe, editor and compiler of *Working Terrier Year Book* and he has no objections concerning a rival book as he is finishing with his publication this year. I really think such a book would be viable and worth while, for *Shooting Times* does not cater for our type of sport.

Mara is lame; a chance meeting with Phoibus and Deimos, aptly named sons of Vampire has rendered her badly bitten. Puppies which "favour" a leg often bend the other pastern to compensate for such an injury until the pastern is nearly on the floor. The damage is seldom permanent and the pastern soon corrects itself when the leg heals and the dog no longer favours the other foot. I know, believe me, that the combination of terriers and lurchers often results in serious fights and lame lurchers.

Tuesday 25

I shall begin work on the new periodical fairly soon—today in fact I shall write to Colonel Walsh, Aubrey Fryer—a fascinating chap as extreme as I am—to get articles from these people. I shall also give an interview with Harry Lees to complete the lurcher scene. Writing stuff myself is not on. I have far too many books in print already. Alan Thomas, Eddie Chapman and Winch will give me all the terrier articles I need or want and I will certainly write up my fascinating interview with Brian Nuttall.

Maurice Bell has been phoning around to get various noted Fell terrier men to stand interview for my book "Fell Terriers". It will not be easy to get many of these men to allow an interview and Bell must be my key to such a door. Fortunately, he is very amicable and more than reasonable about going out of his way to help me. Winch is bogged down with legal cases so I cannot rely on his help with the research. So

Bri, me boy, you are on your own, and the very best of luck. Let's hope Maurice comes up with what I want.

Stoats have taken up residence in the poisoned-off rat holes, so I gether that there are no rats at home. All seem to have left the hedgerow. I like stoats, they represent all that is vital, alive and quicksilver to me, but they have to go, I'm afraid. The land is going to be used to house some poultry chicks and they are hardly likely to thrive while stoats abound. Stoats, unlike ferrets and polecats, rarely attack adult poultry, but they are hellers on chicks. They will probably leave when the rats that have come because of the filth left by the tinkers have (a) moved on or become extinct through the shortage of food, the winter or cessation of rubbish tipping, or (b) the rats become too large for a stoat to tackle, for few stoats, weasels or polecats relish a duel with a big buck or doe rat.

Wednesday 26

My tracking of the working Fell terrier pedigrees becomes more complex than I thought. Hinchcliffe's stock, some of the finest and gamest smooth coated Fells in the country, is descended from local dogs around his area, reinforced with dogs from Bray and Nuttall. Now, Nuttall's dogs did not go to Hinchcliffe directly, but Hinchcliffe bought a trained dog, a dog called Flint from a chap in Glamorgan, and Flint had been bred by Nuttall. Nuttall trained this dog, found it outstanding but far too hard and furthermore, when Nuttall used his dog he found that Flint threw a large proportion of undershot offspring. Hinchcliffe used this dog judiciously, for Hinchcliffe is an intelligent man and is aware of both strengths and weaknesses in his strain. So a minimum of poor malformed stuff was produced, but the craze in South Wales at the time of writing, is to inbreed none too wisely, at that, to Hinchcliffe's strain. The result is obvious. Bayliss of Nantymoel, produced some terrible mouths in his strain by dint of using a surfeit of this line. In the hands of people like Hinchcliffe, or Nuttall (whose practical knowledge of genetics takes some beating) the use of this dog caused no damage, but such men are rare. It will be interesting to see the stuff produced by Welsh breeders in years to come. My own strain also carries some of this blood, so I too must be on my guard against problems of dentition. Jaeger, my Fell terrier

stud, brought in to improve heads on my strain, is a grandson of Flint. Still, the dog bred some outstanding working dogs, dogs of bottomless courage, so I do not regret bringing the line into my strain. I shall use more Patterdale/black Fell blood but I will now seek a slightly related line, one in which Flint does not appear.

Michael Croucher phoned and we are back in business. Filming starts on 20th December 1980 with a hunt with goshawks and Harris hawks. I phoned Granville Maddocks and made the arrangements this evening. On 21st December we ferret the banks of a railway cutting in Leicester with Paul Taylor and finally on the 23rd December, a fox dig in Sutton, Surrey with Doug Cooper, owner of C.T.F. (the field sports equipment suppliers) and then, with luck, we are finished. I've enjoyed the filming but, my God, it is tiring. A month of filming would kill off the average man. My ferrets will be in top shape for the filming and with luck, so will Paul's.

Tonight, I made the mistake of leaving Mara, my beautiful lurcher puppy, loose with Vampire's puppies: they killed her. The end of a fabulous experiment—where will I get her like again? It takes me an age (ten years to breed her and ten minutes to kill her). She had everything, looks, brains, speed, the lot and in ten minutes she was dead.

Maurice Bell's Wensleydale Fox Hounds on the top of Penn Hill.

Thursday 27

I feel sick over the death of my lovely puppy. She would have set the scene for a new strain, an invincible strain I am sure. Now I have nothing. Mick and Roger buried her last night. I was too sick to think about it. Now, I am back to square one yet again. How can I breed another such litter? It took two generations to breed this strain. She was perfect in every way, the best puppy I have ever bred—now I have nothing. Thus ends yet another dream. I shall start again however, and by 1987–1991 I shall have my own strain of lurcher. In spite of this awful setback, I am not beaten yet—another starting point.

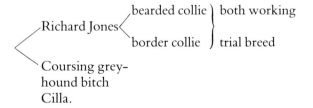

This line mated to Eddie Jones' dog Celt (merle/greyhound) and Guy Page's dog and by 1987 I should

be close. Still, what a tragedy to lose my lovely bitch, but the mark of a first class dog breeder is to get up off one's backside and face reality and start again.

We invited the reporter from the *South Wales Argus* up for a hunt tonight—though whether he will come is a moot point. He seemed enthusiastic on the phone, and very eager to come. We will see if, on reflection, he will.

He came, and even if he didn't enjoy it, he seemed impressed. Not a spectacular hunt—we killed 200 or perhaps a few more for we didn't count the dismembered carcasses—but it was certainly one of the fastest on record. We spent less than forty minutes actually hunting the place, and the rats were running well. Tom Lancaster, our reporter, seemed just a little stunned, but recovered enough to ask pertinent questions about rats and their hunting. My dogs are not even slashed up after their encounter. Anyway, Tom Lancaster, our reporter, seemed to think it would make good data for a half page of his newspaper. I feel we may read about his real opinion of the hunt in a week or so.

Mara aged 14 weeks stalking a bird.

Friday 28

A dead pig dropped by a local farmer and a road casualty cat dropped by a local gamekeeper. Ferrets go wild with delight with cat meat and although it can be a danger as it can carry feline infectious enteritis, it is still an incredibly appetising meat for ferrets. Even sick ferrets are keen to eat cat meat. The tom weighed 14 lbs, a huge and ancient male, but the ferrets went wild with ectasy when they saw him. I always feel a bit ashamed at feeding road casualty cats, as some-where, someone is waiting for their pet to come home, and I felt pretty bad when my own Siamese met his end in a road accident. I shouldn't have liked him fed to ferrets, I must admit.

Maurice Bell has arranged a tour of the Lake district and north to interview the following Fell breeders:-

John Cowen
Walter Parkin
Harry Hardesty
Cyril Tyson
John Winch
Graham Ward
Fred Jenkinson
Arthur Irving
Eddie Poole
George Newcombe.

I take off on 28th December for a two day visit.

Saturday 29

Dawn and a hard, fruitless night behind me—the night was one of the most unproductive ever. I saw seven foxes illuminated by my beam—incidentally, Phillip got me a new cost price 12 volt battery—ran four, missed all of them, with Merle performing like a crass amateur. At no time did he look like taking even one. On his off days, I wonder if he even tries for foxes for last night one of my leggier terriers could have taken the one that scampered into Stone's hollow wall. The ground became frozen hard by 4.0 am and I was glad to return home to the cottage. Poor old Merle, he had icicles hanging from his fur and little else to show for his troubles.

I must start the two helions from Vampire this morning; they attacked the border bitch in whelp to Jackie's dog. It took a hell of a struggle to get these two tiny mites off the bitch, both were hell bent on killing her and their milk teeth made considerable havoc on both her hide and my hands before I had separated the contestants. They are ready for lion, not just rat—never have I bred such aggressive puppies—but aggression is not always the symptom of a good worker, though I'll bet my boots these will catch and work any quarry I want.

I could have used the helions this afternoon for I was called to bolt a fox with Beltane. For one moment only, I toyed with netting the fox and let the babes bay the fox in the net or between the tines of a fork. Still, as luck would have it, it would not only have been foolish to take them but futile since the fox lodged between two huge boulders in the embankment and I had to get Billy Orton to shoot the beast. He was not keen to have the carcass ragged by the babes either, as he is a trophy hunter and has probably only seen a few foxes. No hurry, there'll be other foxes, and time for the helions to rat for a year or so before they see fox. They will go, however, of this I have no doubt.

Sunday 30

A whole pattern of fox tracks (the one-behind-one tracks) on Cope's frosted fields—a vixen and a litter of cubs coming back to the home earth would be my bet. I'd be willing to bet my boots that the whole litter are back at the breeding earths in Barlow's fields, forbidden to me as it is shot over by a syndicate and I have an excellent relationship with the Barlows. Sooner or later, the syndicate will realise the foxes are there and Cymag the earths. It is (so Steele Bodger, my ex-vet assures me) a mistake to think that cyanide poisoning is a painless way of dying. It is a particularly nasty, though I must admit very rapid way of killing below-ground vermin. Everything dies, rats, rabbits, foxes, badgers, the entire occupants of an earth in fact; and dogs which enter recently cymaged earths, often come to grief. Still, that's the way with syndicated shoots.

I ferreted Leveson's holding this morning, and though the earths looked used, Fudge only bolted a stray rabbit from the warrens, a big fat buck which the nets slowed up long enough for Woolly to kill it. These earths, warrens, call them what you will, were once the most productive places I used to ferret. Either it has been poached or myxomatosis has seen off the rabbits in the area. Last year, I took fifteen fine healthy rabbits in less than an hour from these earths. A poor day, but I found a net that Hank lost this time last year. It was a cheap nylon affair which though it looked soiled and muddy, was still usable. The hemp or flax nets weather very badly when left out for an entire year, even if they are treated with linseed oil mixtures, but nylon is indestructible, or nearly so. Yet I don't like nylon nets, for I'm a bit conservative in my tastes.

My Fell terrier is ready for rat, as ready as she'll ever be, that is. She is very aggressive, though not nearly as aggressive as Vampire's two puppies. I will break her to poultry in a week or two and this time next year, she will be ready for fox, no, not just ready, taking them quite readily. Some terriers have an inexplainable look about them, eyes, attitude, maybe, which tells an experienced hunter a dog will make it. Some—Joe Weir for example—used to say he could feel a good terrier as soon as he picked it up; it was as if some magnetic force radiated from it. My Fell terrier has that look and feel that tells me it will be a flyer when it enters to fox. Lunatics (I must admit I was tempted yesterday) would enter this puppy prematurely, having it going to fox at six months and ruined by twelve months.

167

December

Monday 1

The earth is like iron and there is not a chance of running a dog in such conditions—knocked up toes and more serious injuries are certain, so it's lamp on charge and after the fight tonight (Wolverhampton Civic Hall) I shall explore the possibilities of ratting a pig farm near Pattingham. Really, I am spoilt for choice, ratting-wise and rarely leave my beloved poultry farm to forage abroad for new ratting spots.

Cordwell Hylton, the fighter I went to see in Wolverhampton lost, so I returned early to "sus" out my pig farm in Pattingham. There are rats there, have no doubt, but not as many as they seemed to think. Rats often make liars of people. "We have hundreds of rats" often means we have a small colony (4–12) feeding near the house, "overrun" with rats means I've seen six or seven, rats as big as cats means a few average sized bucks and does. Actually, I doubt whether it is worth while hunting this farm, but I must certainly keep the place in mind.

Phoned Peter Whittaker of *Pugs and Drummers* whose booklet on ferreting is a classic even if it is a diminutive piece of work. Whittaker, a no-nonsense, down to earth, ferreting expert who has considerable experience of both rabbit and rat hunting with ferrets. I left a message with his wife, asking him to write an article on any aspect of ferreting. Whittaker has an easy style of writing ideally suited to this sort of Year Book and with luck, he may contribute to the book.

I would like a thinning out of my stock to make way for young hybrid bitches (Patterdale to Russell) but there is little that I can do to thin out the stock—the fox terrier/Russell hybrids are catching, but not as well as I would like. I could put them out to sensible homes or rat them another year and hope they improve. I do not think that they will be top grade in spite of the fact they are bred from my best bitch Beltane. I might breed better stock by using one of the fox terrier bitch hybrids as a brood, but I am very reluctant to use any bitch that is second rate as a dam for future stock. I will find them good homes and begin again, adding only Nuttall's or Hinchcliffe's stock to my strain.

Tuesday 2

A phone call from a man who wishes to breed his own type of terrier, mating spunky, gutsy Staffords to Bedlington terriers. He wants the addresses of any owners of Staffordshire bull terriers who actually fight their dogs or test them at badger baiting. Risky—of course, I know of men who actually fight their dogs and many who still bait badgers with Staffs—but they would certainly not thank me for divulging their addresses. On the subject of creating such a hybrid however, I have seen stock bred like this in my own birthplace and gutsy, ugly hybrids they proved to be. They were used for hunting, ratting and baiting sports that were common when I was a child and are recently experiencing a revival in my valley. The Bedlington/Staffs hybrids resembled blue-black, pot bellied Dandie Dinmont terriers, and I believe that there is still some of this stock bred in South Wales to this day. However, fast Staffords, dogs that would bite a hole in a wall, are getting quite rare and although there is now a club to promote the working Bedlington terrier, many of the hell-raisers of old are now long gone. Personally, I think the breeding of such a hybrid would not only be expensive but a bit futile. There are still excellent, very hard strains of terrier available, very tough Fells and even one or two ugly, useful strains of Jack Russell terrier that might lend themselves to improving and be more than capable of doing anything a Bedlington/Staffs hybrid would do.

As yet nothing from *South Wales Argus*. Perhaps the

subject is not suitable for the newspaper. The *London Evening News* and the Tokyo newspapers both did features on the subject as has the *Walsall Observer*. Still, it's early days yet and Tom hasn't had all that much time.

Wednesday 3

Dawn and the ground is no longer frozen though the temperature is only 4°C. Fathom ran and failed to take a large hare and failed to even turn the brute. She is no hare dog, but lampwise, rabbit wise, pheasant, partridge and whisper it, poultry and she is a world beater. Beige ran her hare for five minutes later, overtook it with flashing speed, turned it in tight circles and eventually took it single-handed in Avery's field—a field off the land where I have permission. She retrieved it however, and we hightailed it home. I can't understand hunters who leave hares to the birds and rats. Within five minutes of coming home, the hare was skinned and soaking in salt water. I never leave a hare to hang (or anything for that matter) for that which is high is rotten and I dislike putrid meat of any sort. Do gourmets actually enjoy vulture-high meat or is it merely an affectation? It's not that I haven't tried it, I have. I find the taste unpleasant. Meat is meant to be eaten fresh, raw, nearly bloody, not flavoured with decay or softened with bacterial action.

Fathom took two rabbits on the way home even as we raced across the field. Whenever she lets me down and she does sometimes—no, heck, quite a lot—she really lets me hit a high spot morale-wise within minutes of a failure. A super hunter, a real all-round lurcher, no speed merchant, but solid and sound, describes Fathom. Woolly is much faster, much more eager to please, and much more amusing, but will he be as good a lurcher?

A letter from Jack Ivester Lloyd of whom I am a great fan, and one whose work has helped me put together a style suitable for writing the books I turn off. I asked him to give me an article for the year book and as I knew he would, he willingly offered his help. Any year book with Jack's articles is on to a winner. It will be a 100-page book, maybe 10 pages of adverts, but the rest stuff from top-grade writers like Ivester Lloyd. This should be the best year book of its kind ever compiled, of this I have no doubt.

Thursday 4

A mixed and curious day. Dawn and four fairly easy runs with the lurchers at rabbits that I considered dead certs. We caught none of them. Returning home, however, Woolly nearly fell on one and caught it. Rabbits are never the dead certs most lurcher men would have you think. They bob, weave, jink and throw off the most persistent and dextrous dog. I haven't seen a hare all morning, not even a distant pair of long ears escaping casually over the horizon. Do they move from season to season or have I harassed them far too hard lately? Foxes are plentiful and the nights are fairly dark.

Richard Jones (the vet, not my collie) dropped some somewhat unpleasant data my way when I went down to get the two hellions their second leptospiral injection. He had treated a pedigree litter of puppies (breed best not mentioned) for parvo virus two years ago and most had recovered. Last week a vet from near Buxton phoned and told him that one of the puppies had recently keeled over and died and autopsy had revealed lesions of the heart. Richard Jones (the collie not the vet) Nightwing, my Fell terrier and two others contracted this deadly infection and lived. Will they, too, die after two years or so? There is so much I don't know about dogs!

No use holding the hellions back much longer. I will enter them to rat this time next week. Breaking them to poultry will be harder than entering them to rat, I fear. I shall enter Nightwing, my Fell terrier as well next week. Type wise, she is a bit long in the back, and small in the head but she is very straight-legged and of good type: a lovely animal bred from some of our gamest stuff in the Midlands, a truly valuable addition to my pack—a dash of this blood might prove exactly what I want. Anyway, testing first, for if she is not utterly game she must not be added to the line. One mistake with the fox terrier hybrids has to be enough.

A poor night's ratting: scarcely more than forty were taken and we had to work to get those. No fault of the dogs—our own fault in fact, for there were too few of us to get to the escape holes quickly enough. They are poisoning on the farm and dozens of cadavers litter the sheds.

Friday 5

A bad, wet morning but a rabbit to show for our troubles. Woolly came upon it by chance, I think, more than by judgment. He bowled it two or three times, failing to pick it up, but Fathom snapped it up under Woolly's nose. Picking up, the actual capture of a rabbit, is a skill some dogs learn quite slowly. Penguin, Woolly's grandmother took many months to learn to pick up and caught her first few rabbits with her paws. I enjoy keeping families of dogs and ferrets. One can actually see family resemblances. Penguin's early days were really a bit of a puzzle. The first rabbit she saw, a tiny drummer, that slid the nets and ran towards her, panicked her and she raced back to the parked van and hid beneath it shivering with fear. Charlie Little, who was hunting with me at the time, shouted for me to "put her down" and I must admit I felt terribly humiliated. Penguin was eight months old at the time and many lurchers are catching well at that age. Yet by fourteen months old, she had foxes to her credit. How curious is the development of a lurcher, what idiots the men are who sell lurchers or, worse still, put them down at the first setback!

Both the border bitches are now obviously in whelp, although the smaller one looks emaciated. She has been kennelled with the border dog and he obviously hogs the food. She needs to be fed separately and well away from the male who bullies as well as wolfs down the food. These will be the only puppies I have sold for eight years. My God, talk about chickens before hatching—I have parvo virus on the premises and I'm talking about selling the puppies—Plummer, you are the born optimist.

Another lunatic phone call (I really must go ex-directory) asking if I would swop him a lurcher (trained) for a broken coated Jack Russell terrier. I felt hurt, the idiot actually thought I'd be in the market for such a swop.

Saturday 6

Dawn and another mistake. For seven weeks, a small colony of weasels has taken up residence in my hedge. They keep down the mice and tiny rats, even if they cannot cope with the adults. Normally, I make a noise as I approach their lairs and they scamper back below ground. This morning they didn't scamper quickly enough, and Omega caught one killing it with a deft flick. Weasels are diminutive, fragile creatures. Locally, some of the village oldies call them minivers—not strictly accurate as miniver is a mixed or variegated fur possibly a partially moulted stoat's fur from the Latin minutus—small, various, part-coloured. Anyway, it died, miniver/weasel. I phoned Roy Lees, a close friend (I dedicated "The Working Terrier" to him) but he was out. A pity, because Roy is getting to be a crack taxidermist and there is a craze for stuffed, glassy eyed horrors at this moment in time. Why, I don't know; a room full of stuffed creatures is rather like a scene from a book by Roald Dahl. Anyway, tomorrow, he will come and claim the little tragedy.

Mick and Roger called after a fruitless day's hunting and so I bolted three rabbits with Fudge for their dogs to chase. They did and didn't catch one—still, it's a good dog that can catch rabbits in this sort of cover. Fudge is on cracking form and though she did dally with a rat in one warren, she pushed out the rabbits in record time. I shall work her sparingly before the hunt on the 21st December, when we shall work before the cameras. Pray to God, Fudge doesn't louse it up like Fathom did. That's all I need now—a ferret that lies up before the cameras and a lurcher that fails to retrieve!

On the subject of ferrets, a chap called Clive Griffiths a computer "what d'ye call it" from Birmingham, came up to buy a ferret—I have one of Paul's I don't want and Paul needs the money at the moment (hell, who doesn't?). The little hob is in lovely condition, but he is undershot or hog mouthed, as they say in ferreting circles and his teeth protrude slightly, a bit unsightly but it doesn't interfere with the work of a ferret. Once, in Doncaster market, I saw a litter of hog-mouthed ferrets, so terribly undershot that they could scarcely use their mouths. I don't like abnormalities of any sort, but I've seen some useful hog-mouthed stock.

Paul Taylor called at seven and left before midnight. He is a bit depressed at the moment and intends to read a degree with the Open University. He would like to write and I doubt if O.U. will help him. To learn to write, one must write and not simply read for a very boring degree.

Sunday 7

I discussed getting Paul to write for my year book and to review books for it. He is widely read and has a collection of sporting books second to none. Ian Niall is his idol (a writer I admire greatly), and T.H. White whom I knew personally. As a writer of sporting books, I detest the "I gave it both barrels" type stuff so commonly published in periodicals. I feel if Paul gets some success as a writer, he will certainly go on to great things.

I met a breeder of soft coated Wheaten terriers—dogs that are still extremely game to the point of insanity—in fact, I have a photograph of one (a macabre photograph) that was such a treasure in its life that its owner had it stuffed when it died: a curious gesture reminiscent of Victoriana rather than the present day. All Irish terriers have a common origin. The Irish terrier, the Glen of Imaal, the furious Kerry Blue, and the soft coated Wheaten are all related and have a common denominator, an extraordinary courage. Show breeding has certainly wrecked the Staffordshire Bull terrier's character, but the Irish breeds are still the gamest things on God's earth. I wonder what a soft coated Wheaten mated to a greyhound might breed—a game lurcher, that is for certain, and one with a fair degree of brain for Irish terrier breeds are incredibly tractable for terriers. Perhaps, someone, somewhere, has bred this incredible hybrid. Such a cross, a greyhoundy specimen perhaps, would be a wicked fox killer.

Near midnight and another request to kill off a fox that has done damage in Shenstone. It is very cold and icy, 4° Centigrade in my bottom shed which is very cold since the tinkers have stolen the lead from the edge of the shed. I was reluctant to turn out to hunt the brute. Still, dawn found one badly bitten Merle and a very dead fox. The skin is poor, for some months ago, it caught a lot of buckshot. Perhaps this crippled a muscle or so and made it incapable of living off rabbits and thus turned to poultry. Perhaps, if left alone, undamaged so to speak, this fox would not have been a pest. I detest guns.

Monday 8

I have slight frost damage to my face and fingers, small insignificant damage but enough to convince me that at forty-three I am too old for the life I lead. Ben Lilly, huntsman to Teddy Roosevelt, hunted every day and slept outdoors from the heat of Carmina Real to the Rocky Mountains until he was well into his seventies, but he was made of sterner stuff. Each winter, I begin to have the first taste of mortality, and by spring I am so bushed and exhausted that I vow this is my last winter of hunting by night in driving sleet, snows and frost, but as summer comes my resolution wavers and autumn finds me eager as ever, awaiting the first really heavy frosts. How much longer will I refuse to admit I am ageing rapidly? I am tired after a hunt that would have scarcely winded me ten years ago. When I came to this district some thirteen years ago, I walked to Lichfield each day and carried a hundredweight of dog food home each night, humping it on my back. I was fit, agile and very strong, but four years later I bought a car and took less exercise and my health began to suffer as a result of my increasing use of the car. As a result of the internal combustion engine, I am only a shadow of my former self.

Checked the nets for the television performance of the 21st—ferreting. To show up well on TV, we will use bleached nets and though they do not blend with the undergrowth, it will make TV viewing better. I only hope the rabbits are equally television orientated and do not stop at the very obvious nets, realise these are a trap and creep back into the warrens. Actually, biologists believe that most animals are colour blind and unable to detect a difference between white bleached nets and dyed nets. Likewise, I do not believe that hanging snares until they are covered with verdigris, or worse still, pickling them in human urine until they turn green, helps much. Snares usually entangle their victims in darkness or just before dawn. The glitter of new snares would not be seen by night and at dawn the hedgerows and fields are so covered with dew that they glisten far more than an unverdigrised snare.

Tuesday 9

I am not going to breed any more Jack Russells until this plague is ended, and I rather regret the border terriers are in whelp when there is still danger of parvo-virus about. Still, I am always going to be on my guard about this dreadful disease. Immunity? Well, how long does a virus live in a dog free establishment? 3 months—one year at the most. In a kennels it can trickle on for far longer until:

(a)   the disease can find no new hosts i.e. puppies, ferrets, etc.

(b)   until the bitches become so immune to the bug that they develop huge quantities of antibodies which give the puppies immunity to the bug.

I'm a bit doubtful about this one for I lost over a hundred puppies to distemper waiting for the bitches to develop immunity. Still, our vet was recently asked to inoculate a pack of fox hounds against parvo and on examining the blood samples of the hounds, found that the bitches had antibodies aplenty and were able to cope with the bug. The disease must have hit the pack at some time to give this immunity to the hounds, but not once had the huntsman seen sickness in his wards, and not one puppy had died or faded. There must be many strains of parvo virus ranging from the relatively harmless to the absolutely lethal.

The chicken raids are over in the district. Albert, the local cowman, has lost no more hens since I killed the fox at Lane end. We skinned the fox this morning. The carcass is peppered with old shot and new. Some fine No.6. shot—not suitable for big quarry has embedded itself in the spine and some recent No.5 shot is, or rather was, festering in the rump. One leg has been broken (and reset) as a result of the peppering. Boy, could this fox have told a tale. After such mangling by gunmen, the *Shooting Times* reviewer has the cheek to say (about *The Complete Lurcher*) that catching foxes with lurchers gives field sports a bad name!

Wednesday 10

Sally Hancock brought a greyhound for Merle to mate, the same greyhound that bred Eddie Jones' Celt and the dog Mick sold to Corporal Hooten, a chap who phoned me from Germany. Stuff from this bitch is top grade, fast, elegant, strong boned and incredibly tractable; the bitch, bred in Ireland from kin of Minnesota Yank was owned by an Oxford Coursing club man and is more than capable of catching hares single-handed. Mick Kirby only reared two puppies from the mating, but both are excellent. Hooten's dog—I saw him at the Game Fair—is a pale fawn merle pied and resembles a very big strong boned whippet. Hooten phoned me two months ago about the dog. He is catching quite well but Hooten cannot get him to jump, a simple mishap in training, perhaps. Still, Sally should breed a good litter of puppies from this bitch.

Harold Hodson Walker, of Tutbury, borrowed my blue coursing bitch Cilla, to breed some lurcher puppies. He mated her to Terry Ahearne's dog Rusty, and bred a good multi-coloured litter of puppies. Cilla is now in season again and I shall mate her to Merle and buy back the litter. If my genetic calculations are correct, I should breed 50% black and 50% merle, for black and blue are simply phases of the same colour. I've bred eleven puppies from her and so has Harold. I have no doubt that there will be some four puppies in the litter as even when mated to a pedigree bearded collie, she has bred some very fast, useful puppies. (Moses' bitch Steel is from this mating.) To Merle, she might be capable of producing a good light- to medium-boned batch.

Harold's other bitch, a rough coated Jack Russell, a granddaughter of my famous stud Rupert, is to be mated to Vampire and once again, I shall buy up the puppies as I am short of bitch puppies. Rupert was the sire of 42 working certificate offspring, a record at the time and his stuff has excellent nose, a quality some of mine lack.

Thursday 11

Thursday and the rat hunt and tonight I enter the hellions. Peter Whittaker phoned about an article for the Year Book, now called tentatively *The Hunters Year Book*. Whittaker's style is to the point and his articles interesting. He will be a priceless asset to the Year Book. This is a genial easy going, cultured sort of chap who is an excellent ambassador for the field sports brigade. I will welcome this article—though

Omega pulls off an incredible snatch.

frankly, I haven't the nerve to edit it.

What a rat hunt, fast, furious and fruitful. We entered the hellions tonight and both went like hell in the night. Both Phobus and Deimos are only half the size of an adult terrier, but they caught and killed the first rat they saw and were hunting like old stagers by the time the pack reached shed two. It was amazing to see these tiny mites—they were born in July—catching large, savage rats. If only I had mated Beltane to Vampire frequently and kept the offspring! Now, I fear she is too old. Her last litter was not reared well and she had ceased lactating before the pups were two weeks old. Next litter—if any? To Vampire again, I think and to hell with keeping chocolate coloured puppies. Anything from the pair looks promising.

The Fell terrier, while it was very vociferous, did not attempt to catch a rat. She seemed to give tongue at anything she saw, rather than come to grips with it. Nuttall of Holmes Chapel, says that this is not uncommon when this line comes in contact with rats for they seem by nature to give tongue at anything they don't understand, in fact Nuttall predicted that behaviour. In a few weeks, no doubt the reaction will be different. I have little doubt she will acquit herself well during the next trip out. My own terriers have been ratted for sixteen generations and ratted hard at that, so I expect early starters. Six weeks from now, I shall compare the performance of both Fell terrier and Beltane's puppies.

The puppies look quite dreadful this morning and their faces are so swollen that they can scarcely open and shut their mouths. First time out, all puppies have swollen faces after mangling several rats, but after a trip or so things are different. They quickly become immune to any infection a rat can offer.

Doug Cooper C.T.F. has arranged a fox dig at Box Hill, Surrey and I shall enter Mick's dog, Toby. With luck, we will film the whole dig from start to finish without upsetting any established hunt or shoot. I shall also hunt the land near my house (Barlow's farm) and dig a fox there but there is a possibility we shall upset our local shoot if TV cameramen tramp across fields that are to be shot only a few hours later. All in all, a TV producer's lot is not a happy one. Croucher must run pussyfoot through life to prevent upsetting anyone. I would love my own TV series but I feel that I could not cope with it. I have offended so many people during my hectic life. I do not have Croucher's panache, expertise or feeling for the media.

Fudge is in terrific shape for Sunday's hunt. I shall keep only this jill and her offspring next year, taking care to use a hob that is not only tame, but from good workers. There is a rash of pet ferret keepers at this moment, and sooner or later it will be difficult to get good sensible ferrets. As yet, any ferret will work, as the instinct to kill is still strong in all ferrets, but it probably pays to use only quiet, tractable, good workers.

I journey north to Kendal tonight, book a room there and meet Maurice Bell to hunt with the Wensleydale Fox Hounds tomorrow at 9.0 am. The Lake District is waterlogged for it has rained heavily this last week or so. The lane around Kendal is under water and the gills (the fast flowing fell streams) are overflowing. Hunting such a land will be messy and cold, but I need the experience of hunting such country if I am to write a book on the Fell terrier.

Drawing a fox at Barlow's earth.

Arrived at Maurice Bell's house in Hawes in driving rain. The day was rained off for it would be lunacy to hunt under such conditions. At 10.30 however, the rain ceased abruptly and we journeyed to the River Ure to hunt the district up to Penhill with the West of Yore Fox Hounds. One fox was put up and leaped the dry stone wall only a yard from me. The hunt lasted some two hours when the hounds lost the scent of the fox. The hounds put up a roebuck towards the end of the day and surprisingly did not riot—I say surprisingly because most hounds find deer almost irresistible. Few hound packs that hunt deer country have not a few mistakes to their discredit.

Frank Buck was out with the West of Yore and had three terriers with him, a black Fell terrier, a black and tan bitch and a border bitch. All three have entered to fox and all three are worked regularly with the packs around Buck's home.

I photographed one of Bell's terriers, an iron hard, rather scruffy Fell terrier, jet black and long coated. The gamekeeper who owned the dog was selling it next day as it was too hard and tore foxes nearly to pieces. If one wanted such iron hard dogs, a visit to Bell would surely provide one. Bell's dog, *Britt*, a famous tough fell terrier of his day (bred from one of Buck's dogs, I believe) sired many of the furious dogs. Many of Britt's puppies went to Scotland and would not only kill foxes but also kill Scottish wildcats. Bell has one bitch from this illustrious dog, a black neat fell terrier aged seven, who unfortunately has a growth and cannot perpetuate the bloodline.

A late night, I'm afraid and not exactly the best of things as I have to ferret several miles of embankment in Leicester. A light rain and some sleet. I am almost hoping Paul will call off tomorrow because of rain.

Drawing a fox at Barlow's earth.

It is not a suitable day for ferreting: driving rain, sleet and howling wind and I am starting out for Leicester. Truly, I must be mad. I glanced out of the window at dawn at the awful weather and was tempted to go back to bed, but at 8.0 am I found myself half way to Leicester through wind and rain. By 9.0 am I arrived in Stapleford at Paul's house and with Clive Griffiths and his wife Lyn, we set out to ferret the embankment in Melton Mowbray.

A poor day: two rabbits taken and three more bolted, escaping through impossible places in the bank. Fudge caught and held a large buck rabbit under a grit tray near the edge of the track, an impossible place to net but certainly the best place to get a run from Paul's dog, Fleet. However, Fudge held the buck and refused to allow it to bolt and I had to reach under the concrete base to pull out Fudge and the rabbit.

Blinding sleet and a very bad place to ferret. Another buck taken and ran by Paul's dogs across the fields near the track. A difficult catch but a spectacular retrieve to hand. By 2.0 pm Paul called off the day and we returned to Stapleford drenched to the skin after ferreting the very worst and most unproductive part of Paul's one hundred miles of railway track. I am soaked to the skin, wet and a bit fed up, but one weekend in the near future, we shall ferret a more productive spot and get a far larger haul.

It will be fairly profitable, though hard-earned money for the warrens are usually in deep cover and thick brambles.

Doug Cooper phoned at 6.0 pm to alter the date of the fox dig. Foxes are using the earths we intend to dig, but the Hunt are due to draw the land the day we planned to dig. I dislike inviting trouble and, while I am not a hunt supporter, in the truest sense of the word, I can appreciate what hunt supporters must feel to have their day ruined. We will change the day and alter the venue.

Alan Thomas phoned at 6.20 pm. He intends entering into hunt service with one of the Southern packs. Jobs in hunt service become vacant on May 1st of each year—a relic of hiring and firing spring fairs. Personally, I do not envy him the job. Hunt service is not simply a day out with the terriers, but messy work cleaning hounds and knackering and boiling fallen beasts. Alan has a profitable local store type of business and he will find the drop in salary (and, whisper it, social status) hard to bear.

I fed the hellions at 7.55 this morning making a note that the facial swellings are now reduced until their faces are almost back to normal, but on returning I found Deimos ears were up in the pricked position and made the dog look like a miniature English bull terrier. Ears rise and fall quite frequently during teething as irritation of the gums produces all sorts of reaction in the muscles that control ear carriage. Their grandsire, Laddie, was prick eared until he was seven months, whereupon his ears dropped and he became a show stopper. Ear carriage alters the appearance of a dog considerably and can ruin a show dog's appearance. Many of the present day smooth-coated Patterdale terriers carry a fly ear, as most of the blacks can trace their ancestry back to Frank Buck's brood bitch Topsy, rated in the Wensleydale area as one of Frank's best terriers. This peculiar ear carriage appeared in some of Hinchcliffe's superb working strain some five years ago, as Flint, the sire of many of Hinchcliffe's terriers, also dates back to Topsy. The ears on the puppy will certainly become dropped as soon as teething stops.

Once again an alteration in the TV schedule. We hunt Box Hill on the 23rd December, the date we had previously allotted to dig. To produce such a programme is a nightmare. I do not envy Croucher. In January, we will piece the programme together and I shall do the narration—voice over, they call it in the trade—a task I do not relish at all. I have no experience of such a task and I wonder if I am up to it.

Ruston is having great difficulty collecting good coursing shots for his book *Pictorial Guide to Hunting*. His other photographs are incredible. Ferreting, ratting, fox digging, badger digging shots have come out fine, but he needs a chance to get coursing shots. Of course, he has had plenty of offers which did not materialise. What incredible liars some lurcher men are; but like all liars, when called to show their skills, they tend to fall flat on their faces.

Another run at fox and a bad miss at that. My beam flickered and failed as Merle closed with the fox and I think he bowled it a few times as it broke into cover. I heard the crashing about in the undergrowth as Merle ploughed in after it. My fault, not Merle's, I'm afraid. I knock batteries and beams around quite a lot and don't really look after my equipment as much as I should. In fact, I ill-treat it.

Harold Hodson Walker is bringing Cilla for mating in a few days—Thursday, he estimates. Hope to God Merle mates her, though his track record has improved greatly recently. He has to date, mated Fathom (Woolly is one of the pups), Steel (Moses' bitch), Mick's greyhound (the dam of Eddie Jones' dog, Celt) and two greyhound bitches belonging to Sally Hancock. Not a lot, I admit and he is a reluctant stud, but his stuff is very good and I've had nothing but good reports about his puppies. As yet, the oldest puppies are not yet a year old, but most of his stock is catching quite well. Cilla always breeds slinky, grey-houndy stuff even when mated to heavy dogs, so I'm expecting quite a litter if she takes with Merle.

A freezing night—driving sleet and wind, an ideal night for lamping, or so it would seem; so with charged lamp battery, I set out and worked the back of the River Tame, Britain's dirtiest river. There just aren't the rabbits about. I saw two and ran one which Fathom took. The area is not well or over-shot, so I can only assume it is being poached. Poaching is on the increase since the spate of unemployment started. I caught sixteen rabbits in a night at this place in December 1979, and I missed far more than I caught. Now there is little to hunt on the water meadows. On returning from the hunt, however, I put up a badger and to my surprise, Fathom ran him, even attempting to lunge at him. Curious—is this the start of a brand new Fathom, not the awful coward of old? Strange—and proof that the lurcher continues to develop for several years.

One of the hellions, Phobus, looks decidedly off colour, a husky cough and a tucked up belly. Last week's rat hunt perhaps. God knows, the rat carries a host of foul infections ranging from salmonella to leptospirosis. Anyway, no point in home diagnosis and treatment. Any good dog deserves good treatment—and a visit to the local vet, Richard Jones. I hope to goodness the puppy makes it. It is a superb hunter already and will contribute a lot to the future team. What rotten luck I get. I am almost afraid to develop an affection for a dog in case it dies. This year, I am certainly jinxed. Every puppy I have fancied seems to have died of something. Are the Chinese right—that certain years are illfavoured. 1980 has certainly been a bad one for me.

Examination revealed swollen glands in the throat and his gums are bleeding badly. Nasal discharge is brown, foul smelling and tinged with blood. Diag-nosis—mine and the vet's—rat bite fever, and this can kill. What will happen to Phobus is in the lap of the gods. I just can't afford to lose this puppy.

I spoke to Doug Cooper of C.T.F. Ltd about fox traps. The present trend with pelt hunters is to trap "pelts" and not to hunt foxes with terriers or lurchers. Foxes taken with catch-alive traps rarely have damaged pelts, but the killing of captive foxes is odious and not pleasant. Last year, I heard of a chap from Leicester who caught 178 foxes in catch-alive traps, baiting them with dead hens and rank fish. Rank meat certainly lures in foxes, and if the trap is left out a few days to accustom the foxes to the presence of the cage, this trap is a good method of taking foxes. I used two such traps five years ago, and caught many foxes (though more cats, I fear). It is amazing that, in spite of the beating the foxes took last year from pelt hunters, they seem as numerous as ever.

Phobus is better this morning and the bloody brown nasal discharge is clearing somewhat. It is standard practice (I think) for a vet in doubt about the true nature of a canine illness to give an antibiotic shot until recognisable symptoms manifest themselves. In the case of a virus, the shot does little good for a virus is not harmed by antibiotics; yet, an antibiotic shot is usually helpful for a viral infection usually opens up

Bedlington Whippet hybrid—a real ferreter's dog.

the system for bacterial attacks. The complications that set in after a distemper attack are often caused by bacterial attack, and an antibiotic invariably sorts out the infections. Let's hope it can do the trick with Phobus.

A letter from Don Bakewell, who breeds useful Bedlington/whippet Bedlington/greyhound hybrids. Roger Parsons' dog, Ben, was bred by him. Also enclosed was a pamphlet advertising the exploits of Tom Withers' dog, Jerry, a twelve pound rat slayer—a prick-eared Jack Russell type with obvious bull terrier influence. Interesting, but then I find anything to do with rats little short of fascinating, in fact. Funnily enough, although London is credited with being the home of the rat pits, the last rat pit exhibition

(or at least the last known rat pit prosecution) was at Leicester in 1912. Rat pits became illegal in 1911, but they were well on the way out, popularity wise, before this date. The rat pits were unpleasant affairs that bore no resemblance to legitimate hunting. And on the subject of rat hunting, tonight is Thursday.

A furious hunt and considerable damage to the dogs. One hundred and fifty plus rats taken, but the dogs look frightful. The border has an inch long gash above his eye and Omega has a very bad tear in the mouth. As yet, the hunting instinct in the Fell terrier is still dormant but early days yet. I tried out photography using a flash but I fear I am a long way behind Keith Ruston. The shots I took will look very amateurish when printed, but I have to begin somewhere.

TOM WITHERS' DOG,
"JERRY,"
CHAMPION RAT KILLER OF ENGLAND

Born August 6th, 1890   Weight in Condition 12 lbs.

Trained

by

R. COX.

Played

by

W. MANSHIP

PERFORMANCES

His First Performance was Aug 2, 1891, when he killed **5** rats in **16** secs.

Next winning a Sweepstake, Whitsuntide, 1892, killed **5** rats in **20** secs.

Next winning a Sweepstake, killed **5** rats in **16** secs.

Bank Holiday, 1892 won All-England Sweepstake, killed **7** rats in **23** secs.

Oct. 1, 1892, won great All-England Sweepstake, killed **9** rats in **30½** secs.

Christmas the same year, at Mr T. Palmer's, Birmingham, All-England Sweepstake, killed **14** rats, in **1** min. **7** secs.

Won, All-England Sweepstake at Birmingham, killed **7** rats in **53** sec

Whitsuntide, 1893, won great All-England Sweepstake, £2 10s. each dog, killed **13** rats in **1** min **4** secs.

Aug. Bank Holiday, won a Sweepstake, killed **4** rats in **10½** secs.

Nov. 27, 1893 won All England at Mr. T. Palmer's Birmingham, killed **6** rats in **16** sec

"JERRY" was debarred from taking in all Handicaps in Leicester and Birmingham from Nov 27, 1893, to Dec 24 1894, on account of his fast time.

Dec. 24, 1894 won All England Sweepstake, killed **7** rats in **27½** secs.

June 1, 1895, won Sweepstake, killing **5** rats in **10½** secs.

Aug. 3, 1895, killed **5** rats in **11½** secs.

Dec. 3, 1895, won another great All-England Sweepstake at T. Palmer's Birmingham killed **7** rats in **27½** secs.

April 6, 1896, won a £20 match, killed against Martin's "Jew," twice its weight, and killed 4 rats extra, rats averaged 15 oz., time **4** min. **35** secs.

Whit-Tuesday, killed **4** rats in **12½** secs.

July 18, 1896, won a £20 match against A. Martin's "Rattler," killed **9** large rats in **40** secs.

Aug. 1, 1896, killed **5** rats in **15½** secs.

Oct. 10, 1896, won All England Sweepstake, killed **5** large rats in **9½** secs.

Feb. 27th, 1897 was to kill **50** rats in **7** min. for a Silver Cup value 10 guineas, he accomplished the feat in **4** min. **49½** secs.

Tom Withers, "Griffin" Vaults, Belgrave Gate, Leicester

Friday 19

Flu, or at least a heavy cold (I hope it is the latter) and I am too ill to go out with the dogs this morning. My terrier team look quite horrid, faces swollen, eyes closed. Omega has a fearful rip in the gums and the border terrier dog looks deformed. His face is ripped and swollen and I feel I should have stitched the wound above his eye.

Phobus is much better and eating quite well, but the infection is still with him. He smells necrotic and the stench of decay almost hits me as I open the door of the kitchen. Another antibiotic shot should clear him up. His saliva smells foul, but his faeces are normal. No doubt the infection is local. Another injection tonight and it should sort things out. Our local vet uses am-

179

phycillin in cases like this. I wish my own illness was this easily cleared up. The next three days with a heavy cold (or flu) will be hellish.

It looks as though Merle is fated not to mate Cilla. He penetrated her yesterday but failed to tie. I doubt if she will take. I've heard of bitches who can conceive without tieing (I've owned one actually) but these are few and far between. Anyway, next season I shall mate her to Richard Jones and try to breed another bitch like Mara. The market in good quality lurcher puppies is apparently still there so Harold might be on a winner selling puppies from this mating. Cilla will be in season in or about June.

A letter from Gerald Jones, who writes under the name of Dan Russell. He has agreed to write an article for the Year Book. It will be a good article: few people have this man's experience with terriers and fewer still have the ability to write about them.

Saturday 20

The flu is still with me, but at 8.0 am I fed Pagan's puppies, noting that there has been savage fighting between the dog and the bitch. Both are straight legged and of good quality and the male, a bull terrier headed dog, is especially well formed. The bitch is a trifle mouse-headed, a common fault of my strain; but she looks very neat and showy. Her ears are a mite suspect, rose rather than pricked. A tricolour perhaps, and not a colour I like, but she is full of quality and mated to my hellions or even Vampire, she will be enough to get my pack to rights again. The male will be the ideal dog to mate to Omega (it is her grandson) or even to Beltane (she is her great-great-grandmother). It may also be just the thing to put spunk into my fox terrier/Russell hybrids. Early days yet, and he will have to prove himself first. Still, the breeding is excellent and I shall certainly repeat the mating.

At 10.30 camera team, Eddie Jones and I arrived at Granville Maddock's house at Wood End, Tamworth for a day's beagling. Cold, wet and miserable and after four hours of tramping over wet fields, I am far from well. Beagling is not the sport for the unfit and my flu has weakened me considerably. It is now 7.10 pm and I am wheezing and exhausted. Yet, tomorrow I am off to Leicester to ferret the railway bank at Melton Mowbray. Granville has promised me country to hunt for rat, rabbit and mink, for Granville has considerable influence around Tamworth. If I get two days' hunting a week, in addition to my Thursday night at rat, I can justify keeping a pack of terriers. A draught beagle or so would help them to pack, but I should need to weed out the fighters. Judicious use (and I should need to be careful not to lose the hunting instinct in my pack) of Alan Thomas' dog, Rollo might possibly do this. I'd have to watch the nose in my pack though. Rollo has no nose to speak of and neither does Omega. Next season, I shall mate Omega to Mick's dog Toby (a pup from Hinchcliffe's Patterdale Jaeger mated to Warlock's daughtert, Battle). Half my litter will be tan but half will be traditional Plummer marked. Toby has an excellent nose, just as good as Beltane's, and this might help Omega's offspring.

A phone call to shift a fox—10.36 pm and I am too exhausted to go. I will certainly lose Astor's land as a rabbit hunting pitch, but I am not up to going out tonight.

Sunday 21

A hellish night with driving rain and a chest infection to accompany my flu. I am in no mood to go out. My temperature is 103° and at 3.0 am when Mick Mitchell phoned about going to Melton Mowbray, I was in no condition to go, but 8.0 am found me at Paul's house in Stapleford waiting for Michael Croucher.

Filming on the railway has its disadvantages. Firstly, we need an escort—a man employed by British Rail to be with us at all times (he has a claxon horn) to alert us in the unlikely event of a train coming. We are also required to wear a near-luminous pink jacket which makes us all look slightly incongruous and very effeminate. Still, this is regulation and without these jackets, we don't go on.

In spite of three hours of ferreting what looked like well filled warrens, we ferreted out (and caught) only two rabbits. I still feel quite desperately ill as a result of the ordeal. No excuses, there just weren't the rabbits available. What looked like good, well-used warrens were ferreted thoroughly and yielded only two rabbits. Perhaps myxie? I haven't a clue, but it was a disastrous hunt.

The filming of the ferreting sequence.

We arrived back at 4.0 pm and witnessed a nasty fight between Vampire and one of the fox terrier/Russell hybrids. The result was predictable and I had to prise Vampire's jaws. Sooner or later, Vampire will break the poor devil's spirit. The fighting between Vampire and the other males—that I can no longer justify taking Vampire hunting. Time for retirement, Vampire. I've long promised it; now it must come. He is still virile and a fantastic stud, but his timing now makes him look ridiculous at a rat hunt. How have the mighty fallen! What a hell of a dog he was, but *was*, not is—and it's time for young stock to enter the ranks of the rat-hunting team. Vampire will still kill a fox stone dead, for he has always been a master at brawling, but he is only a shadow of his younger days.

Monday 22

A tedious day. Spent the morning doing tying in shots for BBC 2 and afternoon in an abortive fox hunt. For once, Barlow's land held no foxes and we spent two hours simply looking for an inhabited earth with Mick Kirby and his dog Toby. Toby, a cross bred Patterdale/Jack Russell terrier, the result of mating Hinchcliffe's dog Jaeger to a daughter of Beltane, is a cracking good rat dog but as yet, he's not encountered a fox. He didn't today either. It's funny, but when a man wants to catch a particular animal before the TV

181

cameras, it's a racing certainty he will fail.

I am putting Vampire out to stud with Mick Kirby. At ten, he is still the best of studs and sires some superb puppies. I feel I shall miss his use in the team, and somehow I feel I have betrayed the old deveil. He has killed many dogs and maimed more, but his haul of rats and foxes is unbeatable. I shall regret his passing, and it will take years to replace him. Breeding wise, he is incredible, 15 generations of Working Certificated dogs produced him, and his only non-working certificated ancestor was a pit bull terrier that was said to have been fought regularly. As a hard case, a hunter, a sporting terrier, for all conditions, I have not had better.

Pete Beddow's bitch (Woolly Bear's sister) has been killed on the A 38. A pity, a useful bitch. Pete seems desperately upset about it. I shall lend him Woolly—it is the least I can do.

Harold Hodson Walker brought Cilla for a mating today and she stood and Merle mated her, tying for twenty minutes. This litter is already ordered and the chances are it will fetch up to £100 a puppy. I've often thought one first rate lurcher puppy is a far better bet than ten indifferent ones, so perhaps £100 is not expensive. Certainly Eddie's puppy Celt (I believe he paid £50 for him) is an exceptional dog and cheap at twice the price. However, the financial situation of the average man is a bit desperate so buyers may be a bit slow in coming. Personally, I would give this price for a suitable dog. I should like to see how puppies from this mating turn out.

Tuesday 23

Alan Thomas has offered me a puppy to mate to Vampire. It is a smart red fawn Patterdale/Jack Russell bitch bred from a hard-bitten, bull terrier-headed dog mated to a first rate Jack Russell bitch. I really need game blood to add to my strain. The bitch is thirteen months old, scarcely a puppy, I suppose, but already entering to fox quite well. Alan has hunted with Eddie Chapman's brother a good unpretentious hunter, who is trying to breed a mink hunting pack by mating a Bedlington type terrier with a beagle. Interesting, but I'd like to see the progeny—they could be hideous, but nature usually exerts an ameliorating influence on the progeny of the most unlikely parents and the puppies don't look as hideous as one would expect.

A fox dig in Box Hill, Surrey—or at least a trip to Box Hill—for in spite of the fact we tried eighteen earths, in fox thick country, we could not find one and returned home dead beat. Mick Kirby is also down with the same flu bug that nearly put me out of action, and after twelve hours of travelling and walking, we were both dead beat.

Midnight and shortage of ferret meat has pushed me out after rabbits. Fathom ran two and caught two. She is in superb form, catching and retrieving well. In a few weeks, I start work on a new book and I'll have little time for lurcher coursing. I shall, therefore, lend Paul Taylor Fathom, the friends of John Benton, Beige and Pete Beddows will borrow Woolly. Merle will not be put out for, like most collie/greyhound first crosses, he accepts change reluctantly. Also, it is a rather stupid thing to lend out a fox-killing lurcher when I shall be pelt hunting after Christmas. On the subject of foxes, I failed to catch in front of the TV cameras, but tonight seven appeared in the beam. Fathom ignored them. Never work with kids and animals!

I am still ill and need the Christmas holidays to recover, but somehow I don't feel I will get that rest.

Wednesday 24

A deep gloom is upon me, the result of a fruitless day's hunting and a racking cough, the remains of the flu infection. At dawn, I fed the dogs and perhaps they were sympathetic to my mood as there was not a single fight.

Food is easily come by over Christmas, as not only are there fallen cattle and pigs aplenty, but there is also a surfeit of poultry waste. I fed forty pounds of duck offal this morning, and while it has a slight emetic effect the dogs look well on it. Of course, there is always the risk of salmonella when feeding duck offal but the risk is slight when one compares the fattening of present day ducks with those of old. In pre-war times, ducks were allowed free range and fed on pond plants and insects—a rich and certain source of salmonella. They also mated on water and some pond organisms entered the cloaca at the time of mating— hence, the "duck egg deaths" of 1948. Modern ducks are fed balanced diets, kept on straw and never allowed to see a pond. Hence, salmonella is practically unknown. I say practically, as I've had a batch of puppy deaths feeding duck offal.

9.30 am: my gloom is dispelled by a letter from Jack Ivester Lloyd praising my book *Nathan*. Praise from a writer of his ilk is praise indeed.

Where are the foxes? I need foxes to photograph and film and for once in my life, I seem unable to find one. Another fruitless day spent sending Beltane through the earths, but not a fox to be found. Doug believes they are living out in cover and not going to ground. This sometimes happens in mild weather for foxes are quite happy about living out in thick undergrowth if the weather is right. A day's frost will put things right, I think.

Work on the *Hunter's Year Book* is progressing nicely. So far, a good set of articles by Mick Kirby, Paul Taylor, Frank Sheardown and a promise of good articles by Dan Russell and Jack Ivester Lloyd. With a few book reviews and a couple more articles, I will have a first class Year Book to be released in October for the Christmas market 1981.

My border terriers are close to whelping and in spite of the mild weather, I shall put them under a heat lamp to whelp. I shan't keep the pups as they are not what I want, although at £70 a puppy, border terriers are worth keeping.

Thursday 25

Caught a large stoat on the edge of Stone's wood this morning and had trouble stopping Omega and Beltane fighting over its ownership. Both are excellent bitches and there is bad blood between them. They hunt together without mishap, but it is nearly impossible to allow them to exercise together in the run. My phone has but to ring and they are at each other's throats as soon as I leave the run to answer the telephone. At one time, I thought it good practice not to stop their battles, but they caused such awful trouble and damage to each other that I now find it expedient not to exercise them together.

I wrote up the research on the origin of the smooth-coated Fell terrier erroneously called the Patterdale, and explored the baffling enigma of the life of Cyril Bray of Kirby Lonsdale, a gentle man, an ex-schoolmaster and son of a clergyman, but who bred some of the gamest, gutsy dogs in the country. He left no records, so unravelling the genetic maze is a gargantuan task. I shall keep accurate records so that when I pass on, any small contribution I have made to the working terrier will be accurately recorded. Vampire's great-grandfather was Bray's doughty grappler Rusty, a red dog as game as a pebble; while Mick Kirby's dog Toby and my bitch Pagan are great grandchildren of Flint, a grandson of Rusty.

The rabbits are back and curiously breeding in midwinter. The dogs chased and missed a small drummer early this morning. Rabbits will breed as soon as the temperature rises a few degrees above freezing so it seems. I hope they are not so inclined in Leicester as I intend to ferret there on New Year's Day and young rabbits (nestling kittens) below ground are a sure bet for causing a ferret to lie up.

Friday 26

Another fruitless dawn hunt for inhabited fox earths. Where in hell are the foxes living? I tried forty-one good earths this morning and not one had a heavy scent, let alone a fox.

I was invited to the Boxing Day meet of the Warwickshire Beagles, but I have declined in favour of going to lunch (called dinner by us commoners) with Moses Smith at Kirk Langley. Steel is near season again, but Moses does not intend to breed from her this time. There is some evidence to suggest that bitches do not suffer from breeding every season, and research had shown that out of condition bitches do not come in season. Personally (although I rarely dispute the findings of American Veterinary Colleges) I think this is a lot of hooey. During a distemper outbreak some ten years ago, one of my bitches came in season when she was desperately ill: she subsequently died. In my opinion, creatures near to death come in season in the forlorn hope of perpetuating the species. Plants certainly do. Four years ago, the drought shrivelled up seedling groundsel on my wall and the plants (merely two seed leaves) came into flower to continue the species. I don't breed every season but I've seen street bitches who are always in whelp and don't look any the worse for it. Not my scene though.

A reasonably standardised type of fell terrier known as "border/lakeland" in the fells.

Pagan's tricolour bitch is a heller, quick to take offence sharp as a razor. Although she is the wrong colour to enter the main pack, she will prove invaluable as a brood bitch to resuscitate my somewhat flagging bloodline. I shall inoculate her and her brother next week.

Moses has a litter of springer spaniel puppies bred from his own bitch mated to another gamekeeper's dog. Every week, one sees hordes of springer puppies for sale in *Shooting Times*. How do they all find homes? There must be a bottomless market for these pups. Moses wants £70 each and seems confident he will sell them.

Saturday 27

Not the best of days. I returned from Cambridge at 1.15 and took Woolly and Fathom to run in the lane. Someone has ferreted the lane edge for rabbits were sitting out in the frozen thickets. Fathom caught two and Woolly ran two more but missed badly and crashed into the rusty wire ripping his legs badly. He is so sore that he screams as soon as he tries to stand. A pity, as I hoped to take him ferreting in Leicester, but he will be very lame by Thursday. Really, he needs a heat lamp to reduce the danger of death from shock, but they are over my border bitches who are due any time now. Poor old Woolly, he looks a hell of a mess.

On the subject of border terriers, both look as full as eggs and very close to whelping. I don't really want these puppies as I dislike winter rearing and I would not breed from my own Russells in mid winter. Whelping a litter without a heat lamp is a bit of a risk, for not only are the puppies likely to chill and die, but the survivors look poor and weedy. Jackie Fallon says borders are fetching £70 a piece—a hell of a price to pay for a pet animal, though I would not hesitate to pay double that price for a working dog puppy— *Chacun a son goût*, I suppose.

Nightwing is maturing rapidly. In spite of the fact she is not killing rats yet, she is very bold and fearless, though she does tend to give tongue at anything strange. Before adding her to my strain, a time of savage testing must take place. By dint of breeding only from game dogs I breed very few quitters, so I am reluctant to absorb a bitch that does nothing. But she has only been ratting twice, so it is ridiculously early to tell if she is suitable. If she is good, I shall mate her to Buck's young dog one day, but that is too far into the future to even contemplate.

Nearer to hand, I photographed Jackie Fallon's border terrier litter tonight, sired by Bugsy, a dog with a damaged front leg, but bred from three generations of border terriers that work—a novelty in these times for quitting, non-instinct borders are a dime a dozen. Bugsy mated a rough coated Russell bitch at the Meynell Hunt and bred a brown, rough coated bordery-looking male that entered to fox at six months. If his track record is good, and it looks as though it might be, I shall mate him on to my strain of Russell, for in spite of his lack of furnishing (what rubbish the show breeders admire) he is of good type and utterly game. Such blood would surely not come amiss in my own strain of terrier. One of (possibly) Pagan's puppies might make a useful "entry point" for Jackie's dog to enter the strain. Furthermore, Bugsy has an excellent nose—the first priority in my strain.

Sunday 28

Sunday dawn, and another rabbit for Fathom, sadly of the litter which lives at the end of my run. Still, it's better than stolen guinea fowl and poultry. Woolly looks better this morning and is rolling in something disgusting in Barlow's field even as I write this. Filth rolling is a habit in which all dogs seem to indulge and it must serve some biological purpose, though for the hell of me, I can't see what. All sorts of absurd ideas are put forward to explain it and none of that stands up to scrutiny. It seems dogs just enjoy rolling in filth— full stop.

A savage fight between Vampire and Rollo (a side contest of the main bout between Omega and Beltane) but one I will remember for some time to come for in separating them—an unpleasant job, as Vampire has a hell of a grip—my hand was seized by him and one finger crushed quite badly. He did not mean to do this, I am sure, but hot from a fight he will strike at any-thing. Little or no damage to Rollo, but my hand is black and blue. Fortunately, I had the presence of mind to keep my hand in Vampire's mouth and not try to pull it away. If I had tried, I would now be minus one finger, at least.

Another instance of Fathom's cunning. Eddie Jones, Pete Beddows (he borrowed Woolly today) Frank Picton and his father were outside my cottage with their dogs. Fathom had been running loose for an hour and returned home to my cottage, small rabbit in mouth. She saw the band outside my house and slipped into the trees, burying the rabbit in some leaves. When they had left, she returned the undamaged rabbit to the house. A true lurcher, sly as a chicken thief and a born survivor, more at home under a Romany vardo than in the house of an unsuccessful school teacher.

My fourth night without sleep, and tomorrow it is north to the Lakes to research the Fell terrier.

Monday 29

There is parvo in the Lake District and few want their kennels visited. Edmund Dargue lost a puppy and an old bitch to this virus only last week. A pity, for I needed to visit him for data on Joe Weir, ex-huntsman for the Ullswater.

I visited Walter Parking at his flat in an old folk's block. Parkin is 71, crippled by strokes and quite ill, but in his heyday he was a great fell man. He once walked sixty-seven miles to hunt with Joe Weir: a great old fell man now sadly without terriers. When he hunted the Lunesdale Fox Hunt, they were a formidable pack. I can remember reading a curious tale

A typical crag earth in the fells.

about him. In the 1950s one of his hounds picked up a dose of strychnine and went into a thrashing fit, finally becoming rigid. Unwisely, Walter tried to resuscitate the hound by giving it the kiss of life. He was desperately ill and nearly died as a result of this act. The Fells will not see his like again, I fear.

Visited John Cowen of Bully House Farm, Embleton, Cumbria. Cowen keeps black-and-tan fells with a dash of show blood to give them class. Unlike many fell terrier breeders, he is quite open about the use of this show blood and his only complaint about pedigree registered Lakeland types is that they tend to fight. I liked Cowen, a straightforward, easy-going chap who kept accurate records of his breeding schemes. Cowen's original stuff was bred by Hardesty's famous Turk—a grand dog, a looker and a great battler. Most quality rough fell terriers (Buck's excluded) date from Turk. Tyson's dog, Rock, Bell's Twist and Winch's Chanter all have Turk in their immediate pedigree.

Arrive home exhausted, noting that yesterday Bill Colclough brought his bitch for mating and I forgot to put in the entry in the diary. The pace is killing me. I am unable to live at this speed.

I shall take a puppy from Bill Colclough's bitch. Her breeding is excellent and the puppies from her and Rollo will do my strain some good. Twice, she has been mated by Vampire, but half her litter was putty nosed. All her pups are dead game, but are inclined to be stock worriers.

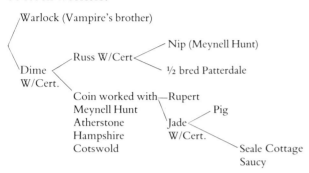

This stuff mated to Rollo (breeding 30th Sept.) will produce a fine dam line to mate to Vampire. Jade was a wonderful bitch who produced 40 working certificate puppies. She died aged 13, a bitch with a wonderful nose. Six of her grandchildren went to the U.S.A. I wonder what has become of them.

Guy Page brought his dog Jude tonight. He is having little success in lamping him: Guy's fault, I fear, for the dog is very keen and quite fast enough for the job. Practice, practice, practice is the only secret of training dogs to hunt. A good, useful dog I think, well trained, keen and a wonderful jumper. Such a dog is a true lurcher and with work will become a good provender dog. If I breed dogs of this ilk from Richard Jones, I shall be well pleased. Guy's dog is in fact Richard Jones' half-brother. Never did two animals look less alike.

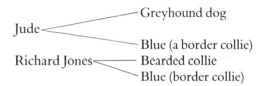

A quiet start to the day—exercise period relaxed and not a single fight. Even Omega and Beltane seem at peace with the world, and more important still, with each other. It will not last. They'll be at each other's throats by tonight. The only way to settle such a bitter hatred once and for all, is to actually kennel them together. They would damage each other quite badly, but once one had established supremacy, this infernal enmity would cease. They no longer exercise properly and merely circle each other waiting for one to put a foot wrong.

I travelled north to Leeds today to take part as Richard Whiteley's guest in "Calendar." I enjoyed the interview great fun and harmless entertainment. Of course, I took a ferret. No Whiteley show would be complete without a ferret. Later, in the bar of Trident House, the Stage Manager of "3,2,1" put the ferret down his trousers—sooner him than me. Trident are a great team with which to work and are hospitality itself.

I must write to Tyson of Egremont for an interview concerning his terriers. Rock, his famous stud, is yet another dog descended from Harry Hardesty's famous Turk. Together with Buck's Viper, Turk must be the terrier that influenced most bloodlines in today's fell terriers. Bell's strain of terrier is a judicious blend of both Buck's strain and the dogs of Harry Hardesty, but the two strains are in my opinion, best kept apart as they represent separate types. Personally, I rather like Buck's type as I find Turk's stuff too big for my linking . Winch swears by the Hardesty line, however, and much of the stuff around Consett is bred from Turk mated to fell type terriers with a strong trace of border terrier—descended from Yak Bob, an early border terrier and a tremendous worker.

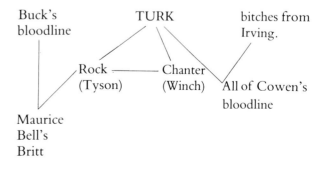